INNOVATION AND PRODUCTIVITY UNDER NATIONALISATION

The first thirty years

CHRIS HARLOW

Routledge
Taylor & Francis Group

LONDON AND NEW YORK

First published in 1977 by George Allen & Unwin (Publishers) Ltd

This edition first published in 2018
by Routledge
2 Park Square, Milton Park, Abingdon, Oxon OX14 4RN

and by Routledge
711 Third Avenue, New York, NY 10017

Routledge is an imprint of the Taylor & Francis Group, an informa business

British Library Cataloguing in Publication Data
A catalogue record for this book is available from the British Library

ISBN: 978-1-138-50336-6 (Set)
ISBN: 978-1-351-06690-7 (Set) (ebk)
ISBN: 978-1-138-47859-6 (Volume 18) (hbk)
ISBN: 978-1-138-47896-1 (Volume 18) (pbk)
ISBN: 978-1-351-06745-4 (Volume 18) (ebk)

Publisher's Note
The publisher has gone to great lengths to ensure the quality of this reprint but points out that some imperfections in the original copies may be apparent.

Disclaimer
The publisher has made every effort to trace copyright holders and would welcome correspondence from those they have been unable to trace.

ROUTLEDGE LIBRARY EDITIONS: THE ECONOMICS AND BUSINESS OF TECHNOLOGY

Volume 18

INNOVATION AND PRODUCTIVITY UNDER NATIONALISATION

Innovation and Productivity under Nationalisation

The first thirty years

CHRIS HARLOW

POLITICAL AND ECONOMIC PLANNING
GEORGE ALLEN & UNWIN LTD

First published in 1977

ISBN 0 04 600003 8

George Allen & Unwin (Publishers) Ltd.
Ruskin House, Museum Street, London WC1A 1LU

Political and Economic Planning
12 Upper Belgrave Street, London SW1X 8BB

Printed in England
at The Lavenham Press Limited, Lavenham, Suffolk.

Contents

The author's thanks are due to the many staff in the New Bodleian who answered frequent calls for material, to the officers of the public corporations who provided comments on the drafts, and to a patient director of research.
The book is dedicated to Shelagh, for her help and support.

1 Introduction

The core of this book consists of five main chapters. Each one deals with a different British public corporation and examines the way in which the corporation has introduced technical change in its capital equipment over a period of approximately thirty years.

The organisations chosen for the study were:
(1) the National Coal Board
(2) the British Gas Corporation (formerly Gas Council and Area Gas Boards)
(3) the European branch of British Airways (formerly British European Airways)
(4) the Central Electricity Generating Board (formerly the generation and transmission division of the Central Electricity Authority)
(5) the telecommunications service of the Post Office.

The industries in which these organisations operate are self-evident from their titles. Four of them actually dominate the industries in which they are located. The NCB, the Gas Corporation, the Generating Board and the Post Office have virtually a monopoly in the sales of coal, gas, generated electricity and telephone services respectively in Britain (England and Wales in the case of the Generating Board). The fifth organisation, BEA from 1946 to 1973 and the European division of British Airways thereafter, maintained a substantial share of the markets in which it operated throughout the thirty years covered by the study.

There are some differences in the corporate structure of the five bodies which need to be pointed out. The NCB is an independent corporation with a Board at its head and an autonomous financial structure. BEA was similar in structure up to 1973, but then became an operating division subject to the British Airways Board and without a separate financial structure. The Gas Corporation for most of the period of the study was constituted as the Gas Council and twelve Area Boards. The latter were autonomous in their finance and management but some functions were co-ordinated through the Council. The Generating Board has financial autonomy in the electricity supply industry and its own Board and management structure, but for the first ten years after nationalisation it was merged with the Central Authority as an operating division of the industry. The telephone service was also originally an operating division of the Post Office. During the 1960s it gained more independence in finance

1

and management, but did not become a separate corporation. In the last part of this chapter these organisations and their development are more fully described.

Four out of five of the corporations came into existence within four years of the end of the second world war, as part of the Labour Government's programme of nationalising Britain's basic industries. The fifth, the Post Office, had already been in the public sector as a civil service department for more than 100 years.

For a variety of reasons, during the years following the war the five organisations were each separately launching upon technical policies and programmes which were of great importance for their techniques of production and the productivity with which factors of production were employed. In part, re-organisation and concentration consequent upon the transfer of the industries to public ownership brought about a scrutiny of the technology used by the industries. The wording of the Acts of nationalisation typically included at some point the duty 'to develop and maintain . . . secure and adequate supplies of (coal, gas, electricity, etc.) in an efficient manner'. Rationalisation of the provision of public utility services had already been used by the Government and Parliament in one or two instances as a means of promoting greater efficiency in supply, which provided a precedent for the postwar corporations.[1]

In addition, the condition of working methods and capital employed in some of the industries was such as to make men experienced in their operations more than ready to look for change. The transfer of the industries to a single controlling authority (or in the case of gas, to a small number of regional authorities) provided a structure within which it was easier to effect technical changes which were already felt necessary. Some of the technical changes described in the chapters which follow thus have their origins further back than the postwar period; but that is not to say that these technical changes raise issues of policy which were only relevant to the 1940s and 1950s, or which have long since been resolved. The technical programmes examined in the research for this book were programmes which were reaching a stage by the late 1960s where the results would be expected to be observable and the problems of managing technology which are demonstrated by the policies adopted have a continuing relevance.

The programmes which the corporations embarked upon were as follows:

(1) The National Coal Board's major pre-occupation was, and still is, to raise manpower productivity in the underground mining industry which produces over 90 per cent of coal output. During the 1960s and 1970s it sought to do this by introducing innovatory machinery at the coal face in order to achieve very high rates of production at each face being worked.

(2) The gas industry was faced in the 1950s by stiff competition from electricity and steadily mounting costs caused by dependence upon coal. After a long period of experimentation, the industry developed

a process based on oil in the mid-1960s which completely changed the economics of gas production.

(3) British European Airways was in the difficult position of trying to operate profitably over stage lengths which were on average much shorter than those of its competitors. BEA therefore devoted much attention to developing, with the British aircraft manufacturers, specifications for profitable short haul airliners to be built by the British industry.

(4) With the aim of improving fuel and capital productivity in generation, the Generating Board (and the generating division of the CEA before it) has steadily increased the size and thermal efficiency and advanced the technical characteristics of generating plant. In the mid-1960s the development of advanced gas cooled nuclear reactors (AGRs) was added to the development of conventional plant to further this objective.

(5) The switching technology employed in the vast majority of Post Office exchanges was, and still is, Strowger switching. First installed in the UK in 1912, Strowger switching requires a high labour input and is technically unsatisfactory for many modern telecommunications applications. In the latter half of the 1940s the Post Office engineering department began to consider what type of switching should replace it, and there followed a thirty-year programme of development directed at the solution to this problem.

There are three main objectives of the research upon which this book is based: first, to examine how each technical programme came to be incorporated and associated with the organisation's more general business objectives; secondly, to look more closely at the decision points at which the organisations became further committed to the techniques which had been under development; thirdly, to consider the means by which the technical programmes were pursued. Overall the purpose is to show how technology was applied to the problem of factor productivity, to seek understanding of why objectives were not always reached, and to assess the contribution made by the innovations described.

In each of the five chapters which follows the procedure adopted has been to sketch the industry's circumstances during the late 1940s and to show what pressures were working upon the corporations to introduce technical change. This is followed by a narrative of the main technical developments which were sponsored by the corporations, paying attention to the role of internal agencies, such as research and development laboratories, and to the contributions of the manufacturers supplying the capital equipment. Short sections of discussion are included in the narrative, which analyse the factors bearing upon important decision points.

In the typical case there might be a number of such points. First of all there is the need to analyse correctly what the technical problems are which confront the industry, and this would be followed by the choice, in the area of technical policy, of a strategy which would enable the organisation to identify possible solutions. Thirdly, experimental development would be needed to establish the probable operating characteristics and economics of solutions. The fourth stage is to determine on full development of the new technique and, finally, there has to be a decision to invest in it.

Not all these stages of decision are distinguishable in the technical programmes described below, but it is helpful to consider each of the policies against such a pattern of decision procedure. If, for instance, the organisation appears to be starting at stage three, by concentrating development upon one line of technical advance, it is useful to examine the whole programme by considering what the technical problems were and what alternatives had been rejected, even if these were not explicit decisions made by the organisation. Stages four and five also may not be separately distinguished. The organisation may fuse the two decisions by placing a commercial order for a technology which is not developed to a commercial stage.

It was noted above that all the organisations studied are in the public sector of the economy. In principle there are no reasons for supposing that technical change would be managed in a systematically different way by public corporations, but it was actually the case with the organisations studied here that public ownership created special conditions. In the first place, the corporations have had to cope with the influence of government in the formation of general policies for the industries concerned. At some times this took the form of direct intervention in decisions upon technology. At other times government influence acted so as to reduce investment plans, restrain price increases or otherwise affect the business planning of the corporation. In the second place, the corporations operate in a special market structure. Conditions approaching monopoly in the markets for the products of the corporations are paralleled by conditions approaching monopsony in the markets for the capital equipment bought by the corporations. It is argued here that these conditions give the public corporations more power to determine the rate and direction of technical change.

In a more fragmented industrial structure different technical solutions may be adopted by different operating organisations. The successful solutions tend to become distinguished by market forces. Where one major corporation embraces virtually the whole industry, this regulating influence is absent. As a consequence, much more responsibility rests upon the corporation to ensure that it chooses new techniques carefully.

There are some features of the public corporations which made them especially attractive for a study of this nature. In spite of some structural change during the period studied, the management and control of the organisations remained conveniently stable, embracing approximately the same range of operations at the end of the thirty years as at the beginning. This stability allows the development of long-term technical policies to be traced more easily than would be the case if continual changes in management and scope had taken place. The statistics applying to the industries are readily available, comprehensive and generally consistent over time, a feature which applies to few other industries. Finally, there are regular records of the activities of the corporations presented in the *Annual Reports,* originally published as Parliamentary Papers.

Although subject to the shortcomings which formally compiled reports demonstrate, these *Reports* far exceed in their standard of disclosure anything which is available in the private sector.[2] They were used as one of the main sources of material for the study, which relied almost exclusively on published information. The other major sources were special publications of the corporations, the journals of engineering institutions and technical magazines.

THE CORPORATIONS

National Coal Board
The Coal Board started off as one of the largest employers in Britain, with over 700,000 on the payroll in the postwar period. Subsequently, retrenchment in coal output and the increasing productivity of the employees cut the total to 250,000 by the mid-1970s. It was difficult at the outset to know what type of structure to impose on this size of organisation. In fact the Board chose to set up a headquarters with three, and often four, levels of responsibility below it. Below HQ there were eight Divisions, geographically spread over the main coalfields. The Division was in turn divided into anything from four to ten Areas, each Area containing a number of collieries which were relatively close to each other. There were originally approximately forty-five Areas with an average of 20 collieries each; in many Areas there was a further level of responsibility between Area and colliery, because groups of collieries would be further allocated to Area agents.

Within this structure, the main functions of the Board, such as production, marketing, planning, investment and technical development, were directed from headquarters. However, with so many levels of responsibility a good deal of executive authority had to be delegated to the Area management or below to the agent or the colliery manager. The determination of a research programme and the establishment of objectives for technical development were the responsibility of headquarters. An establishment at Stoke Orchard near Cheltenham was set up for research, while the development of mining techniques was at first conducted in the field. As the years went by, new R and D facilities began to take a lead in the conduct of the technical programme.

In 1967 a three-tier organisation was substituted for the previous five-tier one. Seventeen Areas were created with an average of about twenty collieries each; each Area reported directly to the headquarters. This was the main change during the first thirty years of the Coal Board's operations. Most of the Board's functions continued to be directed centrally from Headquarters or from agencies responsible to headquarters and the effect of the re-organisation was to improve control. There had been frequent criticism of the Coal Board's management organisation in the first ten years of its existence, and a series of changes took place in the methods used to formulate general policy and to control the performance of the industry. However, the overall nature of the organisation, with its emphasis upon centralised management, remained largely unchanged.

Gas — the Council and Area Boards

Up to the year 1973 the gas industry under public ownership consisted of a central Council and twelve Area Boards. The production and distribution of gas before nationalisation had been in the hands of nearly a thousand local undertakings. The effect of nationalisation was to introduce concentration, but on a regional basis, so that the federal structure was somewhat in contrast to that of the Coal Board. Each Board was responsible for gas supply in its area, and thus each Board managed the production and distribution of gas as an autonomous body. Each Board operated its own production processes, purchased its own supplies of coal and other feedstocks, set its own prices and was responsible for maintaining its own financial viability. The whole industry employed 140,000 in 1950. By 1974 this had shrunk to 103,000, even though output had increased by a factor of five.

At the head of the gas industry was the Gas Council. Composed of a chairman, deputy chairman and twelve others who were members by virtue of being the chairmen of the Areas, its role was to co-ordinate gas supply and its executive functions were few. With a small administrative staff, the Council considered issues of national policy and represented the industry where matters of interest to all the Boards were concerned.

Thus it was the Council's business to conduct negotiations with the sponsoring Ministry. For instance, in the field of investment, Area Boards prepared their plans for new plant and equipment and then passed them on to the Council, which put together a programme for the industry. The overall level of expenditure had to be agreed with the Ministry and it was the Council's task to present the industry's requirements. In addition, the Council kept a watch on the overall financial position of the industry and composed consolidated accounts as part of the Annual Report. Discussions over price changes or any questions about the statutory role of the Boards were also negotiated under the auspices of the Council. During the period of fuel shortage, coal allocations to the industry were agreed between the Ministry and the Council.

Perhaps the most important executive function of the Council was the supervision of the industry's research programme. There were three main areas of work, production processes, utilisation and appliance research and, later on, transmission research. The Council established the research facilities, agreed the research programme and provided the budget. However, the Area Boards also participated in the development of new processes for making gas and other research. Some Boards funded their own programmes of work. The Council's research and development facilities were actually managed by the Area Board in whose district they lay and the Council's Research Committee, which drew up the programme, included senior representatives from the Area Boards.

The structure described was finally superseded as a result of the widespread use of North Sea gas. With the existence of centralised sources of supply and a national pipeline grid, decisions on production methods, new plant and other investment, marketing, contracts, distribution, etc., passed to a new central body, the British Gas Corporation, in January 1973. The Areas continued in existence as geographical divisions of the Corporation, but without corporate status and operating largely as retailing organisations.

British European Airways
BEA was very much smaller than the other four public corporations. It started off after the war with about 7,000 employees, but staff numbers grew steadily with the high rate of growth of air transportation. Even so, at approximately 25,000 in the early 1970s, BEA was only one tenth the size of the Coal Board or the telecommunications side of the Post Office and it was considerably smaller than the gas and electricity industries.

Alongside BEA's much smaller number of employees went a much simpler structure. Most of the organising and running of services could be directed from a single site, BEA's main base at London, with the assistance of staff at destination airfields. Even servicing and maintenance of the aircraft were very soon centralised when the airline moved into new quarters at Heathrow in the early 1950s. Sales, marketing and commercial policy were also directed from the London base, although naturally much of the selling devolved upon ticket agencies throughout Europe and further afield.

Co-ordination of main-base functions at BEA was achieved through a committee structure and informal contacts between departments. For the most important decisions there was a Policy Board, consisting of the Chairman and Deputy Chairman (and in the later 1950s the Chief Executive), along with the heads of major functional departments, the commercial director, chief engineer, financial controller, flight operations director, etc.

By 1966/7 the diversity of BEA's activities and the different standards of performance which might appropriately be required of them were placing strains on this type of structure. Re-organisation took place over a period of two or three years and resulted in a division among the different services into separate operating organisations. Thus the main business of scheduled European flights became distinct from the charter operation, from cargo services and from the services to outlying parts of the United Kingdom.

There was little precedent, at the time of the formation of BEA, for airline research into the problems of the industry. Although BEA in its early years did undertake a certain amount of work, covering upper atmosphere flying and helicopter operations, the airline had no statutory responsibility to develop or monitor a research programme. The technical responsibility for the most important function, the development of new aircraft types, rested with the aircraft manufacturers.

BEA's role in aircraft development was confined to its influence as a purchaser. Such a position was not without considerable importance in the determination of which aircraft types would be developed. BEA purchasing decisions were, of course, ultimately the responsibility of the departmental chiefs in committee, but much of the work of developing the BEA 'aircraft requirement' for submission to manufacturers was done by a branch of the engineering department, the Project and Development Group. Information about the airline's need for new aircraft of a certain size and operating speed would come from the commercial department and the flight operations department. The desired technical characteristics, particularly with reference to servicing frequency and specification of equipment, were generated from within the engineering department, particularly from the maintenance section. Within the constraints of operating cost and purchase price imposed by the Corporation's financial and sales position, the Project and Development Group then had to select a new aircraft and recommend it to the management.

The Generating Board
The structure of the Central Electricity Generating Board is not essentially complicated, but the Board emerged with corporate status only in 1958 and some explanation is required of the organisation which preceded it. Some form of public control over generation and power station building can be detected as early as 1927, when the Central Electricity Board was formed to build and run the National Grid. Working alongside the Board there were also the Electricity Commissioners, who had the power to control annual investment in new large-scale generating equipment. However, electricity supply came into full public ownership only in 1948; for ten years after that the industry was run by the British Electricity Authority, consisting of the Central Authority (headquarters) and Area Boards.[3]

The Central Authority was responsible for generation and main line transmission, while the Boards were responsible for local distribution, for marketing and servicing the consumer, for retailing appliances and for collecting revenue. Thus the Boards had to pay the Authority for electricity supplied to them.

The Central Authority, as well as undertaking generation of supply, was also charged with responsibility (like the Gas Council) for regulating the affairs of the industry in general, negotiations on level of investment and prices, administering the research programme, handling labour relations, etc. In 1955 the Herbert Report[4] concluded that the mixture of supervisory and executive functions was undesirable; as a result of its recommendations, generation was split off as a separate function and the Generating Board established to supply the Areas. The industry was also provided with a regulating council, the Electricity Council, whose functions, not unlike the Gas Council's, were to monitor investment, pricing, labour relations, etc.

The industry had consisted of about 160,000 employees in the mid-1950s, but only 53,000 of these were transferred to the CEGB in 1958. The Board contained five geographically dispersed generating divisions, running the power stations; the planning and building of new plant was also divided on a regional basis, but the three functions of generation, transmission and installing new plant in the various regions were in reality directed and closely controlled from the headquarters departments in London. The numbers of staff expanded slowly during the 1960s, but fell back slightly to 64,000 by 1974. The system of central direction and control altered little, although some departments moved out of London.

The formation of a research programme was at first the responsibility of a Research Council reporting to the Central Authority. This function was also transferred to the Electricity Council, although the Generating Board staffed and administered the laboratories. The main research facility at first was the laboratory of the former Central Electricity Board at Leatherhead. A good deal of work on electricity supply problems was undertaken at small laboratories attached to some of the power stations and in the late 1950s a facility was established for nuclear research. Central facilities for generation research were not established although the engineering laboratories set up at Marchwood had some functions in this area. The large manufacturers of boilers, turbines and alternators were expected to cover this area of technical development, although co-operative committees were convened from time to time between manufacturers and the supply industry to determine priorities for work.

The Post Office
The Post Office is the oldest of the organisations studied. Responsible for posts, telegraphs and telephones, its structure had been evolving over a long period before 1945, but at that time it was in the process of digesting some important changes which had been recommended by a pre-war committee of inquiry, the Bridgeman Committee. Before Bridgeman there had been a postal service with a regional and subregional system of posts and postmasters, into which the telegraph service was reasonably well integrated. The telephone service, developed during the last twenty years of the nineteenth century and coming fully into Post Office control only in 1912, had a semi-autonomous structure in the regions, and was largely independent of the postal management in London. Alongside the three services was the engineering department, controlled more by headquarters than by the regions, and having more to do with the telephones than the posts.

Set over all these branches of the Post Office was a senior department staffed by the administrative class of the Civil Service and similar to the top echelon of civil servants in ordinary Ministries. It was known as the Secretariat. The changes induced by Bridgeman included the replacement of the Secretariat by the Post Office Board and the reformation of the regional structure; the posts and telephones departments gained more local control over their separate functions outside London through newly appointed Regional Directors, and the engineering service below the headquarters level was more closely integrated with the postal and telephone functions of the regions.

During the immediate postwar period the Post Office was thus managed by executives at headquarters in the major areas of the services provided. They reported to the Post Office Board. The structure was largely centralised; decisions affecting the provision of service, pricing, marketing, technical change, personnel and investment were taken for all regions by the headquarters staff and implemented on their instructions.

In the late 1950s the Post Office's financial and accounting status began to shift away from the revenue department model which it had previously reflected; the establishment of a corporate structure in all the spheres of its operations followed by stages during the 1960s. As this process took place, the centralised form of management and control was maintained, but the Board came more to reflect executive functions. The number of departmental chiefs and Board members involved in decision making was increasing and becoming unwieldy; thus a new top management structure was developed. In 1969, when the Post Office achieved the legal status of a public corporation, these management changes were formalised by setting up a new Post Office Board composed of a Chairman, Chief Executive, Deputy Chairman and six members, whose titles reflected the major functional activities of the Post Office.

Throughout the postwar period, as before the war, research and technical direction were the preserve of the engineering department. The main research establishment at Dollis Hill had been founded in the 1920s and it had a high reputation for its work on transmission techniques. Research and development of exchange switching techniques was initially conducted largely by the equipment manufacturing industry, but the Post Office as a major buyer had an increasingly powerful role to play in determining what equipment was developed. Various co-operative arrangements for technical development were evolved with the industry, reflecting the Post Office's interest as a major customer.

NOTES

[1] The long distance telephone service had been placed under public control in 1895 and in the 1920s statutory provision was made to control the installation and operation of main electricity generating plant through the Electricity Commission and the Central Electricity Board.

[2] In 1972, for reasons which are wholly obscure, these excellent reports were demoted from their status as Parliamentary Papers. They are now published in a glossy format, with more obvious appeal to good public relations, by the corporations themselves, instead of, as previously, by HMSO. It is too early to tell whether this will permanently affect the standard of information which is publicly available regarding the public corporations, but it is an ominous trend.

[3] The north of Scotland, and after 1954 the south of Scotland also, had their own separate arrangements for generation and distribution.

[4] *Committee of Inquiry into the Electricity Supply Industry,* Cmd 9672, HMSO, 1955.

2 Aircraft Innovation and its Effect on Productivity in BEA

Summary

The cost problem affecting British European Airways was the need to bring down the cost of providing each unit of output, the capacity ton mile (CTM). While the ratio applying between the cost of providing each ton of capacity and the revenue received from it was more than the proportion of total capacity sold, the airline would make a loss. Profitability depended upon purchasing new types of aircraft, which could operate at lower costs than those which were available in the first years after the war.

The direct operating costs of an aircraft are made up of crew costs, fuel, landing fees and the cost of engineering maintenance and repairs (mostly labour costs). Other costs include capital charges and the overheads of administration, sales, ground handling and station costs. The bigger aircraft which were introduced, and which incorporated engine and airframe improvements, made little difference to the capital or fuel costs of each unit of output. The advantage which they provided was that in an era of rapidly growing demand they created huge savings, resulting from scale increases, in the productivity of labour employed in airline transport. The larger and faster aircraft produced many times more CTM per hour but the aircrew hours, engineering hours and ground personnel hours needed to support each aircraft flying hour increased only marginally, in spite of the large increase in output. Thus specifying the largest possible aircraft which was consistent with the growth of traffic densities was the airline's route to productivity improvement.

The difference between BEA and the other organisations studied is that the airline did not conduct its own research and development to produce new aircraft types. Its influence on development was thus confined to that which it could exercise as a customer in its choice of new equipment, but due to the innovative approach which the airline adopted that influence was considerable. It may be argued that the influence exercised by BEA as a customer on the development of aircraft was as significant in determining the choice of techniques as that which the other corporations exercised as major performers of research and development.

However, the technical decisions which BEA took were inseparable from the decisions made to purchase new aircraft. There was from the time of the airline's formation an established procedure for arriving at decisions to invest in new equipment. Forecasts of the anticipated level of traffic on each route were prepared by the commercial department and their implications for scheduling and service frequency were worked out with the flight

11

operations department. When, as happened at regular intervals, the growth of traffic indicated that larger aircraft were required, discussions were begun, involving the engineering department, in order that a recommendation about the new type required could be made to the Board.

Demand was thus the main determinant of the need for new aircraft, but the operational costs of the aircraft were also of great importance, since the airline had a commitment to operate profitably. The agency which was responsible for formulating an aircraft requirement in response to information from other departments was a group located in the engineering department. The department's experience of the cost of maintaining and operating existing types was fed into the purchase decision, to establish that the aircraft would be economically viable, as well as being of the right size and type.

The major new techniques incorporated in transport aircraft in the period 1945–75 had been invented before the second world war or else were developed during the war. The exceptions were the turbo-propeller engine, the fan jet engine and the various types of electronic navigational aids. The aircraft manufacturers and the various national governments undertook development; the airlines were called upon to exercise their judgment on the question of when these new techniques could be applied to civilian transport planes and what increases in scale could be attempted. The very large increases in the scale of output of individual aircraft, which multiplied the capacity ton miles produced per hour by the average airliner twenty or thirty times, did not always produce improvements in the capital productivity of the equipment. Where the scale increases benefitted efficiency was in cutting labour costs drastically.

BEA's policy was to innovate by introducing new types of aircraft of the largest size that was commercially prudent and to order them from the British industry in order to foster its commercial development. The results in the first fifteen years were satisfactory; the airline achieved profitable operation and the British industry produced its most successful transport aircraft. But the decisions involved in the transition from turbo-props to pure jets proved less happy and resulted in the airline having a number of aircraft during the 1960s which were not wholly suited to the routes on which they had to operate.

The advantage of using pure jets was that aircraft output could be trebled or quadrupled, compared to the piston engined and turbo-prop types which preceded them, while direct operating costs were slightly reduced and overheads, particularly labour, were substantially reduced, due to scale increases. The pure jet made possible the increase in scale which allowed labour productivity to improve. However, it appeared at first that the cost advantages would accrue only to the very large aircraft, such as the Boeing 707 and Douglas DC-8, which were being developed for longer hauls. Short-haul routes in Europe did not have the traffic density to allow the use of planes of this size. BEA decided to retain turbo-props for the shorter routes and introduce jets fairly slowly on the longer hauls. The jet which they chose, the Trident, did not have the increase in capacity and reduction of operating costs necessary to short-haul operation and which were demonstrated by its contemporary, the Boeing 727. The turbo-prop, the Vanguard, had to be moved on to secondary routes as it encountered jet competition.

The Trident and Vanguard were not positively unsuccessful in the BEA fleet, but they were not well suited to the traffic and competition in the 1960s. BEA's next major purchase decision resulted in the airline opting for American aircraft. Although the government did not allow the order to proceed, the decision to choose the Boeing 727 and Boeing 737 marked a major change in policy. It raises the question of whether the 'Buy British' policy had previously exerted an unfortunate effect upon the process of deciding the requirements of future purchases.

BEA's innovative role had been directed at sponsoring new aircraft for the British industry to manufacture. It was tacitly hoped that they would prove to be attractive to the world's airlines in general. However, when the 'Buy British' policy involved not considering projects from foreign manufacturers, the airline was in danger of becoming isolated, of being prevented from recognising how foreign manufacturers and foreign airline operators were thinking about their market needs. With projects from abroad excluded from BEA's detailed negotiation and specification procedures, the airline was less likely to arrive at a correct judgment of the type of aircraft which would satisfy world demand. This may have represented the greatest hindrance to the successful pursuit of the policy of innovation. It remains a moot point whether BEA had been best serving the interests of the British manufacturers by refusing to buy foreign aircraft, or whether, by evaluating the full range of alternative types, BEA would have come closer to agreeing with the industry on aircraft specifications which were also attractive to other airlines and which would thus have raised the sales of aircraft manufacturers.

The European routes served by British European Airways (BEA), now the European division of British Airways) were earlier under the control of British Overseas Airways; the latter was the nationally owned air corporation formed in 1939 to succeed Imperial Airways and the various short-haul carriers. Imperial Airways covered Europe as well as the other continents, but there was considerable precedence for developing European air routes separately from those longer distance aerial communications which were associated with the Empire. In 1946 this view, that European routes be developed separately, prevailed and the European airline was formed; this was in spite of the fact that continued efforts by the government to encourage cross-Channel and short-distance air transport with continental Europe since 1918 had met with little success.[1]

BEA came into being on 1 August 1946, as a result of the Civil Aviation Act, 1946, charged with the duty to develop air services in Europe as one of the exclusive scheduled carriers. This duty, it might fairly be said, the corporation has fulfilled with a thoroughness which would surely have surprised pre-war observers of civil aviation shortcomings. The route mileage served by the corporation grew rapidly from a few thousand miles in the first year to approaching 100,000 miles by 1975.

During this time the physical output of the corporation rose from just over 20 million to nearly 900 million capacity ton miles (CTM), as is shown in Tables 2.5 and 2.11. (One CTM is the provision of aircraft capacity sufficient to carry one ton for one mile.) World demand for air transport has regularly grown at around 10 per cent annually, at least until the oil crisis of the 1970s. By contrast BEA's capacity grew at approximately 13 per cent per year.

Much of this growth has been achieved by the airline in an environment of severe competition. During the early period, up to 1960, the competition was provided mainly by the flag-carrying national airlines of other European countries, Air France and Lufthansa being two of the main rivals, with Sabena of Belgium, Scandinavian Airlines (SAS) of Denmark, Norway and Sweden, KLM of Holland and Swissair following close behind. Rivalry for passenger traffic between these carriers, and others that operate in Europe, has always been strong. In the early 1960s the competition which BEA faced was increased by the new policy of the British Air Transport Licensing Board, allowing independent airlines to fly on domestic and foreign scheduled routes. In 1970 competition was again increased by the formation of a second force airline from two independent operators, British United and British Caledonian.[2]

However, airline competition is a regulated form of rivalry. Both fare structures and route flying rights are controlled by national and inter-national regulatory agencies. The intention of the regulation of fares is that no single airline on scheduled services should be able to attract extra passengers by cutting its price for air transport; this can be done only by the industry as a whole. The right to fly over certain routes is a matter for bargaining at government level; each nation reserves its power to grant route rights and usually allows foreign airlines to operate in exchange for equivalent reciprocal rights.

As a result, it may not be obvious in what direction competitive activity can be directed. The price is fixed, the product is undifferentiated except by minor variations in presentation. It is almost the classical economist's case of pure competition. However, with fixed fares and a standard product, the industry concentrates a great deal of attention upon attracting the customer by fringe benefits, by the frequency of services and the convenience of their timing. It is accepted within the airline industry that one of the major factors which influences customer choice is the standard of the equipment (the aircraft) operated by each airline. Apart from the more material consideration of speed of travel, quietness and comfort in the aircraft, customers are also attracted by sheer novelty.

Since there is little that the individual airline (outside the context of the International Air Transport Association, which regulates fares) can do to attract passengers by reducing prices or stimulating demand, it is vital from a competitive point of view that no airline allows its equipment on scheduled routes to appear less modern, slower or less comfortable than that of its rivals. Further restraints on competition are often provided by pooling agreements, which affect frequency of service and timing. These operate between two or more airlines which have equivalent rights to fly over certain routes (e.g., Air France and BEA on the London to Paris route). The airlines make agreements about the amount of capacity each will provide in terms of seat-miles per day. They then share out the proceeds of the services. In these circumstances, if one operator has a turbo-prop and the other a jet to use on the route, the latter will get most of the traffic. Thus regulation of competition affects the type of aircraft operated.

The premium on new aircraft types can accelerate the process of adoption of new technology. It stimulates the airline into ordering new equipment, in an attempt to be a monopoly operator until other airlines catch up. It ensures that, if one airline successfully introduces an advance in techniques and achieves it without raising costs, other competing airlines will soon be forced to raise their equipment to the same standard to avoid losing customers. Seen against a background of rapid technical development in aviation since the second world war, the regulation of air transport appears to be a force working towards rapid technological change in the air transportation business.

Background technical developments in aviation were much accelerated by the war. Considerable increases in loads carried by aircraft and in the speeds at which they flew resulted from military needs. The basic invention of the jet engine in Germany and in England was hastened in its development by the availability of finance from war budgets. The aerodynamic theory of wing design for aircraft approaching the speed of sound benefitted greatly from German research before and during the war years. One or two important techniques for the postwar period derived from the 1920s and earlier. Different types of flaps for the trailing edge of the wing and slots for the leading edge were developed and patented from 1919 onwards. Stressed skin metal construction for the airframe, first perfected for the DC-1 and DC-3 by 1935, came from a series of earlier developments and has subsequently been used by all advanced commercial airliners. Probably the most important change which came from the postwar years, on the other hand, was the fan-type jet engine and its development, the high by-pass ratio engine, introduced in Britain and America in the early 1960s.[3]

The race to incorporate all these techniques in new airliners was one which occupied the thirty years after the war and involved some half-dozen governments as well as a score of aircraft manufacturing companies. BEA, as a major British customer for aircraft, was in a position to help determine the outcome of the race. The airline was an enthusiastic proponent of new aircraft and new techniques. It did not stand in the way of innovation. But it had a number of corporate objectives: development of services, profitable operations, support for the British aircraft industry; and it had a complicated relationship with the British government. The airline, as it existed before the merger with British Airways, was also an oddity among European international operators; having no services outside the continent, its route structure gave an average length of journey stage of 250—300 miles, where its rivals were operating at average stage lengths of 500 to 1,300 miles.

BEA's corporate objectives in the postwar context and its special position as a short-haul operator took its technical policy in one major direction, towards the introduction of a commercially profitable and fully competitive short-haul airliner. The aircraft sought had to operate profitably well below the 300 miles stage length, in order to make most of the airline's routes pay. The other stipulation, partly self-imposed and partly imposed by the government, was that the aircraft had to be British. The story of how BEA tried to introduce such an airliner and what prevented it from achieving it occupies the remainder of this chapter.

THE ECONOMIC SHORT-HAUL AIRCRAFT — SUCCESS IN THE 1950s

The decade of the 1950s was a successful one for British European Airways. Success came in three major areas of endeavour. As a British public corporation, it began to operate in surplus and to provide a small but steady return on capital; as a major international air carrier, it attracted an increasing share of passenger traffic; and as an industrial producer of air transportation, BEA managed to increase output per employee, to reduce costs and to follow a vigorously expansionary policy, both opening up new routes and introducing new aircraft.

These achievements should not each be viewed in isolation, even though it is more convenient to describe them singly. Profitability, commercial policy and technical change are merely different aspects of corporate strategy and as such the objectives set in each area are best co-ordinated with those of other areas. Thus gaining the right to fly over new routes and introducing more advanced aircraft are the two classic forms of competition open to airlines. Profitability depends upon, first, the new aircraft being so specified and operated that their actual revenue-earning capacity is properly related to the investment which they represent; second, it is dependent upon the airline correctly judging how much capacity to provide for the traffic anticipated, having regard to the cost of providing each unit of capacity and the revenue which selling each unit will produce. Technical changes in aero engines and airframe design, when embodied in new aircraft, provide the opportunity to lower costs, improve productivity and increase the earning power of the airline's stock of capital equipment. Thus innovation may provide a source of competitive strength and of improved profitability at one and the same time.

FINANCIAL PROFITABILITY

Table 2.1 provides some overall figures covering BEA's financial performance as a public corporation up to 1963. Profits were first earned during the year ended 31 March 1955 and during the years 1956 to 1961 a consistently profitable record was maintained. The capital assets which BEA took over in 1946 had a low monetary value and were quickly and easily phased out, leaving the airline free to replace them wholesale with newer and more productive capital equipment.[4] Thus the historic capital embodied in capital equipment at 31 March 1947 was insignificant in relation to the airline's development. The airline business was expanding

Table 2.1   *BEA's Operating Revenue and Return on Capital, 1948—63*

Year ending 31 March	Operating revenue (£m.)	Surplus on operations[a] (£m.)	Capital employed[b] (£m.)	Return on Capital[c] (%)	Net profit (£m.)
1948	4·1	−3·3[d]	3·7	nil	—
1953	13·1	−1·2[d]	16·0	nil	—
1956	21·6	1·2	16·6	7·2	0·6
1957	24·0	0·8	24·7	3·2	0·2
1958	28·3	1·9	32·7	5·8	1·1
1959	31·8	1·4	39·2	3·6	0·2
1960	36·5	3·2	51·7	6·2	2·1
1961	42·3	2·7	65·2	4·2	1·5
1962	46·4	0·5	83·2	0·6	−1·5
1963	51·2	2·8	87·1	3·2	−0·3

Source: BEA, *Annual Reports.*
Notes: [a] After deducting depreciation, but before deducting interest on capital.
   [b] Capital liabilities plus reserves.
   [c] Operating surplus as a proportion of capital employed.
   [d] Losses in early years were substantially covered by an exchequer grant.

so rapidly that BEA was able to change its stock of aircraft every few years, and aircraft were the major part of the capital stock.

In those industries where much of the capital equipment lasts five or ten times as long as its gestation period, it is difficult to associate a specific set of technical decisions with overall corporate performance, but in the airline business the turnover of items of capital equipment is much quicker, and is more closely related to the gestation period. For instance, the main development of the Viscount was from 1945 to 1952 and the first version, the V701, saw service with BEA from 1953 to 1963. During its years of service it was supported by the derivative Viscount, the V800 series. Gestation periods for the aircraft which followed the Viscount — the Vanguard, the Comet 4B and Trident 1 — were from 1955 to 1960, from 1956 to 1960 and from 1957 to 1964 respectively.[5] These three types then saw mainline service for about ten years each. The financial and operating results of the aircraft's period of service can be related to the decision to purchase it and used as one criterion to judge its success.

In Table 2.2, BEA's performance is measured against that of the other major European carriers.[6] The number of passenger miles, or kilometres, carried is not of course a comprehensive measure of the competitive strength of an airline. International operations are highly regulated, traffic rights between major centres being a matter for careful bargaining and negotiation by airlines and governments. Thus traffic growth for each airline reflects, as well as airline competitiveness, the comparative importance of the airline's airports as arrival and departure points. There is, however, a strong element of competitive strength determining the passenger loads carried, in that a successful airline, expanding its services

Table 2.2   *European Airlines and International Traffic: Traffic Carried 1948—60* (million passenger seat kilometres p.a.)

Year	KLM	SAS	Sabena	Swissair	Air France	BEA	Totals	BEA share (%)
1948	721	341	173	54	815	243	2,347	10·4
1950	1,251	509	478	147	1,118	417	3,920	10·6
1955	1,484	1,086	579	465	2,225	1,108	6,947	15·9
1960	2,660	2,199	1,264	1,138	3,953	2,132	13,346	16·0

Source: International Civil Aviation Organisation, *Digest of Statistics,* No. 90, 'Traffic 1947—61'.

and using new equipment, will attract more passengers to use its airports as staging posts.

BEA's success as a carrier in the 1950s was considerable, and it is understated by the table. To begin with, BEA was relatively little involved in pooling agreements during the 1950s; its rate of expansion is more attributable to its policies and less explicable merely in terms of a favourable build-up of traffic at the airports where BEA operated, than would have been the case if pooling were in effect for most of the period.

BEA was distinctive among major international airlines as being the only one to operate largely short-haul routes. Table 2.3 shows that there was a gap of about 50 per cent between the average journey length of BEA passengers and that of the nearest airline, Swissair. BEA's European rivals were operating both in the short to medium-range market, where BEA was competing, and in the long-range market, particularly the North Atlantic routes, where BEA had no operations at all. For BEA to have increased its market share of the passenger kilometres carried by the six airlines of Table 2.2 argues that the British airline was expanding its share of the short-range routes rather faster than its overall share was increasing, given that the long-range traffic of the others was not declining. From 1958 onwards, when the long-range jets were being introduced on the

Table 2.3   *International Airlines: Stage Length and Journey Length*[7] (*late 1950s*)

Airline	BEA	BOAC	Swiss-air	SAS	KLM	Air France	PAA	TWA
Mean stage length (miles)	263	1,048	660	n.a.	n.a.	937	1,440	n.a.
Mean journey length (miles)	329	2,929	489	671	1313	763	1,306	893

Source: BEA evidence to the Select Committee on Nationalised Industries, *The Air Corporations,* HMSO, 1959.

Table 2.4   *British European Airways: Average Stage Distance, 1957—65*

Year ending 31 March	1957	1958	1959	1960	1961	1962	1963	1964	1965
Stage length (miles)	260	266	278	285	288	289	291	299	315

Source: BEA, *Annual Reports.*

Atlantic routes, BEA suffered as far as market share was concerned in not being able to participate in the upsurge of demand for longer distance travel.[8]

BEA incurred cost disadvantages as a result of the very short stage lengths which its aircraft flew. Short stage lengths decrease the utilisation of the aircraft, thus increasing overheads, and they increase the incidence of landing fees and handling costs; they also make for a higher level of fuel and maintenance costs per aircraft mile.[9]

The introduction of pure jets into airline service between 1958 and 1968 saw an operating cost reduction for medium- to long-haul airlines of 40 to 50 per cent at constant prices. An airline with a mean stage length of 1,000 miles operating at 30d per CTM in 1958 could expect to have reduced those costs to 15—18d per CTM at constant 1958 prices by 1968.[10] On short-haul routes, such as those operated by BEA, operating costs were reduced by a smaller proportion, from about 39d in 1962 to 33d in 1970 (constant 1958 prices), which was the period during which pure jets took over on the shorter journeys. For short-haul work the economies of speed and increased capacity which the pure jets provided were marginal, because the distances involved were not great enough to give more than a slight increase in the rate of utilisation (aircraft hours per day) and the rate of aircraft output (CTM per hour) compared to turbo-prop aircraft.

INNOVATION IN AIRCRAFT

BEA successfully introduced into service four new types of aircraft during the first fourteen years of operations: the Vickers Viking, Airspeed Ambassador, Vickers Viscount and Vickers Vanguard. All four aircraft were pioneered by BEA, being adopted by the airline before any other commercial user was in sight and in some cases being modified or designed to suit the airline's particular view of the type of aeroplane which would be most successful commercially. What is more, the choice of these British aircraft was made at a time when the acknowledged lead in civil transport aircraft was held by American types. The obvious choice of commercial airliner during the late 1940s was one of the American designs, such as the Douglas DC-4 or DC-6 or the Convair CV-240. The two latter aircraft were brought into service in the United States in 1947 and proved popular choices for many commercial airlines, but BEA did not buy them.

The Vickers Viking was ordered before the formation of BEA by the Ministry of Supply. Its appearance and design were similar to the DC-3, except that it initially had fabric-covered wings. These were later changed to metal stressed skin construction. The engines, 770 hp Bristol Hercules, were 25 per cent more powerful than the DC-3s and its cruising speed was nearly 200 m.p.h. compared to 167 m.p.h. for the DC-3. The Viking which BEA bought, altered to suit the airline, had twenty-seven seats; forty-eight of these aircraft were at one time or another owned by BEA between 1946 and 1954.

The other aircraft with which BEA built up its operations was the DC-3, known to BEA and the British public as the Dakota. Once the Viking was over its introductory troubles, the DC-3 was used mainly on British internal flights. In 1949 the DC-3 was already fourteen years old, and although an extraordinary and versatile aircraft, could not be expected to serve as mainline type for very much longer.[11] But BEA could not find a replacement which was sufficiently reliable and as cheap to operate. The airline's engineering department decided to extend the DC-3s life by redesigning it and substantially rebuilding the fuselage, making it into the thirty-two-seat Pionair. It was intended that the Pionair should stay in service until 1956, but, for various reasons, the DC-3 type did not leave BEA's routes until 1962. During the years 1948—50, BEA also increased the DC-3 fleet size from twenty-two to fifty aircraft, by buying surplus aircraft from a variety of sources.

BEA's second aircraft type of new design was the Airspeed Ambassador, known in BEA by its class name, the Elizabethan. Although the airline expressed itself well satisfied with the Elizabethan's performance and operating economics, it does not seem to have been a very successful aircraft. Designed by a small company, Airspeed Ltd, in 1945/6 as a DC-3 replacement, it would have had to approach the performance of its American equivalents in order to provide the airline with a reasonable rate of revenue earning.

Airspeed was taken over by de Havilland in 1948, before the first Elizabethan was delivered, and de Havilland completed the order for twenty aircraft. Technical difficulties with performance and reliability delayed introduction by a year, and it was underdeveloped when finally brought into service during 1952. In spite of having engines rather more powerful than the Convair CV-240, the Elizabethan seems to have suffered from airframe drag, and its cruising speed was lower.[12]

Following hard on the heels of the Elizabethan came the well known Vickers Viscount. During the war the Ministry of Aircraft Production had at its head for a brief time Lord Brabazon of Tara. He had been associated with powered flight from its very earliest days and was personally acquainted with a number of the aircraft industry's great men, some of whom he had known since his youth. In the latter half of the war Brabazon convened the most eminent industry leaders in a series of semi-formal Brabazon Committee meetings, to discuss what aircraft Britain should build to catch up with the American lead in transport aeroplanes. The result was a large number of ideas for projects. After the war about £40m. of government finance was made available for eight aircraft types, developed in the late 1940s and early 1950s. The Viscount was the one successful project which owed its existence, at least partly, to this policy mechanism. Vickers and Rolls Royce were the companies which provided the initiative, basing their project proposal upon a Brabazon suggestion.

Work started towards the end of the war and a test prototype, the V630, was flying in 1948. No other turbo-prop airliners were in existence and its operating performance was something of an unknown quantity. BEA had examined the anticipated economics of turbo-prop transport and had concluded (in 1948) that the gain in output and reduction in running cost which resulted from higher speeds and lower fuel consumption at an expected height of 20,000 feet would be offset by the time taken to reach that height on short stage lengths and by air traffic control delays. However, the prototype, the V630, did a world proving trip which had an impressive effect. Vickers, Rolls Royce and the Ministry of Supply continued to back the project.

The V630 seated thirty to thirty-five passengers, which was probably too small a number to make costs competitive and to handle the growth of passenger traffic. By 1949 BEA had begun to find that traffic was building up on its longer routes, on which the turbo-prop characteristics of height and speed gave greater advantage. Vickers had also announced the forty-passenger (forty-seven by the time it went into service) development of the prototype, known as the V700 series. In August 1949 BEA decided to order twenty V701s, and they came into service during 1953. Over 440 of this aircraft and its derivatives were built, of which three-quarters were for foreign airlines; the government received a levy on sales and recouped about double its initial outlay, although it lost heavily on most other aircraft projects of the early postwar period.

In 1953 and 1954 BEA negotiated a larger Viscount model with Vickers, the V800 series. By the time BEA's competitors had brought their V700s into service, BEA was preparing for this development version. Using the same Dart engine, developing about 20 per cent more power, the V800 series carried fifty-seven and later seventy-one passengers. Its cruising speed was slightly reduced compared to the V700, because of the drag of the extended fuselage.

OPERATING ECONOMICS

The DC-3, the Viking and the up-rated DC-3 Pionair had direct operating costs per seat mile which were very similar.[13] All three aircraft returned reduced costs per seat-mile for longer stage lengths up to about 600 miles, at which distance the Viking was cheaper to operate than the DC-3. The DC-3 had the best economics up to stage lengths of 350 miles. When converted to the Pionair it had several advantages over the Viking, including five extra seats and lower capital costs, and it appears to have been more economical to fly over most stage lengths than the Viking, although of course the thirty-two-seat conversion could not be considered as a mainline aircraft.

The Elizabethan represented primarily a step forward in carrying capacity. Its direct operating economics were no worse than those of the previous types of aircraft, and, given general inflation in prices and wages, this represented an improvement. Even so, the Pionair showed up in *Annual Reports* with slightly lower direct seat mile costs between 1953 and 1955. Allowing that the Pionair was being used on the unprestigious routes, the comparison shows that the scale increases of Elizabethan aircraft had their effect on direct operating economics reduced by airframe inefficiency and engineering costs. The advantages of the aircraft were that its larger size allowed increased passenger traffic to be carried at no greater direct cost than before and at a reduced overhead cost.[14] The aircraft was also popular with passengers. Having a high wing it allowed a good view to everyone with a window seat. In those days of predominantly petrol engined aircraft, operating heights were often around 5,000 feet and the view was a saleable commodity.

The Viscount's direct operating costs per seat-mile were lower than those of the Elizabethan throughout the years 1953/8, during which they were operated together.[15] This was in spite of the fact that the Viscount was about 25 per cent more expensive, in the initial capital cost of the aircraft with major spare parts, and was basically more expensive to run. Standing charges and promotional costs were higher, fuel and oil were consumed in larger quantities by the four engined Viscount; fixed costs, such as landing fees, handling charges and insurance, tended to be higher.

Although it was a commercial and technical success, the Viscount did not represent the type of breakthrough in aircraft efficiency or operating economics which its reputation and widespread adoption would have caused people to expect. It did not halve operating costs in the course of a few years as had the DC-3 in 1935.[16] The improvement in airframe efficiency was probably negligible, compared to previous types from the DC-3 onwards. The only significant improvement in efficiency came from the turbine-drive propeller engine. Because the Viscount produced substantially more power from its four turbo-props while cruising than the Elizabethan did from its two petrol engines, the Viscount was able to travel at 316 m.p.h. compared to the Elizabethan's 240 m.p.h. This resulted in average speeds over the same stage lengths of approximately 230 m.p.h. and 185 m.p.h. But this advantage had to be paid for in higher fuel consumption.[17] This factor, together with the other costs mentioned above, meant that the Viscount was more expensive to operate per revenue flying hour than the Elizabethan. Had the Elizabethan been able to maintain its best performance for most of its operating life, this gap in costs, amounting to as much as 30 per cent in favourable circumstances, would have substantially overcome the Elizabethan's disadvantage of a slower cruising speed. In the American airlines' operating experience of the more developed Viscount models during the late 1950s, the direct operating cost advantage of the turbo-prop over conventional petrol engined equivalents was no more than 5 per cent.

How was it, then, that the Viscount did actually operate more cheaply than the Elizabethan, and how did it turn out to be a success? The answer is that the Viscount, like the DC-3 before it, was a carefully balanced mixture of available techniques, which were both the most advanced at the time yet fully enough developed to be used without incurring heavy development costs while the aircraft was in service.

Table 2.12 shows that, in terms of capital cost per unit of annual output, the Viscount had a slight advantage over the Elizabethan. This is in contrast to the capital costs per unit of output of successive propeller driven aircraft in the United States at the same period. The combination of a fairly small turbo-prop engine with a relatively cheap and light airframe proved a happy one.[18]

The Viscount gained a bigger advantage because of its reliability, lower servicing costs and better state of development when it entered service. Turbine engines are simpler and easier to maintain than piston engines, and having less vibration they place fewer strains on the airframe. The Dart engines used in the Viscount 700 and 800 series eventually reached overhaul lives of 5,000 hours, but a good piston engine only averages 2,000—2,500 hours. The result was much lower engineering costs; engineering related charges can account for 30 per cent of overall airline costs.

Finally, there was the effect of stage length. BEA calculated in 1954 that the Elizabethan would be cheaper per seat-mile than the Viscount up to about 350 or 400 miles, but the shortfall in performance of the former and improved performance of the latter make it doubtful whether the piston engined aircraft would have really been more economical beyond 250 miles. Nevertheless, the Viscount's operating costs were undoubtedly helped by the fact that it was usually flying over average stage lengths of 400-plus miles, where the Elizabethan was used at 300 mile stage lengths on average.

THE VISCOUNT AND PASSENGER APPEAL

The factors discussed above show what caused the Viscount to be an economical aircraft. What caused it to be a success was passenger appeal. When BEA judged in 1948 that the turbo-prop would not be able to operate with advantage on their routes, they had probably not been able to allow for the effect upon passengers of speed, comfort and novelty. The travelling public was found to discriminate between different aircraft on the same route, even where the time saving was as little as ten minutes in an hour's flight. Thus the Viscount was a success on the London—Paris route, for which it had not been designed.[19] The lack of vibration compared to a piston aircraft proved very popular, and the plain fact that the Viscount was observably novel also attracted passengers. As a result, BEA's competitors also bought Viscounts, even though most had previously operated American aircraft.

Thus the major gains of the period 1946—60, which reduced BEA's airline costs per CTM by half at current prices (Table 2.5) and to about one-third of their 1948 level at constant prices, were only partly achieved by reduced direct operation costs.[20] The contribution made to direct operating costs just about kept pace with inflation, which averaged 4 per cent annually over the period. Most of this improvement should be attributed to advances made in techniques which allowed aircraft to carry larger loads, rather than to innovations which improved the efficiency of an aircraft of the same size as its predecessor. The larger part of the reduction in airline costs per CTM came from savings in overheads. Although organisational changes, improvement of ground handling facilities and of airport traffic control procedures helped to create these savings, they should again mainly be attributed to scale increases. Overall labour productivity was increasing very quickly at this period (Table 2.13) and it seems probable that the output efficiency of airport facilities was also improving.

THE DETERMINANTS OF PROFITABLE OPERATION

During 1959 BEA's fleet consisted of 109 aircraft. Sixty-three of them were Viscounts of the various types mentioned, Britain's most successful transport aircraft, and forty-one were the converted DC-3/Pionair, up to that time the most successful transport aircraft ever produced.

The financial success and competitive strength of BEA in the period 1956—61 is very closely associated with the performance of these two aircraft. In terms of financial success, the bulk of the capital employed in the business consisted of aircraft, and the economic performance of the aircraft used in carrying passengers and freight was the factor which fundamentally determined whether or not the airline operated profitably. BEA's policy had been to develop profitable air services, and, with one important reservation, this objective had guided its choice of aircraft.

In the years before the arrival of the Viscount, BEA had made fairly heavy losses, although these were gradually being reduced as the volume of traffic grew and the system of organisation improved. The airline's management explained the economic constraints which determined for them the limits of profitability in successive issues of the *Annual Report*. Fundamentally, the problem was that before 1953 the operating costs of the aircraft BEA had available were higher than their capacity to generate revenue. In fact, BEA might well have faced increasing losses during the 1950s as the traffic built up, were it not for the fact that there are increasing returns to scale with increased airline output.[21]

Nevertheless, BEA faced the problem that early aircraft had direct operating costs which were fairly close to the revenue received per seat sold. As a consequence, it was only when most or all of the seats were sold that the aircraft contributed to overheads.[22] To add to the problem, the general trend of fares, which determine the revenue rate per seat-mile, was downwards, because the rate-fixing body, the International Air Transport Association, was concerned to stimulate traffic growth. Operators which were using cheaper aircraft than BEA and which had a higher proportion of longer and better paying routes in their route structure, were able to counter declining revenue rates by cutting direct operating costs.

On the face of it, total costs could be met by improving the load factor or by cutting the overhead. But, in fact, the first course of action would have meant running only the popular services, and thus losing on the total number of passengers and suffering increased overheads. The second course of action was actively pursued by trying to improve the efficiency of the centralised facilities and staff. It was easiest to achieve through expansion. With more capacity ton miles being performed each year, the fixed overheads of administration and central facilities could be spread over a greater number of units.

REDUCING COSTS

Table 2.5 shows the slow progress made towards reduced costs per CTM during the years 1947 to 1955 (column 4). During that time the number of seat-miles sold went up by five times, a factor which helped to reduce costs and provided the expansion necessary for the introduction of larger aircraft. An indication of this is given by showing what happened if aircraft capacities did not keep pace with demand. From 1948 to 1952 the number of seats per aircraft varied between twenty and twenty-five, but it reached thirty-three in 1953 (the effect of full introduction of the Viscount and Elizabethan) and forty-seven by 1958, when the fleet was substantially Viscounts and Pionairs. Between 1951 and 1952 the expected introduction of the Elizabethan was delayed. The airline had to increase its seat-miles sold by 20 per cent without being able to use larger aircraft (columns 2 and 3 of Table 2.5). Costs per CTM rose rapidly, both because of increases in input prices (wages, fuel, etc.) and because of the inability of the existing aircraft to cover overheads.

Table 2.5 also illustrates the relationship which exists between costs and profit. By comparing the figures in column 6, the ratio of capacity available to the load carried (the load factor), with the figures in column 7, the ratio of the costs of each unit of capacity to revenue obtained from each unit sold, it can be seen that where the load factor (column 6) is greater than the cost to revenue ratio (column 7), the airline makes a profit. Losses occur when the load factor is less than the cost to revenue ratio.

HOW PROFITS CAN BE REACHED

It can quickly be seen why this happens. No airline can expect to sell all the capacity it produces. It is regarded as quite acceptable to sell between 50 and 70 per cent of the CTMs produced each year by scheduled passenger and freight services. Statistically, this can equally well be considered as the airline selling a proportion of each unit of capacity. Provided that the proportion of each unit sold is not less than the ratio between the cost of providing a full unit and the revenue receivable from a

Table 2.5 *BEA Output, Costs and Revenue, 1948—62*

1	2	3	4	5	6	7	8	9
Year ending 31 March	CTMs offered (m.)	LTMs sold (m.)	Total costs per CTM (d.)	Traffic revenue per LTM (d.)	Ratio of CTM/LTM (overall load factor) col. 2/col. 3 (%)	Ratio of cost/CTM to rev./LTM col. 4/col. 5 (%)	Passenger load factor (%)	Profit[a] (£m.)
1948	21·6	13·5	83·6	73·3	63	114	69	−3·3
1949	28·6	17·9	67·8	72·8	63	93	65	−2·8
1950	40·2	24·8	49·2	66·5	62	74	63	−1·3
1951	52·9	30·6	45·2	70·6	58	64	59	−1·0
1952	56·7	36·7	51·8	70·8	65	73	67	−1·4
1953	69·2	43·5	50·6	72·4	63	70	65	−1·5
1954	83·6	53·6	47·5	66·2	64	72	66	−1·8
1955	98·3	63·6	41·7	64·6	65	65	68	
1956	124·5	78·7	40·5	65·9	63	62	69	0·6
1957	139·1	98·7	41·0	64·1	65	64	70	0·2
1958	160·3	102·1	40·9	66·6	64	61	69	1·1
1959	181·1	109·4	41·8	69·7	60	60	63	0·2
1960	192·0	130·0	43·1	67·5	68	64	69	2·1
1961	237·4	154·8	41·4	65·6	65	63	68	1·5
1962	282·0	169·0	41·0	66·4	60	62	61	−1·5

Source: BEA, *Annual Reports, 1952—62.*
Notes: [a] Losses during 1947—54 were largely covered by an exchequer grant.
         [b] Net profit after interest in 1954/5 was £63,000.

full unit, then losses will not be sustained. Thus if a unit costs 6·5d to provide, including direct and overhead costs, and can be sold for 10d then the cost to revenue ratio is 65 per cent. Sales of 65 per cent of units are needed to cover costs. The airline's load factor must be kept above this level or costs per unit must be reduced.

BEA's policy in choosing aircraft throughout the early years of its operations reflected the urgency of bringing costs into a better relationship with the revenue obtainable. The 1949/50 *Annual Report* expressed concern at the adverse trends in traffic revenue, and in the following year the relationship between operating economics and larger aircraft was stressed. In 1953/4 the *Report* pointed out that, although the load factor had been improved and the cost per CTM had fallen by 6 per cent, the revenue rate had gone down by more than 8 per cent as a result of the introduction of tourist fares by IATA. Profitable operation was still a year away.

The Viscount and Elizabethan were fully introduced into service by 1954. With their arrival BEA had aircraft which were large enough to operate at no higher direct cost and to bring down the overhead cost. The ratio of airline costs per CTM to revenue received per LTM fell below the load factor and profits were recorded in 1955.

With the operation of the Pionair, BEA faced a different set of constraints. By the late 1950s this aircraft was being used on domestic routes, where the revenue rate was lower than for international flights. But the Pionair could not be expected to achieve lower total costs per CTM than the newer aircraft. By producing direct operating costs of only 5·0d per seat-mile, compared to 4·4d per seat-mile for the Viscount (1956), the DC-3 Pionair was doing as well as could be expected. The ratio between costs per CTM and the revenue rate on domestic routes could not be expected to fall below any achieveable load factor. The Pionair's CTM costs were starting to rise because of its age and its use on shorter routes. There was little more that could be done to improve the aircraft's productivity.[23] The load factor which would have been required to make the Pionair profitable in the late 1950s was in the region of 85 per cent and there was no way of achieving that on scheduled services.

In spite of making a loss, the Pionair was indispensable to the task of making BEA profitable. The airline accepted the obligation to run low density unprofitable routes around Britain's coasts and there was probably no other aircraft which could have done this and lost money only at the rate of 20 per cent of full costs. BEA had spent a good deal of time looking for an aircraft to make the low-density domestic routes pay. Several aircraft were proposed but not built; the best configuration for these routes may have been similar to the Britten Norman Islander, which was developed much later.

The Pionair was the 'least unsuccessful' candidate of the 1950s because it combined the operating capacities of a reasonably large aircraft with very low fixed costs. DC-3s in the period after the war were changing hands at prices around £5,000. BEA's Pionairs stood in the books at

£20,000 capital cost each, after conversion. Thus interest, depreciation and other standing charges were extremely low, while fuel and most running costs per seat-mile were at least no higher than for any practicable replacement and not much higher per seat-mile than those of the Viscount. Where the Pionair lost out was in flying crew pay, engineering costs and in bearing its due share of BEA overheads, but an airline which was much smaller than BEA and was organised on different lines to carry very low overheads might have been able to make the DC-3 routes pay in a good year.

The purely rational principles behind the aircraft procurement policy of any airline in BEA's position were thus those of trying to achieve a ratio of costs to revenue rates which was lower than the load factor at which the aircraft were likely to operate. The revenue rate being strictly beyond the airline's individual control, after the attack on costs there remained the load factor as the third element in the relationship which affected profitability. Obviously advertising, reputation, service and other intangible factors affect the public's desire to travel by a particular airline, but these are difficult to analyse. Airline experience is that the load factor carried on passenger services is observably affected by aircraft qualities, particularly speed, comfort and novelty.

BEA had pursued a cost reduction objective in aircraft choice and had clearly exhibited a reluctance to purchase or operate any aircraft which had costs above the rates obtainable in revenue, or which failed to contribute to the overall aim of reducing the airline's average costs per capacity ton mile. But there was one proviso which at first sight detracted from BEA's determination to lower seat-mile costs, and become a profitable airline. This was the policy of buying British aircraft, first publicly stated as a commitment in the *Annual Report* of 1950/1.

'Buy and fly British' appeared to be in contradiction to the airline's avowed intention to become profitable, because the British aircraft of the period were more expensive to operate than American ones. For short-haul operations BEA could probably not have bettered the DC-3/Pionair which served it from 1947 to 1962, as many other airlines found. But for BEA's longer hauls, of stage lengths between 300 and 700 miles, cheaper aircraft were passed over in order to fly British. Neither the Viking nor the Elizabethan compared favourably in cost or performance with the Convair 240 and its derivative, the Convair 340. Many of BEA's competitor airlines in Europe were flying Douglas DC-4s and DC-6s by the end of the 1940s. Although not strictly comparable with BEA types, both were well developed and highly competitive aircraft. The Viscount was the first aircraft which achieved cost and performance figures which were close to American transport aircraft. Although not an aircraft which reduced operating costs dramatically, the developed Viscount V800 probably gave better cost and performance figures on European stage lengths of 500 miles than Douglas aircraft would have done.

In operating British aircraft on its route structure of comparatively short stage lengths, BEA was involved in a risky enterprise which had its penalties. According to the figures which were produced for the Select Committee of 1958/9, BEA's average cost per CTM in 1956 and 1957 was rather higher than that of most of its European rivals, even though the Viscount had been in service for three years by that time.[24] If other airlines had had higher operating costs, BEA might have been able to pay for its innovatory approach by persuading them to raise general revenue rates. As it was, the internationally agreed revenue rates were more likely to suit BEA's rivals than BEA.

BEA did not only face extra running costs through choosing innovatory aircraft. There were also introductory costs and they could be heavy. The airline calculated that it had lost about £½m. of potential revenue as a result of technical deficiencies in the early months of the Viking's service (1947/8). Modifications to the Elizabethan were expensive to perform and the shortfall in its performance delayed introduction by more than a year. No figure was set on the revenue lost, but the cost of providing the extra planned services with equipment which was less economical to operate, and of carrying out engineering development, was estimated at £225,000. There were also introductory costs associated with the Viscount, but that aircraft was brought into service fairly well up to time and in an advanced stage of engineering development, so that these costs were not heavy.

Against these extra costs, BEA had to place the advantage of being the monopoly operator of a number of aircraft types which were distinctly different from the competition on European routes. The Viking had a slight lead in the short-haul transport field during 1946 and 1947, being available before the Convair 240 and Martin 202, and being faster than the DC-3.[25] The Elizabethan, with its high-wing design and more than usually comfortable interior, was also thought to have special passenger appeal.[26] With the Viscount, BEA had for over a year a complete monopoly of turbo-prop aircraft operation. The Viscount built up a reputation for quietness and comfort, and was considerably faster than the aircraft it was competing against in Europe. It appears to have started off by operating at even higher load factors than were common for new aircraft upon their first introduction.[27]

BEA argued that the policy of operating advanced or novel aircraft resulted in higher load factors. The London to Paris route was cited as an example to the Select Committee of 1958/9. If higher load factors were achieved, they would balance to some extent the higher costs which an innovatory policy on aircraft procurement seemed to imply.

The evidence about load factors is difficult to interpret, and points to no definite conclusions. On the one hand, the Elizabethan in its first year of service achieved a passenger load factor of 63 per cent, which was no higher than that of the older BEA aircraft in service at the time, while the Viscount started the following year with a passenger load factor of 69 per cent. On the other hand, both aircraft were introduced rather later than the build-up in traffic demand would have justified and the load factor achieved may have represented the relationship between exogenously determined demand for travel and the aircraft capacity available to meet it.

Table 2.6 shows the load factors for passenger services in the main European airlines from 1950 to 1961. BEA's figures are considerably higher than the others from 1954, the first full year of Viscount services, to 1957, by which time many airlines had equipment which was as good. Air France is the exception, approaching BEA's figures in 1955—7, but Air France had also ordered Viscounts and 1955 was the first full year of that airline's operations with the new aircraft. Both BEA and Air France were well above the world average for load factor during the first four years of the Viscount's service.[28]

Table 2.6 *Airline Load Factors, 1950—61 (passengers)*.

Calendar Year	World Average[a]	Air France	BEA	KLM	Sabena	SAS	Swiss-air	Alitalia
1950	n.a.	64	60	61	49	55	58	52
1951	64	69	66	63	52	58	63	68
1952	64	66	65	63	51	57	65	71
1953	62	64	66	63	50	52	63	64
1954	61	62	68	57	47	49	58	54
1955	62	67	70	60	52	54	64	55
1956	63	69	70	62	54	57	64	55
1957	61	69	70	60	57	56	62	57
1958	59	63	63	53	56	55	59	55
1959	60	63	69	54	53	58	60	56
1960	59	62	68	55	53	56	68	58
1961	55	55	63	50	54	50	61	54

Source: International Civil Aviation Organisation (ICAO), Series T.19.
Note: [a] All airlines reporting to ICAO.

The evidence is not inconsistent with the Viscount being an aircraft of high passenger appeal, and BEA may well have done better by having bought the Viscount than it would have done with any other equipment available at the time. But it seems more likely that the innovatory policy succeeded because it was contained by strictly commercial constraints on the aircraft's specifications and performance, not because it placed invention and novelty at the head of the airline's priorities. The constraints imposed on the specification, size of aircraft, seating capacity, range, power, etc., meant that the V701 Viscount turned out to be the right size for the market of the 1950s, where the V630 prototype would have been a failure. The actual specification also meant that the larger aircraft had slightly reduced direct costs, where a smaller aircraft would have been more expensive to operate.

THE AIRCRAFT OF THE 1960s

The new aircraft, such as the Viscount, which BEA operated during the 1950s were conceived as basic types during or immediately after the war;

they were developed into commercial machines during the late 1940s. By ordering a stretched version of the Viscount, BEA was able to operate profitably without introducing a new mainline aircraft between the start of Viscount services in 1953 and the end of the decade.

However, even before the Viscount began its working life in April 1953, events were taking place in aircraft technology which were to make the choice of aircraft for the 1960s very much more difficult. Long-range transport aircraft with turbo-jet engines had become a reality with the introduction of the Comet by BOAC in May 1952. Initially the pure jet aircraft appeared to offer few advantages and to pose little threat in the short-to-medium-haul field, mainly because of its higher costs. Whereas the aircraft designer of the 1930s produced innovations in order to make transport aircraft more efficient, the designers of the 1940s and 1950s wondered whether jet engines would make airlines less efficient.[29]

The problem was essentially whether an increased rate of output would pay for increased costs. On short stage lengths the increase in costs per flying hour for a jet was even steeper compared to other types than on long hauls; its increased output per hour, which depended upon average speed and size, was more difficult to achieve. A brief comparison with a turbo-prop can illustrate this. The Viscount 701 operated at a total cost to BEA of about £180 per flying hour during the early years (1953—6). The early pure jet transport type, the Comet 1, if operated over BEA's longer routes, might have achieved total hourly costs of £360—400. But given the slightly smaller pay load of the pure jet, approximately 9,800 lb compared to 11,800 lb for the Viscount, the increase in speed would scarcely compensate for these higher hourly flying costs. Over stage lengths of 1,000 miles the Viscount was producing 1,350 CTM/hour (5·2 tons carried at a block speed of 260 m.p.h.) where the Comet would have produced at best 1,850 CTM/hour (4·4 tons carried at a block speed of 420 m.p.h.).[30] The difference in productivity was less than 40 per cent, whereas the cost differential was of the order of 100 per cent.[31]

THE BIG JETS

The breakthrough in jet transport economics had to await the time when engines were powerful enough to lift airframes carrying payloads of over 16 tons. The big jets of the late 1950s, the Boeing 707 and Douglas DC-8, had operating costs per flying hour 2 and 3 times as high as their immediate predecessors, propeller aircraft such as the DC-7C, Constellation, Viscount and Electra. But their rate of production, carrying 120—140 passengers at block speeds approaching 500 m.p.h., was at least three times as high as the long-range propeller aircraft and four or five times as high as the smaller and shorter-range ones. Production of 6,000 or 7,000 CTM/hour was fairly typical of the big jets, where long-range propeller aircraft were achieving just over 2,000 CTM/hour and the shorter-range types only 1,000 to 1,500 CTM/hour. However, such was the increase in capacity that economic operation of the big jets had to wait not only for engines, but also for the build-up of passenger traffic in sufficient numbers for a reasonable frequency of services to be offered.

The main decisions to go ahead and develop the Comet were being taken in 1946 and 1947, but BEA had little reason to fear that the Comet would invalidate its 1949 decision to buy the Viscount. The Comet was not designed for short-haul routes and competitor airlines were unlikely to buy it. But during the 1950s it was a completely different story. The early years of the decade saw important decisions being made to develop a range of jet airliners, and the effect of these decisions was ultimately to force BEA to consider jets for its own operations. The three big American plane makers, Boeing, Douglas and Lockheed, had been discussing commercial jets with the airlines in the late 1940s. Neither side was prepared to go ahead until 1952, for reasons that were a combination of uncertainty on the technical issues and caution about the operating economics. In April 1952 Boeing decided to build a jet transport prototype, named the B367-80, in the hope of attracting orders both for civil aircraft and for a military tanker to refuel jet bombers.[32] The prototype flew in July 1954; the airlines were seriously interested. In September and October 1955 Pan American and United Airlines ordered the Boeing 707 and its competitor, the Douglas DC-8.

Most of BEA's competitors in Europe were intercontinental airlines which had entered the North Atlantic market in the postwar years. They thus had a need for the big jets which could fly the North Atlantic non-stop. The trans-Atlantic 707 and DC-8 were not going to be in service until 1960, but BEA was afraid that the big jets would be operated between European capitals on the short leg of an intercontinental journey and thus provide a faster and more attractive service which the turbo-props could not match.[33]

SHORT-HAUL JETS

Meanwhile in France the short-haul jet transport was emerging as rapidly as the big jet in the United States. A French government-sponsored design competition for a jet airliner was held on the basis of specifications drawn up in 1951. In 1953, the Sud-Est Caravelle won the contract for two prototypes and in May 1955 the first of these flew. Air France ordered the production model six months later and in 1956 used the second prototype to run trial freight services to Algeria and demonstration flights in Europe. Orders came in 1957 from SAS and other leading European airlines. In May 1959 Air France and SAS started Caravelle jet services and by 1960 short-haul jet operators were flying on a number of BEA's European routes.

The original Caravelle was not as fast as the first Comet, cruising at rather less than 450 m.p.h.; the developed models coming into service by 1961 achieved 490 m.p.h., as a result of having more powerful engines. On the other hand its payload, even for the first model, was nearly double that of the early Comet 1 at over eight tons or seventy passengers. Given a block speed of 360 m.p.h., the rate of production was about 3,000 CTM/hour and the later models, which could achieve block speeds of up to 400 m.p.h. on longer stages, were producing nearly 3,500 CTM per hour. The direct operating cost of a Caravelle in 1960 was estimated at about £360 per flying hour, at a time when BEA's first jet was costing about £380 and the later Viscounts some £150 per flying hour.[34] A comparison of the Caravelle's direct operating cost per CTM with that of the other two aircraft is hard to obtain, because it is difficult to compare aircraft costs when they are incurred in the service of different airlines. The cost structures, accounting conventions used and nature of cost categories are sufficiently varied between airlines to make such comparisons suspect. However, the indications are that its costs might have been within the range 30d to 38d per CTM, which would have been required by BEA.

BEA'S POLICY, 1953—6

BEA was monitoring the development of jet transports, but the airline was also still concerned about costs. Although the Viscount had helped the airline to run profitably, the problem of profitable operation below the 300-mile stage length still remained. Extracts from statistics derived from operations in the 1954/5 financial year (Table 2.7) show the contrast between the route results.

Table 2.7 *Traffic Results 1954/5, BEA Aircraft* (BEA average stage length 255 miles)

	Viscount	Elizabethan	Pionair
(1) Aircraft type			
(2) Average stage length operated	484m.	299m.	155m.
(3) Cost per CTM (including overheads, etc.)	39d	43d	41d
(4) Revenue per load ton mile	65d	65d	58d
(5) Load factor achieved	67%	63%	63%
(6) Cost per CTM as proportion of revenue rate	60%	66%	71%
(7) Profit or loss on type	+£714,000	—£304,000	—£512,000

Source: BEA, *Annual Report*, 1954/5, Appendix 7.

The Viscount, averaging over 484 miles per flight, was producing a profit at a level of 11 per cent of the capital cost of the fleet. This was because the load factor achieved was considerably higher than the ratio of costs to revenue (lines 5 and 6). The Elizabethan, at 299 miles average flight, had both higher costs and a lower load factor, the latter being well below the cost-to-revenue ratio. The Pionair, at half the average flight distance of the Elizabethan, was able to return a lower cost per CTM, but it also worked at a lower revenue rate (line 4), because of the lower level of domestic fares.

What BEA needed was aircraft whose costs per CTM on short journeys of 200 and 300 miles would be low enough to give a cost-to-revenue ratio well below the load factor which could be expected. It was in consequence that the airline specified the stretched Viscount V800 series. The V800s had 20 to 30 per cent more payload capacity than the V700, created by an enlarged fuselage and more powerful engines; operating costs per flying hour were increased by only 15 per cent, in spite of the fact that the stage lengths flown were reduced to near 300 miles and that the capital cost was higher (Table 2.12). The result for the V802 was that costs per CTM fell to about 38d, while the rather more expensive V806 still managed to hold costs per CTM at about 40—42d per CTM, in spite of increases in wages, materials, landing fees, insurance, etc. However, the 802 and 806 were intended only as interim types to cover the late 1950s and early 1960s, while a major new aircraft was being developed.

BEA's objectives during the mid-1950s were to expand air transport services and to extend them to as many consumers as possible, to operate profitably and to develop the British aircraft industry. Cost reduction flowed naturally from these. In earlier years the general lowering of air fares had made the airline's task of getting cost and revenue into line more difficult, but, once established, the airline accepted the IATA's aims as its own. As long as traffic growth was stimulated by lower fares, BEA could continue to operate increasingly larger aircraft and thus achieve the cost reduction sought. Believing that jets would have the effect of raising costs on short-haul routes, BEA decided that there was time for one more round of turbo-props.[35]

This helps to explain how it came about that BEA, while well aware of the fact that many world airlines and some of its main competitors were ordering jets, in 1955 went ahead with a major new turbo-prop, the 100-seat, 13-ton payload Vickers Vanguard. If the BEA view of the world had been accurate, and the best interests of the air transportation industry had truly lain in the direction of ever cheaper fares, made possible by ever more productive aircraft, then the Vanguard would have been a step in the right direction. Intended to cruise at 425 m.p.h., with a block speed of over 300 m.p.h. and a payload approaching 13 tons, the Vanguard would have been producing 3,900 CTM per hour. Unfortunately, the design speed was never attained and the large turbo-prop engine developed especially for the Vanguard, the Tyne, had a number of engineering problems, making the aircraft rather more expensive to operate than had been anticipated. Nevertheless, while in BEA service on fairly short stage lengths, averaging 350 miles, the Vanguard was regularly turning out 3,500 CTM per hour and was the most productive of BEA's aircraft right up to 1968, when the Trident 2 was introduced.

Several factors intervened to prevent the Vanguard from becoming the aircraft which BEA originally hoped it would be, economical over all routes and able to operate profitably on the short high-density stages, such as London to Paris, Heathrow to Manchester and other popular routes of 200—250 miles. It was not a cheap aircraft to develop, having to bear the development cost of a new engine (the Tyne turbo-prop) as well as a completely new airframe.[36] Thus, whereas it might have been expected that it would have been priced at about 50—75 per cent more than the last Viscount, model V810, which was in production at the same time, the Vanguard appears to have been sold at 140 per cent above the V810's price.[37] There is a tendency for the airline's standing charges on each aircraft to follow the trend of capital cost, and the Vanguard turned out to be three or four times as expensive on these standing charges as the Viscount V806 (BEA did not buy the V810). Had it been outstandingly reliable the Vanguard might have overcome these disadvantages, because of its very high rate of production. But engineering development costs continued to be high for the first four years of service (1961—4).

The Vanguard's costs per CTM did not fall below 35d until after it had been in service for two years; developments on the revenue side were disappointing also, because the rate of growth of world demand for air transport was less buoyant in 1960 and 1961.[38] This dip in the trend coincided with increases in world capacity of the order of 14 per cent per year, the result of the jet-ordering boom of 1955—7. Load factors fell (Table 2.6). BEA had predicted this, but was unable to do anything about the consequent surplus capacity. The new Vanguard was being used on continental routes, where there was competition from jets, and on the domestic ones, where the revenue rate was low.

The Vanguard's passenger load factor suffered and was only just above the BEA average for the early years of service, even occasionally below. The revenue rate achieved, because of concessionary fares and low domestic rates, was around 55d per LTM, when the BEA average was 63d. These figures meant that the Vanguard did not turn out to be the profitable short-haul aircraft BEA wanted.

THE NEW JET

The ordering of the Vanguard kept turbo-prop aircraft in BEA service well into the 1970s, and turbo-props were the types which had made the airline successful. But competition from jets could not be met except by the use of other jets. Thus jets came to dominate the 1960s, as turbo-props had dominated the 1950s. BEA had led Europe by its innovatory policy in specifying and operating Viscounts, but its experience with the pure jet Trident, the main fleet type from 1965 to 1975, was very much less happy.

The idea of having the Vanguard as the mainline short-haul high capacity aircraft was under consideration from 1953 to 1955, and the order was finally placed in 1956, after several months of contract negotiations. By that time active discussion was taking place about the need for a jet.

In July 1956 requests went out from BEA to five aircraft companies for jet transport project proposals based on a preliminary requirement. Vickers, de Havilland, Bristol, Hawkers and Handley Page were the companies chosen, but it is believed that Handley Page did not submit a design. On the basis of the companies' proposals and traffic forecasts by BEA's commercial department, the Project and Development Group within the airline drew up proposed specifications for the Policy Committee's deliberations. There was some internal disagreement about the right size for the Trident. With the Vanguard already being developed for the shorter and higher density routes, there was a certain amount of pressure from the Commercial Department not to have a large aircraft (i.e. of 100 seats). At the time BEA had fifty-two new aircraft on order (V802s, V806s and Vanguards), with a combined total capacity rather larger than the whole of the then current fleet. Adding a larger aeroplane would exacerbate a tendency to over-capacity. After twelve months of preliminary studies, a BEA requirement was agreed in July 1957 and issued to the aircraft industry.

Several contenders were still in the running after some months of project studies and twenty-three designs from four manufacturers were considered between July 1956 and January 1958.[39] BEA's Policy Committee and the Board determined on an aircraft well below 100 seats. The new jet was to have capacity for seventy to eighty passengers on normal services, ninety-five with six-abreast tourist seating, and was planned to be able to carry the full payload for 1,000 miles at 600 m.p.h. On the assumption that there were nine passengers to the ton on normal services, the payload may be estimated at 20,000 lb or slightly over. The rate of production at block speeds of 400 m.p.h. could be expected to be 3,600 CTM per hour or above.

A month after this specification was issued, BEA asked for approval from the Treasury through the Ministry of Civil Aviation to place the order with de Havilland for the DH 121 design, eventually known as the Trident. There was then a year's delay before full approval from the Government was gained, although a Ministerial announcement in the Commons in February 1958, followed by a Letter of Intent to Purchase from BEA to de Havilland, meant that the other manufacturers knew how matters stood.

The reason for the delay in 1957 was the Government's desire to bring about the concentration of the British aircraft industry. The industry had great traditions, established during the second world war, and there were still nineteen companies operating in 1957 (fourteen airframe and five aero-engine), in spite of the fact that the numbers of aircraft built had declined from tens of thousands in wartime to about 2,500 in 1952 and less than 1,000 during 1957. Many of the firms were fairly small and most were dependent on government orders or R and D contracts for survival. What the Government wanted was a much smaller number of firms with larger financial and technical resources.

To achieve this policy objective the Government was prepared to use its position as the main customer of the industry and as the patron of the nationalised airlines.[40] When BEA requested permission to order from de

Havilland, the Ministry of Supply saw the order as an opportunity to bring about mergers through the exercise of purchasing power. Contracts were to be placed not merely on the grounds of a winning design, but also with companies of sufficient financial and technical strength to make sure the project was carried through quickly and without Government assistance.

De Havilland had suffered disaster only three years before with the Comet 1 which had been withdrawn after a series of fatal accidents. The Ministries of Supply and of Transport and Civil Aviation, which had responsibility respectively for the aircraft manufacturers and for the airlines, tried to persuade BEA to accept other aircraft. They encouraged other manufacturers, Bristol and Hawker Siddeley, who were ready to merge, to put up projects which would be acceptable to BEA.[41] The Ministries were unsuccessful, probably because BEA's project and development department had evaluated the other aircraft carefully and because of the determination of the Chairman, Lord Douglas, to resist pressures which he thought contrary to BEA's interests.[42] The airline knew which project was most suitable after studying so many competing designs, and was not prepared to take the Bristol aircraft, the Hawker Siddeley one or any combination of other designs.

These negotiations, conducted in the winter of 1957/8, took until the end of February. The Ministers' objections were finally resolved by de Havilland forming a project company, called Airco, with Hunting Aircraft of Hurn on the south coast and the Fairey aircraft company. Permission to negotiate a contract was given and BEA and Airco began to draw up the precise specification for the Trident. Financial approval for the project did not come until August 1958, but it is probable that BEA and Airco had not sufficiently defined the contract for the order to have been placed before that time.[43]

During July 1958 the Trident design became fixed at an eighty-seat aircraft with three Rolls Royce Medway engines at the rear, but there is a normal tendency for projects to increase during developments. The Medway, RB 141, had an expected static thrust of 12,000 lb per engine, and was likely to grow by 10 or 15 per cent while under development. The power available, at 36,000 lb static thrust, and the aircraft's maximum payload were both likely to be greater than BEA had intended.

The year 1958 was a bad one for air travel. BEA's load factor dropped 5 per cent, from 68 to 63 per cent. In addition to the Vanguard, BEA had ordered six Comet 4B aircraft in 1957, in order to cover the gap between 1959 and the service date of the Trident. Over-capacity seemed unavoidable. Pressure built up for a change of specification and early in 1959 a new proposal for a smaller engine, the RB 163 Spey, came from Rolls Royce. It was expected to develop about 10,000 lb thrust, instead of the 14,000 lb which was by then predicted for the Medway. This was the kind of design change which the airline was looking for and BEA asked Airco to fit the Spey engine and reduce the size of the aircraft correspondingly. In the summer of 1959 a contract was signed on this basis for twenty-four aircraft.

OPERATING RESULTS: 1960 ONWARDS

The aircraft on which purchase decisions were made in the latter half of the 1950s remained with the corporation for most of the period from 1960 up to 1973, when the merger with BOAC was completed. The Comet entered service first and was phased out in 1969 and 1970. The Vanguard remained in passenger service from 1960 to 1970/1, after which it was used mostly for cargo operations. The Trident, which did not reach service until 1964, was still with the fleet in 1975.

During the thirteen years 1960 to 1973, BEA's profitability record did not maintain the promise which it had shown during the 1950s. Although there were a few years in which profits were made, there were more in which the operating surplus was insufficient to cover interest charges. The airline's finances became complicated after 1964 by the adoption of various accounting practices which were designed to reallocate the extra costs incurred in using innovatory aircraft. Because BEA bore extra costs during the introductory period into service of new types, which would not have been incurred had the airline used established types, it had become the practice during the 1950s to capitalise extra engineering expenditure and other costs considered to be attributable to the new type. The effect was to remove extra costs from the operating account and add them to the capital liabilities of the corporation, just as if these costs had been part of the purchase price of the aircraft. Without this expedient the operating account would have been unduly burdened by extra expenditure when teething troubles were experienced with new aircraft. Indeed, in the year 1961/2 the operating account would have been in deficit, owing to the combination of costs attributable to the Vanguard and a difficult year in other ways, had £1·35 million not been transferred in this way.

By 1965 the financial picture had become more complex. Capitalised introductory costs were continuing to be carried as capital liabilities and the process of writing them off against the operating surplus began. Introductory costs, however, were by then being incurred on the Trident. The operating surplus was adjusted, first positively to remove these extra costs, then negatively to write off previously capitalised costs. In Table 2.10, the net effect of these adjustments is shown in the second division of column 3. In 1968 a special capital account of £25 million was set up as a capital reserve to compensate the airline for the use of higher cost aircraft. Drawings against the account were made in the following four years to make up the surplus on operating account and cover capital charges. Table 2.10 shows the level of net profit before the drawings on this special account were included.

From the fact that these accounting practices were used, it can be deduced that the innovatory aircraft which followed the Viscount were not able to bring the airline much success in terms of financial return.[44] The formula for financial profitability in the 1950s had been: first, specifying aircraft whose direct operating costs were at least no higher than their predecessors' in current terms, thus representing an improvement when taking account of inflation; secondly, achieving lower airline costs per

Table 2.8 Traffic Results of BEA Aircraft, 1964/5 and 1965/6 (BEA average stage, 315–320 miles)

Aircraft type Year		Trident 1 64/5	65/6	Comet 64/5	65/6	Vanguard 64/5	65/6	Viscount[a] 64/5	65/6
Average stage	(miles)	541	411	627	723	365	362	228	225
Cost per CTM	(d)	45	49	33	31	31	33	44	44
Revenue per LTM	(d)	80	84	61	57	54	54	73	73
Cost/revenue ratio	(%)	56	58	54	55	57	61	60	60
Load factor achieved	(%)	58	60	57	62	58	59	62	62
Profit	(£m.)	0·140[b]	0·688[b]			0·468	0·602	0·706	0·415
Loss	(£m.)	1·060[c]	0·712[c]	0·825	1·831				

[a] Sixty-six-seat Viscount 800 at lower standard of comfort than main services.
[b] After deducting introductory costs.
[c] Before deducting introductory costs.

Table 2.9 Traffic Results, BEA Aircraft 1969/70 and 1970/1 (BEA average stage 357 miles)

Aircraft type Year		BAC 1-11 1969/70	1970/1	Trident 2 1969/70	1970/1	Trident 1 1969/70	1970/1	Vanguard 1969/70	1970/1	Viscount 1969/70	1970/1
Average stage	(miles)	262	262	810	837	427	431	414	406	174	169
Cost per CTM	(d)	46	52	36	38	55	60	36	46	64	75
Revenue per LTM	(d)	88	96	72	74	98	104	62	67	91	101
Cost/revenue ratio	(%)	52	54	50	52	56	57	56	70	70	74
Load factor achieved	(%)	52	52	55	50	63	59	60	60	65	62
Profit	(£m.)	0·040		2·419		3·957	1·264	0·978	2·868	0·952	2·514
Loss	(£m.)		0·861		0·668						

Table 2.10   *BEA Operating Revenue and Return on Capital, 1961—3*

1	2	3		4	5	6
Year ended 31 March	*Operating revenue (£m.)*	*Surplus on operations (£m.)*[a]		*Capital employed*[b] *(£m.)*	*Return on capital*[c] *(%)*	*Net profit (£m.)*
1961	42·3	2·7		65·2	4·2	1·5
1962	46·4	0·5		83·2	0·6	(—1·5)
1963	51·2	2·8		87·1	3·2	(—0·3)
1964	59·9	5·9		88·7	6·7	3·0
1965	65·9	3·4	4·2	92·1	4·6	1·3
1966	76·3	3·6	4·5	98·5	4·6	1·3
1967	86·4	4·6	4·3	105·1	4·1	0·7
1968	92·3	3·1	2·0	121·5	1·6	(—1·8)
1969	108·4	4·6	3·2	135·5	2·4	(—1·5)[d]
1970	126·0	10·4	11·0	140·7	7·8	2·5 [d]
1971	133·4	0·3	(—0·8)	167·7	—	(—7·5)[d]
1972	154·7	2·5	1·2	206·2	0·6	(—7·8)[d]
1973	179·6	10·9	9·4	212·2	4·4	(—1·2)

[a] Two figures are given for the surplus on operations from 1965 onwards. The first is before removing introductory costs from expenditure and writing off a portion of capitalised costs; the second shows the surplus after these adjustments have been made.
[b] Capital liabilities plus reserves.
[c] Based on the operating surplus after write off.
[d] Payments of £5m., £4m., £8m. and £8m. in these years from the Special Account made recorded profits, where the profit and loss account showed a loss after payment of interest.

CTM produced, by spreading overhead costs over an increasing volume of traffic handled; and thirdly, returning load factors which were higher than the achieved ratio applying between the cost of providing each ton of capacity and the revenue received from it.

For a number of reasons, this formula was not as successful in the 1960s and early 1970s as it had been in the 1950s. The reasons fall into three broad categories. First, there was the strength of the competition faced by BEA; secondly, there was the relationship applying between BEA's costs and revenues; and thirdly, there was the nature of the aircraft which were being used.

Competition on European and domestic routes became more severe in the 1960s and the forms of competition which mainline airlines faced became more varied. The European flag-carrying airlines stepped up their rate of expansion on European routes somewhat later than BEA, so that they were experiencing in the early 1960s the growth achieved by BEA in the late 1950s.[45] The anticipated operation of jet trans-Atlantic services between one or two European airports at the start or end of their journeys also took place. It will be remembered that the big jets, mostly 707 and DC-8 aircraft, had passenger carrying capacities which were about twice those of the aircraft operating within Europe in the early 1960s. Although these flights by trans-Atlantic aircraft were not frequent, the available seat capacity on some routes rose rapidly. BEA's passenger load factor had averaged 66 per cent in the 1950s, but during the 1960s the average fell to 63 per cent and the trend was towards a further decrease (Tables 2.5 and 2.11). BEA's share of the traffic on its main European routes dropped from 54 per cent in 1960/1 to 49 per cent by 1962/3. At home, independent carriers were licensed on BEA routes from 1960.

Competition, and the increased capacity available on many routes, must be held partly responsible for the other declining trend affecting BEA, the decreasing rate of revenue return. During the 1950s BEA's revenue rate per LTM sold had averaged over 66d; it had been no lower at the end of the decade than at the beginning (Table 2.5, column 5). During the 1960s it went from 67·5d in 1960 to 62·2d in 1965, and did not turn upwards again significantly until 1968 (Table 2.11, column 5). The causes were the steady pressure among IATA operators for lower fares in order to stimulate demand, and BEA's need to adopt a marketing response to competition at home and abroad. Special tourist rates and reduced fares for particular services were introduced. The Vanguard, BEA's lowest cost aircraft, was particularly affected by the reduction in revenue rates; in the mid-1960s it was operating at 15 per cent below the BEA average and considerably below the rates applying to the Trident and Viscount (Table 2.8).

Against declining load factors and a falling rate of revenue per LTM carried, BEA would have had to reduce its cost-to-revenue ratio further than in the profitable years of the 1950s in order to remain profitable. In the last years of the 1950s the cost-to-revenue ratio averaged 62·4 and in the first five years of the 1960s it was 61·2. The reduction in costs achieved in 1960—4 was not quite great enough to cope with the adverse conditions. The cost-to-revenue ratio achieved was not below the overall load factor in 1962 and 1963. During the period 1965/6 to 1972/3, although the revenue rate had begun to improve, costs were increasing faster; the cost-to-revenue rate was equal to or more than the overall load factor in 1968, 1969, 1971, 1972 and 1973, which resulted in losses being sustained.[46]

THE AIRCRAFT OPERATED, 1960—73

Mention has already been made of the difficulties experienced with the Vanguard. The Comet 4B was an interim aircraft, which BEA never intended to use to provide a major portion of its capacity. The Trident had a long and difficult gestation period. Subsequent purchases by BEA included the Trident 2, the BAC 1-11 500 and the Trident 3. The Trident 2 was ordered in 1965, the others two years later. The Trident 2 was a long-range derivative of the original Trident for BEA's Middle East flights. The BAC 1-11 and the Trident 3 were purchased by BEA after requests by the airline for permission to order American aircraft had been turned down. The BAC 1-11 500 was a derivative of the earlier 1-11, and the Trident 3 of the Trident 1. Thus the only two innovative aircraft being operated by BEA during 1960—73 were the Vanguard and the Trident.

Table 2.11 BEA Output, Costs and Revenue, 1960–74

1 Year ending 31 March	*2* CTMs offered (m.)	*3* LTMs sold (m.)	*4* Total costs per CTM (d)	*5* Traffic revenue per LTM (d)	*6* CTM/LTM overall load factor (%)	*7* Cost per CTM/revenue per LTM (%)	*8* Passenger load factor (%)	*9* Profit[a] (£m.)
1960	192·0	130·0	43·1	67·5	68	64	69	2·1
1961	237·4	154·8	41·4	65·6	65	63	67	1·5
1962	282·0	169·0	41·0	66·4	60	62	61	(−1·5)
1963	327·9	106·4	37·7	62·6	60	60	61	(−0·3)
1964	378·8	227·1	36·0	63·2	60	57	63	3·0
1965	435·6	254·2	35·6	62·2	58	57	61	1·3
1966	480·9	289·5	37·5	63·3	60	59	63	1·3
1967	547·5	324·8	37·6	63·8	59	59	63	0·7
1968	569·6	330·7	39·6	67·0	58	59	60	(−1·8)
1969	590·5	349·0	44·5	74·5	59	60	62	(−1·5)
1970	661·3	385·0	43·9	78·6	58	56	62	2·5
1971	699·0	378·6	48·7	84·5	54	58	60	(−7·5)
1972	782·7	411·8	50·2	90·2	53	56	58	(−7·8)
1973	803·2	432·1	48·8	89·6	54	54	57	(−1·2)
1974	883·7	501·4	51·2	94·7	57	54	61	n.a.[b]

Source: BEA, *Annual Reports*, 1964–74. (1975 is not available on a comparable basis.)

Notes: [a] Transfers from a Special Account, set up to compensate BEA for not being able to order the aircraft of its choice in the 1960s, made the losses of 1969–72 into profits.
[b] Not available on a comparable basis. Regional air services transferred out of the European divisions of British Airways. Probably a net profit of about £5m. would have been earned by the former BEA routes.

The use of two derivatives of the latter meant that much of BEA's operational performance during the 1960s and early 1970s was determined by the airline's decisions in 1955—9 to buy these two aircraft. It is therefore important to ask how much the design and performance of these two aircraft contributed to BEA's difficulties in the period up to 1973.

The Vanguard had a high rate of output, nearly three times as many CTMs per hour as the Viscounts, and was capable of achieving low operating costs. But it arrived in service at the end of the turbo-prop era. During the two years in which it operated mostly against the Viscounts of other European fleets it could have returned good profits, but it was plagued by high costs and low availability attributable to introductory difficulties. By the time that the aircraft's costs per CTM were falling to the level of 30—35d, jet competition, particularly from the Caravelle, was building up on the main European routes on which the Vanguard operated. To use the capacity represented by the Vanguard, BEA had to offer concessionary fares and transfer the aircraft to other routes, where the revenue rate was lower, with the result that the profits made by the Vanguard were still low (Table 2.8). As an innovatory aircraft the Vanguard's worst faults were that it just missed its market and that it marginally failed to perform on cost as it should have done.

The Trident did not improve upon the Vanguard in its rate of output. It was also more expensive to buy, and perhaps 50 per cent more expensive to fly per CTM produced. However, when BEA ordered the aircraft it was intended to provide jet capacity on the airline's longer haul routes of stage lengths averaging 600 miles. When it came into operation, the Trident had to be put into service on some of the shorter high-density routes such as London—Paris (in mid-1965) and as a consequence it was averaging stage lengths of 400 miles. Had the Trident been used on longer routes, its costs would have been lower and their relation to the revenue rate would have produced better profits. The Trident was the aircraft which should have been making most of BEA's profits during the latter half of the 1960s. That it failed to do so was due to the fact that it was not designed to be used for the routes on which BEA was forced, by the competition from other jets, to operate it.

Although BEA ordered no innovative aircraft after the Trident, the airline made several more efforts to agree on specifications with the British industry for a high capacity jet aircraft to operate on short European routes at low costs. Between 1963 and 1965 negotiations went forward on aircraft of about 150—190 seats, using advanced technology engines of the high by-pass ratio type. The proposals made failed to come to anything, because of the difficulties over finance. In the two main aircraft companies remaining, the constituent companies had backed transport aircraft in the period 1955 to 1964 which had failed to produce profits. Neither the VC-10, the Vanguard nor the Trident had produced a reasonable profit for the manufacturers, even though each had government finance behind it, as well as company money. Government support also ceased in 1965, with the introduction of the policy that all aircraft projects were to be pursued in partnership with European countries. Partners could not be found for the new projects and each proposal had to be dropped.

By 1965 BEA was concerned about the potential of further jet competition in Europe. The Boeing 727 had been ordered by Air France. It not only offered higher capacities and lower operating costs than BEA's aircraft, but also more flexibility.[47] By exchanging some of the fuel load on take-off for extra passenger load, the aircraft could be made to operate over short high density routes at a direct cost not significantly worse than on longer routes, where the traffic was more sparse. The airline had finally rejected the idea of retaining the turbo-props in mainline services beyond 1967, and therefore needed a considerable addition to jet capacity for 1968 onwards.[48]

In June 1966 BEA requested permission to order eighteen Boeing 727-200 and twenty-three Boeing 737-200 aircraft. The 727 was already in airline service; the 727-200 series was a stretched version planned for 1968, with a capacity of around 150 seats. Deliveries could therefore be expected within about two years. It would have been able to take over many of the high density routes of 300—600 miles which the Trident 1 was operating. The 727-200 would also have been used on the highly competitive routes such as London—Paris and London—Amsterdam. Air France was reported to be introducing 727s on its prestige routes in the late 1960s.

Boeing's 737 aircraft, a type based on the use of many 727 components, but having only two engines, had not flown in 1966. Lufthansa had ordered the 737-100 and was expected to bring it into service, on German internal routes particularly, during 1968. The 737-200 series had a slightly larger passenger capacity (113 maximum where the 100 series maximum was just over 100 passengers), but its attraction for BEA lay in the fact that it was also a flexible aircraft, using the same Pratt and Whitney engine, the JT 8D-9 turbo-fan, as the 727-200.

However, the Government was not prepared to allow BEA to buy American aircraft, even though BOAC had done so a few years earlier. The airline found a British alternative to the 737 within a few months of being refused permission. The aircraft ordered was a stretched BAC 1-11, with two rear-positioned up-rated Spey engines and a seating capacity of nearly 100. The 1-11 series 500 was expected to have rather higher costs than the 737 which BEA had wanted, but its actual performance in service (Table 2.9) compares well with the other aircraft operating in the late 1960s and early 1970s. Although flying over very short stages for a jet aircraft (average length 260 miles), costs per CTM were well below those of the Trident 1 flying an average stage of over 400 miles. The 1-11-500 was probably the first BEA aircraft to show an overall profit, although a very small one, on the operation of stage lengths below 300 miles. It was a well developed aircraft by the time it reached BEA service, with a fairly low capital cost and consequently low fixed annual costs. The introductory costs of the type had been borne by earlier operators and thus the 500 also had low engineering costs.

The requirement for a larger aircraft, which the 727 would have filled, took longer to be satisfied. The Government, in refusing permission for American aircraft, had indicated that launching aid would be available for a British alternative. Further design studies by BEA's project and development department indicated that a new proposal for a BAC aircraft would suit their needs for a large capacity jet in the early 1970s. Called the BAC 2-11, it depended heavily on the BAC 1-11 design and some components, but used a new engine from Rolls Royce; this engine, designated the RB 211, and having a high by-pass ratio, was considerably quieter than previous jets. It was eventually used for the Lockheed 10-11 Tristar airbus. The BAC 2-11 was to have about 190 seats and was estimated to be a few per cent cheaper in seat-mile costs than the 727-200. However, the development costs were estimated at £110 million; subsequent experience with the RB 211 was to show that this had been an optimistic figure. It appeared to the Government that it could not justify the expenditure of launching aid on this scale, as well as the support possibly to be given to the joint French/British/German airbus. Consequently it appeared cheaper in the short run to agree with BEA upon some form of state subsidy to compensate the airline for being forced to accept a second Trident development, the Trident 3B, instead of the 727-200 or BAC 2-11. The launching cost for the 140-seat Trident 3B was expected to be under £20 million, since it used the engine and much of the technology already developed for the Tridents 1 and 2.

CONCLUSION: THE ECONOMIC SHORTHAUL AIRLINER

BEA introduced into service during its twenty-seven years of independent existence a total of five completely new types of aircraft, as well as a number of more established types. The former were the Viking, Elizabethan, Viscount, Vanguard and Trident. The Viscount was an outstanding success. The other four were technically satisfactory, making great advances in the rate of aircraft output and in the speed and comfort of air travel. Table 2.13 gives a measure of the increases recorded in labour productivity, much of which is attributable to more efficient aircraft.

The policy of flying new types worked well for the airline at first. Airline costs were reduced reasonably quickly and some evidence suggests that the achievement of high load factors, a most important consideration, was attributable to the new aircraft. However, the airline faced one particular problem, that it operated short stage lengths. It was not unique in this aspect, because many American domestic carriers were operating over similar average stage lengths, but it was unique among its competitors in Europe.

For most of the airline's existence its aircraft were only able to operate profitably while being used on stage lengths which were above the airline's average at the time. Tables 2.7, 2.8 and 2.9 show that the more profitable aircraft had above average stage lengths; profitable operations depended

Table 2.12 *Costs of Productive Capacity, BEA Aircraft*

Aircraft	Date of introduction	CTM per hour[a]	CTM per year (m.)[b]	Capital cost (£m.)[c]	Capital cost per CTM/year (d)	Typical overheads per flying hour[d]	Overhead cost per CTM (d)
Elizabethan	March 1952	890	1·78	0·30	40·5	£76	20
Viscount 701	April 1953	1,200	2·40	0·31	31·0	£73	15
Viscount 800	February 1957	1,300	2·60	0·46	42·3	£96	18
Comet	April 1960	3,550	7·10	1·26	42·5	£202	14
Vanguard	December 1960	3,850	7·10	1·15	35·9	£230	15
Trident 1	March 1964	3,200	6·40	1·51	56·6	£293	22
Trident 2	May 1968	4,450	8·90	2·22	60·0	£300	16
BAC 1-11	October 1968	2,750	5·50	1·55	67·5	£250	22
Trident 3	March 1971	4,750	9·50	(2·40)[e]	60·6	£313	16

[a] Estimated average in BEA mainline service.
[b] On annual utilisation of 2,000 hours.
[c] Purchase price to BEA at 1968 prices.
[d] Estimated cost at 1968 prices of headquarters staff, fixed equipment cost and sales costs, as allocated per aircraft.
[e] Estimated purchase price in 1971 of £3·1m.

Table 2.13   *Labour Productivity of BEA Staff*

Year ended 31 March	CTM (m.)	Employees	Output per employee (CTMs)	Year ended 31 March	CTM (m.)	Employees	Output per employee (CTMs)
1948	22	7,249	2,984	1964	379	16,688	22,701
1950	40	6,459	6,225	1966	481	18,790	25,592
1952	57	7,945	7,136	1968	570	21,414	26,599
1954	84	9,020	9,268	1970	661	23,228	28,471
1956	125	9,570	13,007	1972	783	25,348	30,970
1958	160	10,933	14,660	1974	884	23,608	37,432
1960	192	12,190	15,750				
1962	282	14,493	19,460				

upon the revenue surpluses from the longer routes being higher than the revenue deficiencies from the shorter ones.

Even the longer routes were not always profitable, in spite of BEA's strict attention to reducing costs and keeping them as low as possible. For instance, the Viscount V802 made small losses in the revenue year 1958/9 at stage distances 50 miles above the BEA average, and the Trident 2 was unprofitable at 837 miles in 1970/1; but these losses were part of the risk of an expanding air transportation business. Airlines were not in general very profitable at the time.[49] The factors which affect the airline's profitability are long-term trends in aircraft productivity and the level of fares. These are not matters which the airline can influence in the short term of a year's operations; the load factor, on the other hand, may drop below the level needed to cover the cost-to-revenue ratio in a very short period, as demand fluctuates.

Some of the airline's difficulties in the 1960s stemmed from having the wrong aircraft, or from being forced to operate the aircraft it had over routes for which they were not suited. It is arguable that this state of affairs came about because the airline's policy of introducing new types encouraged it to think of its own needs as special. The actual difference this made to profits may have been marginal, but, more seriously, there are grounds for questioning whether the methods used to support the domestic aircraft manufacturers were of real assistance to the innovative performance of the industry. Finally, the policy of introducing new aircraft types did not result in the aircraft that BEA really needed, one that would operate profitably over stage lengths of about 250 miles, and it is worth examining the reasons which may account for this.

The important decisions to examine are the decisions to purchase the Vanguard and the Trident. It has already been noted above that other airlines miscalculated the life expectancy of the turbo-prop. Having done so, however, they were revising their opinions by 1960s, when the popularity of the Caravelle and the prospects of the Boeing short-haul jet were making themselves felt. BEA took another few years to adjust its aircraft procurement policy.

The order for the Vanguard had a profound effect upon the specifications of BEA's order for the Trident. The Vanguard's capacity was approximately double that of the Viscount V800 series, and the latter had only begun to be delivered to BEA in 1957. Thus while BEA's Board and Policy Committee were debating the size which the new jet ought to be, capacity increases were anticipated in the airline which would rapidly increase the total output of CTMs offered in the early 1960s. The routes on which higher levels of traffic were forecast, such as London—Paris, were expected to be served by the Vanguard. Thus BEA's view of the market dictated that the Trident should be specified to suit longer hauls and it resisted the tendency of the project to grow from the 75-seat, $3 \times 10,000$ lb thrust, 1000-mile stage length aircraft into the 110-seat, $3 \times 14,000$ lb thrust, 1800-mile aircraft which de Havilland wanted to build.

There was a view put forward by Hawker Siddeley that the original DH

121 project specification, with over 100 passenger seats and three engines of 12—14,000 lb thrust, would have rivalled the Boeing 727, which had seating for about 120 passengers and three 14,000 lb thrust Pratt and Whitney engines, in a way that the reduced Trident 1 of 1959 could never have done. Market research in the 1950s had led de Havilland to forecast sales of 500 aircraft like the early DH 121 during the 1960s, a prediction which in the 727's case proved in no way optimistic.

However, the interpretation that BEA caused de Havilland to miss building a competitor to the 727 is probably over-stating the case. The DH 121 had an interior body diameter which gave about 6 inches less total width at passenger shoulder height. Boeing claim that this would have made American carriers unwilling to accept the six-abreast seating needed to give a capacity of over 110 passengers in the tourist configuration. Most importantly, the Trident did not have the advantage of the 727's very efficient high-lift wing, which enabled its performance to be acceptable to many domestic American carriers. This was a feature which the Boeing company were able to develop with their 707-prototype for the 727, but for which no requirement was stated for the Trident. It is, on the other hand, possible that if BEA had wanted to buy the larger DH 121 project and had ordered it in 1957, the resulting aircraft might have sold well in Europe in the early 1960s.

Aside from such speculations, what is more interesting is whether the Trident which BEA specified was really the right aircraft for the airline to order. The airline needed a jet aircraft to counter the Caravelle and the jet capacity which would be coming on to the European market from international operations. The obvious choice was the Caravelle itself, but it was ruled out by the policy of buying British aircraft.[50] While the specification of the Trident was still being thrashed out, BEA actually purchased an aircraft to perform this stop-gap role, the Comet 4B. It is difficult to find an explanation for the decision to specify the Trident so that it fulfilled the same role as the Comet 4B. It would have been easier to understand if the airline had been seeking in 1958/9 to order a 90—95-seat jet aircraft for stage lengths of 300 miles with costs as low as the Vanguard's. That was the type of aircraft which American operators of stage lengths similar to BEA's were seeking at that time. It was also the type of aircraft which BEA could have used in the mid-1960s.

One explanation of the Trident's specification is that BEA's Board during the late 1950s did not expect that jet aircraft could operate profitably at stage lengths of less than 600 miles. Thus they planned for a world in which jet operations within Europe would be confined, as far as the next aircraft generation was concerned, to longer hauls only; they expected neither that the Trident would return lower costs than any current aircraft, nor that they would wish to operate a jet at short stages so soon. If this was the view that prevailed in the case of the Trident order, it was one which the airline found even easier to argue given its policy of not seeking foreign aircraft projects as purchase proposals. The comparative isolation of negotiations only with the British industry allowed BEA's policy of introducing new types of aircraft to reflect a narrow view of what was required.

The policy of introducing new British aircraft lapsed by default before BEA was absorbed into British Airways. The immediate reason for this was that development finance from the aircraft companies and the Government dried up. One underlying cause was that the majority of transport aircraft manufactured in Britain had failed to produce profits. Popular wisdom has attributed the lack of success in selling aircraft to the smallness of the domestic market. The Viscount is one example which contradicts this, but the argument about market size has diverted attention from the question of whether the real failure has been in the decision processes used in choosing projects.

BEA's experience with the Trident provides a paradoxical example, in which the airline might have been able best to support the British manufacturing industry by being open to proposals from foreign manufacturers as well, thereby ensuring that when a British project was chosen it would stand comparison with all the alternatives.

NOTES

[1] *Report of the Committee of Inquiry into Civil Aviation* (Cadman Report), Cmd 5685, HMSO, 1938.
[2] Surface transport must also be regarded as competing with air, particularly on domestic services, but not in the sense of supplying the same product.
[3] Ronald Miller and David Sawers, *Technical Development of Modern Aviation*, Routledge, London, 1967.
[4] The actual fleet taken over when BEA started operations in 1946 consisted of Dominies, Avro 19s, Junkers JU52s and Douglas DC-3s. The first three types were uneconomic in commercial service and only the DC-3 remained in use in the long term. The earliest 'BEA' aircraft, the Vickers Viking, was initially only rented from the Ministry of Civil Aviation; after considerable modifications had made it more economic to use, BEA bought a number of the aircraft.
[5] The Comet came into service earlier and had a shorter gestation period, because a similar aircraft was also ordered by BOAC and both were derived from the ill-fated Comet 1 (which BEA did not use).
[6] Lufthansa did not resume operations until 1955.
[7] Stage length is the distance between landings.
[8] R. Davies (*History of the World's Airlines*, OUP, 1964) put BEA's share of intra-Europe traffic at 29 per cent in 1955 and 30 per cent in 1960. BEA in its 1961/2 *Annual Report*, claimed to carry 46 per cent of UK—continent traffic in 1960/1.
[9] In 1953 BEA published comparative figures to show the extra costs of short stage lengths:

Aircraft type	Route	Distance (miles)	Direct seat/ mile cost (d)
Viking	London—Paris	250	2·15
Viking	London—Nice	760	1·80
DC-6	London—Nice	760	1·59
DC-6	London—Athens	1,560	1·38

(*Annual Report*, 1952/3, p. 64.)

[10] BOAC, the long-haul British carrier, with an average journey of nearly 3,000 miles and mean stage of 1,000 miles, reduced costs per CTM from 40d in 1956 to 17d in 1966 (at 1958 prices). But the 1956 figure was well above that of comparable airlines and a larger reduction was to be expected.

[11] There will never be another aircraft so fabled. Its feats include: losing 12 feet of wing against a mountainside, but completing its flight and landing safely; having one wing replaced by a DC-2 wing, 5 feet shorter, and still flying satisfactorily; and taking off with as many as seventy-four people on board (nominal capacity was twenty-one seats) in China. About 13,000 DC-3s were built from 1935 to the late 1940s. No other aircraft has equalled this quantity of production. In 1976, forty-one years after its first flight, it was still performing sterling airline service all over the world.

[12] The Elizabethan was described as a burden to the engineering department in a frank *Annual Report* during its introduction — but so could have been most new aircraft. Its nearest American equivalents were probably the Convair CV-240 and the Martin 404. Each had about forty seats, two engines of approximately 2,400 hp and cruising speeds above the Elizabethan's 240 m.p.h.

[13] The main categories of direct costs were fuel and crew costs, aircraft landing fees and engineering overhaul and maintenance.

[14] Overhead costs cover aircraft depreciation, interest on capital, staff costs at base airport, sales costs and the running costs of ground operations.

[15] The Elizabethan class was withdrawn during 1957—8.

[16] The trimotor aircraft of 1928 operated in the US at about 2·6 cents per seat mile; their twin engined successors at about 15 per cent less. In 1936 the DC-3 in its first full year of operation seems to have reduced this to about 1·25 cents.

[17] Turbo-props and pure jets both use more fuel per passenger seat mile than piston engined aircraft, the advantage of the piston engine being less when compared with the pure jet. But the fuel used by the turbine, kerosene (paraffin), is of lower grade than aviation petrol and consequently is usually cheaper. Comparative fuel costs are thus dependent on the price ratio between kerosene and petrol and are particularly sensitive to the question of what taxes are levied on aviation fuels. In Britain the fuel and oil costs of the Viscount were some 40 per cent above those of the Elizabethan in the years 1954—7, per aircraft flying hour, while the Viscount produced about 25 per cent more seat miles per hour. Thus fuel costs were measurably higher for the Viscount. In the United States the Viscount returned lower fuel and oil costs per passenger seat mile than its piston engined competitors.

[18] Capital costs (depreciation and interest on the price of the aircraft and major spares) represented only about 5 per cent of total aircraft cost per flying hour, but other standing charges and fixed costs tend to follow the trend of capital costs. Fixed costs which follow the trend of capital costs can amount to as much as 25 per cent of costs per flying hour. The speed increase (and capacity increase) of Douglas aircraft which had approximately the same block speed as the Viscount took their weight up to 100,000 lb and over. The Viscount, at 57,000 lb, was only 9 per cent heavier than the DC-4 of 1942; it exceeded the Elizabethan's weight by only 2,000 lb, yet carried the same load nearly twice as far and nearly 50 per cent faster. The later Viscounts, of the same capacity as the DC-6 types, were 40 per cent lighter and cruised as fast or faster.

[19] Davies, *History of the World's Airlines*, op. cit.

[20] In constant price terms, the reduction in airline costs per CTM between 1948 and 1958 averaged nearly 12 per cent annually.

[21] The Edwards Committee, 1969, estimated that, even with identical organisation, hourly flying costs would be reduced by a figure in the region of 14 per cent merely by scaling up operations from five aircraft to fifty aircraft.

[22] Between 1950 and 1954 BEA would have had to operate at load factors of 75 per cent to achieve a profit.

[23] The basic productivity of the DC-3 type was 320 CTM per hour at stage lengths of up to 250 miles. The Pionair conversion managed to produce 370 CTM per hour; but BEA had to maintain standards of comfort rather higher than the seventy-four-seater DC-3 reported in China (see note 11 above) and thus further loading of the aircraft had to be ruled out. (Viscounts averaged 1,250 CTM/hour and the Trident 3 (1972) over 5,000 CTM/hour.)

[24] Select Committee on Nationalised Industries, *The Air Corporations*, HMSO, 1959.

[25] P. Brooks, *The World's Airliners*, Putnam, London, 1962.

[26] H. A. Taylor, *Airspeed Aircraft*, Putnam, London, 1970.

[27] P. St John Turner, *Handbook of the Vickers Viscount,* Ian Allan, London, 1970. Reported load factors were 80 per cent at start of services, a figure which could not be expected to hold for long.

[28] Achieved load factors are determined by the relationship between capacity and the level of demand. High load factors may be indicative of an airline's tendency to underestimate demand growth and thus to order less new capacity than is required. Both Air France and BEA were above world averages for passenger load factor throughout the 1950s. During the early years of Viscount operation, all the airlines shown were increasing their load factors; Air France and BEA were not unusual in this respect. Finally, load factors reflect the popularity of routes and, in an age when intercontinental travel was opening up, Air France and BEA undoubtedly benefitted from having their bases at Paris and London, where much intercontinental traffic started or finished.

[29] Davies, *History of the World's Airlines,* op. cit., and Miller & Sawers, *Technical Development of Modern Aviation,* op. cit.

[30] These figures for the Comet 1, estimated by the author, may tend to favour that aircraft.

[31] However, the Comet operated profitably for BOAC, partly because the competing long-range piston engine aircraft were much nearer in costs per flying hour to the Comet, between £250 and £300 compared to the Viscount's £180, and partly because the Comet operated at 75—80 per cent passenger load factors for the two years before it was withdrawn. The unusually high load factor would probably have disappeared once BOAC had ceased to be the monopoly operator of the type.

[32] H. Mansfield, *Vision — the Story of Boeing,* Popular Books, New York, 1966, by arrangement with Duell, Sloan and Pearce, New York. Boeing was able to take this risk, with $16 million of its own money, on the basis of profits from the B47 and B52 bombers built between 1951 and 1954.

[33] *Annual Report,* 1956/7, p. 51. It appears from the *Report* that jets were envisaged as offering serious competition to turbo-props only on the longer routes. BEA also talked about a fare differential; they anticipated no cost reduction from jets.

[34] The Caravelle's costs were estimated by P. W. Brooks, in *The World's Airliners,* op. cit., by the use of a standard formula. The costs given for the Comet 4B (a development of the Comet 1 and BEA's first jet) and Viscount 800 series are derived from BEA operational results. If used in services such as BEA's aircraft provided, the Caravelle's costs per flying hour could have been higher than £360 and the effective block speed lower.

[35] It was by no means alone in the conclusions it reached. During 1954 and 1955 American Airlines was actively seeking a larger turbo-prop and ordered seventy-five of the eighty-five-seat Electra from Lockheed in June 1955. More than 200 Electras were sold, partly because it was developed much more quickly than the Vanguard. Brooks (*The World's Airliners,* op. cit.) reports that there was also a widespread view among American operators that jets would be difficult and expensive to operate on short-haul routes. When Boeing came to sound airline opinion on the 727 project, the potentially high costs of jets were a major airline pre-occupation.

[36] The government contributed £4m. to the Tyne, but its total development costs were considerably more.

[37] This was natural enough, since the V810 was bearing a diminishing share of the original development costs of the Viscount and Dart (engine). For the operator, however, it was a poor deal, since the ratio of productivities was 1:2·2 (V810 first) while the price ratio was 1:2·4. The Vanguard also seems to have been priced higher than the Caravelle. According to Brooks (*The World's Airliners,* op. cit.), the latter was £900,000 in Autumn 1959, while the Vanguard was £980,000.

[38] Growth was 14 per cent over the previous year in 1959, 12 per cent in 1960 and 8 per cent in 1961. The decline from 1956 to 1958 had been much sharper (ICAO, *Digest of Statistics* No. 90, 'Traffic').

[39] R. H. Whitby, Lecture to Southampton Branch, Royal Aeronautical Society, 24 November 1965.

[40] K. Hartley, 'Mergers in the Aircraft Industry, 1957—60', *J. Royal Aero. Soc.,* December 1965. The Select Committee on the Estimates of 1956/7 had warned of these intentions and the Defence White Paper of 1957 underlined them.

[41] Hawker Siddeley and Bristol formed a consortium, preparatory to merger, in order to tender to the BEA requirement, and the Ministries favoured this project.

[42] Estimates Committee, *Transport Aircraft,* HCP 42, Session 63/4, Q. 365.

[43] In 1966 the Board of Trade indicated that financial approval was delayed twelve months by the cut-back in 1957 on public corporations spending (Select Committee on Nationalised Industries, 1966/7, *BEA,* HMSO, 1967).

[44] During the six years 1960/1 to 1966/7 a total of £8 million was capitalised as introductory costs, but the real costs of innovatory aircraft may have been twice as much. BEA estimated costs of £6·1 million up to March 1963, mostly attributable to the Vanguard, but the Trident, which was about to start service, also had heavy introductory costs.

[45] Lufthansa resumed operation in 1956, providing a major new competitor for BEA.

[46] In defence of the airline, it must be said that the losses might not have occurred if it had been allowed to order the American aircraft it wanted (see below).

[47] The flexible aircraft is usually one with an excess of power for its designed most economical range. It can thus lift off the ground an increased fuel load for longer range flights without an equivalent decrease in payload and thus without too severe a penalty in seat-mile costs. Conversely, a higher payload than designed can be carried on shorter stage lengths, by using higher density seating, again without too much penalty. 'Flexibility' thus indicates a relatively flat curve of seat-mile costs plotted against range.

[48] The Comet, too, was due for replacement. It had been intended for service from 1960 to 1964 only, but had been retained because of the swing to jets. Only the Trident 1 was to be kept from the existing fleet, and no pre-1964 aircraft were to remain on mainline services after 1970.

[49] The top thirty international airlines showed recorded profits of 3 per cent of revenue in a good year. (Davies, *History of the World's Airlines,* op. cit.)

[50] However, Air France had bought the Viscount and the Caravelle was half British, since it used Rolls Royce engines.

3 Power Station Performance: Policies for Development 1945-75

Summary

The most important cost problem which affected the electricity supply industry at the time of nationalisation was caused by the price of coal. Coal prices had been rising steadily since the 1930s and fuel costs had increased from about one-third to over a half of the industry's total costs. With fuel forming such an important input to production, the generating industry, like the gas industry, became extremely sensitive to further price increases. Although coal for electricity generating was not in such short supply as gas coals, its price nevertheless rose by about 75 per cent up to 1960. Increased costs from this source alone were sufficient to make price increases of approximately 40 per cent necessary for the industry, had there been no opportunity to improve efficiency.

There were, however, substantial opportunities for improving the generation process. The coal-fired boiler, steam turbine and electrical alternator had been used for generation since the early 1900s. Thermal efficiency, which is the inverse of fuel productivity, is dependent upon the application of various technical improvements to each of the components of generating equipment (such as the addition of a steam re-heat cycle), and is also more generally dependent upon operating steam temperatures and pressures. At the time of nationalisation average thermal efficiency in the generating authority's stations was 20 per cent and there was a preponderance of older plant in which thermal efficiency was well below this level. Technically it was feasible at the time to install plant which would operate at 28 to 30 per cent, using techniques and steam conditions which were already established in practice. Further advances made by the generating authority during the 1950s and early 1960s, both in the application of improvements to turbo-alternators and in the raising of steam conditions, brought thermal efficiencies up to 35 per cent.

Of only slightly less importance than fuel costs were capital costs. The constant-price costs of building power stations had shown a declining trend during the earlier part of the twentieth century, due to improved technical efficiency and larger scale of units. The pace of technical change had then begun to slow in the 1930s and the cost of building new stations failed to decline further. With the effect of wartime and postwar inflation, building costs began to rise steeply. At the stage of technological development reached in the 1950s, and as a result of scale increases, the capital costs of generating equipment showed a further marked tendency to decline, as power stations advanced in size from 200 MW to 2,000 MW and individual generating units grew from 30—60 MW to 500 MW. The decline in costs was assisted by the improvement in thermal efficiency. In terms of constant prices, power station building costs declined from about £90 per kW in the late 1940s to around £40 per kW in the early 1960s.

One of the most important new techniques of the postwar period was the development of electricity generation from nuclear power stations. In this technique only the heat source is radically different from conventional methods. Steam produced in a heat exchanger is still used to power a turbine for the alternator. The nuclear power station contributed neither to improved thermal efficiency nor to reduced capital costs in the first twenty-five years of its development. The building of some fifteen Magnox and AGR stations in Britain was initiated as a programme from which economic benefits were expected in the long run. Magnox stations were launched as a measure to safeguard fuel supplies and the later AGR stations were begun in the belief, not unfortunately borne out, that they would be cheaper overall than conventional power stations.

The generating industry's organisation for bringing about technical change was uneven, both in its pattern and in its performance. Before nationalisation, ownership of the industry was fragmented, but there were several outstanding companies which acted as industry leaders. The generating companies entered very little into research and development on generating techniques, but acted as informed and discriminating customers of the equipment manufacturers. Techniques were generally advanced through the process of one generating company agreeing to the purchase of an advanced design of plant from a manufacturer and operating the design somewhat experimentally. When the new techniques involved were established as practicable, further orders based on the design principle would follow. However this informal process had failed to produce a rate of technical advance commensurate with that in other countries for some years before nationalisation, partly through fragmentation and the small size of many companies, which led to them being unwilling to invest in advanced or large-scale designs, and partly through the low rate of investment in new plant, which resulted in the opportunity for experimental plant being limited.

The industry had a strong professional association in the Institution of Electrical Engineers. The Institution provided a useful forum for the discussion of technical developments. One of the major pre-war changes had been the construction of the Grid by a specially created public corporation, and in this venture leading engineers in the profession had played a major part, in both planning and execution. Interconnection of the main centres of electricity demand through the Grid provided the opportunity to build much larger power stations. The means of planning for the installation of large central power stations was provided when the supply industry came under the management of a single national public corporation.[1]

Although rising costs provide a sufficient explanation of the ensuing changes in scale and techniques, the strength of demand for electricity proved an equal or greater force in causing those changes to be adopted rapidly throughout the system. Demand grew at rates between 6 and 10 per cent annually for most of the years 1947—65, and during much of this period the capacity of the system was less than the potential simultaneous maximum demand. Additional capacity was installed as rapidly as the physical constraints imposed by planning and construction would allow. Initially the technical characteristics and steam conditions of new plant installed were conservative, but the generating authority's engineers pressed for rapid technical change. Major advances in generating equipment were made between 1951 and 1966, at first very successfully; in later programmes of new plant, particularly those involving the 500 MW generator and the AGR, performance to design and time schedule was not maintained. Technical failures, cost increases and delay affected both the conventional generating programme and the nuclear one. The effects were less severe than they might have been, because the growth of demand had slowed down by the time that the main difficulties were being experienced.

At the time of nationalisation the generating authority had not undertaken a thorough overhaul of the supply industry's arrangements for the advance of techniques. On the transmission side, central research facilities existed prior to public ownership and they were added to by the new public corporation. On the generation side the authority did not set up central facilities for comprehensive research into advancing techniques. Although laboratories existed on a small scale at some power stations, and tests were carried out on new equipment, the major responsibility for research remained with the manufacturers.

Responding to the pressures of demand and of rising costs, the generating authority tried to speed up the process of advancing techniques and of raising unit sizes, but the informal procedures which had previously been accepted for promoting technical change proved inadequate to their new task. The first major change, from a standard of 60 MW to turbo-generators of 100 MW capacity, was accomplished successfully. It was, however, assisted by the fact that the change in scale was fairly small and did not stretch existing techniques very far. Sets of 60 MW, 75 MW and 100 MW outputs had previously been operated, although the last size had been of rather different design from that which the authority proposed in the early 1950s. Steam pressures were advanced from 900 lb/sq. in. to 1,500 lb/sq. in., and temperatures from 900°F to 1,000°F, but again these were not far above the levels of some previous sets of advanced design. The second change, to 200 MW 2,350 lb/sq. in. and 1,050°F, was used very successfully in one application but was not adopted as a standard. Then half-a-dozen larger sizes of an experimental nature were ordered without pause to consolidate the techniques being employed. They culminated in the 500 MW size, which was adopted as a standard but which had a troubled career.

The increases in scale and operating parameters involved in the AGR programme were even more drastic. The 600 MW reactors ordered were based on a research prototype only one-twentieth the size and working at much lower temperatures and efficiencies. The AGR design was not fixed and was not commercially developed when ordered. In consequence its progress was beset by technical snags, delays and cost increases.

Inquiries into the failures in the 500 MW generator programme laid the blame partly upon the quality of management applied by the CEGB to progress these large projects, and partly on shortcomings in the design capabilities of the manufacturers. While both these criticisms were no doubt justified, they tended to divert attention from the more important issue, of whether the arrangements for research and development and the application of advanced techniques in the generating industry were such as to make the failures which occurred more likely.

The CEGB pointed to the responsibility of the manufacturers for some of the design failings. They in their turn argued that the CEGB, as a monopoly buyer, had squeezed profits and contracts so much that it was not surprising that the research, experimental work and designs which were necessary to such advanced programmes were not always to be found in the developments which followed public ownership.

The truth seems to be that the industry and the Board were together attempting to achieve a fairly complex technical objective, but that neither singly nor collectively did they give its difficulty proper recognition. The research, technical development and consolidation of advanced techniques which were needed for success were not planned for. Investing in new plant for the system was a function not separately distinguished from running the development programme, and the needs of one activity clashed with those of the other.

In the nuclear plant programme also, it appears that technical developments were pushed forward much faster than was justified. The AGR design‘ was so little developed that building a full-scale station would have been desirable only in order for it to act as a commercial demonstration plant for the principles involved. The Generating Board and the Atomic Energy Authority did not see the necessity for this step.

POWER STATION SIZE

Since the end of the nineteenth century the general trend of development in power stations has been to build larger and larger concentrations of generating equipment. The earliest electricity supply power stations were conceived as local units and were designed to provide lighting and power for a district which might have a radius of no more than a mile. However the engineer in charge of one such station in central London, just off Piccadilly, had noticed the tendency of gas companies to close their smaller works and relocate production in larger-scale gas making plants on cheaper land and nearer to cheap supplies of fuel as their total demand and area of supply increased. He decided that the same policy would confer the benefits of scale and of optimising costs upon electricity supply. The young engineer, Sebastian de Ferranti, chose a site at Deptford where space was not constricted, coal could be transported cheaply and water for cooling was abundant. There he started to build in 1888 a power station which would have had an installed capacity of steam engines totalling 120,000 hp had it ever been completed, and which could perhaps have supplied the lighting needs of the whole of central London at that time.[2]

Although the Deptford station was never completed as planned, the policy of establishing large central stations was one that was increasingly adopted by electricity authorities in the years that followed. However, there were many different supply companies, and although it became technically more economical to produce electricity on the scale envisaged by Ferranti, and beyond it, in the early 1900s, little progress was made to integrate and concentrate electricity supply until after the First World War.[3]

Considerable interest was taken in electricity supply by Government and Parliament. The reports produced and legislation based upon them created a climate of opinion favourable to more co-ordination, within which first the Electricity Commissioners (1919) and later the Central Electricity Board (1926) came into being.[4] The former had an advisory role in trying to promote the re-organisation of supply on a rationalised basis, but the CEB was given technical functions and administrative powers by the Electricity (Supply) Act of 1926.

The Weir Committee, whose report in 1926 led to the creation of the CEB, found that there were 572 supply undertakings running 438 generating stations. At the time about 5,400 million kWh of electricity were generated annually, an average of over 12 million kWh per station per year. The CEB was set up to concentrate supply upon stations selected as the most efficient ones, and to establish a national system of distribution; low-cost electricity from the more modern stations would then be available to most electricity undertakings at the lowest possible price. In this way the National Grid, a network of transmission lines for distributing electricity to all parts of England and Wales, was authorised and constructed. Between 1931 and 1938 the Grid was gradually extended over the country by the CEB and from 1933 onwards the Board traded in electricity supply, buying units from the selected stations and selling them to the public undertakings.

By 1948, when the generating industry became nationalised, there were just over 300 generating stations, 143 supplying to the Grid with a further 55 for peak loads. By contrast the number of supply undertakings had dropped by only 12 to 560.

The trend towards concentration of output continued when the British Electricity Authority (BEA) took control. The average size of power stations increased, because of the policy of expanding capacity by adding ever larger units to the system (Table 3.1). The largest power stations in the 1880s were about 1,000 kW, equal to one megawatt (1 MW). By the 1920s power stations were coming into operation at over 100 MW of installed capacity.[5] Barking, opened in 1925, eventually had 120 MW of capacity provided by four separate generating sets, and was planned to reach 540 MW when completed in the early 1940s. By the time that the British Electricity Authority took over the system there were three stations, Barking B, Fulham, Hams Hall B, which approached or just exceeded 300 MW each. Half-a-dozen other stations had output capacities exceeding 200 MW. Twenty years afterwards, in 1968, at West Burton on the River Trent there came into operation a single station served by four generating sets with a total output of 2,000 MW.

Table 3.1 *Power Station Size and Output, England and Wales*

Year	Number of power stations[a]	Electricity generated[b] (m. kWh)	Capacity installed (MW)	Supplied per station (m. kWh)	Capacity per station (MW)	System load factor (%)
1925	438	5,742	(3,700)	12	8	n.a.
1935	(350)	15,863	(7,100)	45	20	n.a.
1945	(320)	33,545	(10,900)	104	34	n.a.
1955	273	75,561	18,951	276	69	48
1965	233	160,360	37,076	688	159	48
1975	168	227,226	63,135	1,327	376	41

Sources: CEA, CEGB, *Annual Reports* and Electricity Council, *Handbook of Electricity Supply Statistics*, 1966.

Notes: [a] Figures in brackets are estimates. n.a. = not available.
[b] Number of sites up to 1945.
In financial year starting in recorded year.

THE SIZE OF GENERATING SETS

Early generating sets were small, but here again there have been continued efforts by generating engineers to go to larger sizes of generator to meet electricity demands. A Cambridge graduate, Mr J. Gordon, astounded the electrical world in 1882 by constructing an alternator for generating electricity with an estimated output of 350 kW. Ferranti's machines at Deptford would have had a far higher capacity.

The first generator of 1 megawatt size was built by Parsons, the inventor of the turbo-alternator, in 1900 for a public utility in Germany. By 1904, Parsons was installing 3·5 MW sets at Newcastle and in 1912 a 25 MW set constructed by his company was exported to the USA.[6] During the 1920s it became increasingly common for new power stations in areas of heavy demand, such as Birmingham and London, to have generators installed of 30, 40 or 50 MW rating. The largest set built before the war in Britain was a 105 MW turbo-alternator commissioned at Battersea A power station in 1933. It was at the time the largest generator in Europe and was not exceeded in size in Britain until the 1950s (Table 3.2).

Table 3.2 *Scale Changes, England and Wales, 1900—70*

Period	Largest stations opened in period	Largest generators commissioned in period
1900—19		11 MW at Carville B, 1914
1920—39	Hams Hall A 250 MW, 1929—39	105 MW at Battersea A, 1933
1940—59	Castle Donnington 627 MW, 1956—60	200 MW at High Marnham, 1959
1960—75	West Burton and others 2,000 MW, 1968—75	550 MW at Thorpe Marsh, 1963

Under the British Electricity Authority, generating sets increased in size from a norm of 30 and 60 MW to the 100 and 120 MW sets which were brought into operation in the late 1950s. High Marnham power station in Yorkshire had a 200 MW generator operating by the end of 1959. During the period 1957 to 1963 there were a number of different sizes of generating set under development, at 275, 300, 350, 375, 500 and 550 MW. These experimental generators led to the adoption by the generating authority (which had become the Central Electricity Generating Board in 1958) of the new standard 500 MW set, first commissioned in 1966 at Ferrybridge power station in north Yorkshire.

The next size of generating set, at 660 MW, began operating at Drax power station in 1974. Studies were carried out during the 1960s on single units of generating equipment working at over 1,000 MW, but it was decided not to proceed with them.

TRANSMISSION TECHNIQUES

The two conditions which have made possible steady growth in the scale on which electricity is generated are the growth of demand and the development of transmission techniques. It was a German, Oskar van Miller, who first demonstrated in 1891 the feasibility of long distance transmission of electricity. He used a three-phase a.c. supply at 25,000 V to supply Frankfurt from Lauffen, 110 miles away.

Transmission difficulties played a large part in delaying the start-up of the power station which Sebastian Ferranti built at Deptford, the forerunner of the large modern central station. The engineer finally overcame the inadequacy of existing transmission techniques by designing and constructing his own cable, which came into operation, also in 1891, at 10,000 V. Until the setting up of the CEB, the extension of transmission networks was limited, although some power companies achieved a fair amount of integration of supply. The Central Electricity Board was responsible for choosing the National Grid voltage and after studying a number of systems determined on 132,000 volts (132 kV).

Subsequently a transmission research laboratory was established at Leatherhead in Surrey. Under the CEB and BEA its work was directed at raising voltages still further. During the 1950s the Grid was being converted to 275 kV and in the late 1960s a Supergrid was established at 400 kV. In order for the benefits of cheaper sources of fuel and the enormous scale of operation to be extended to the consumers, who needed the power in the big conurbations, transmission methods of very high capacity and comparatively low cost had to be available.[7] It was fortunate, therefore, that the raising of voltages to higher levels brought increasing returns to scale. The 132 kV transmission lines of the period before the war were capable of transmitting a power output of about 100 MW. They were thus appropriate to the largest power stations of the time being built outside the conurbations. In 1953 the 275 kV grid system began operating. It had a capacity for transmission of about 600 MW, six times the load of the 132 kV line and very much in keeping with the output capacity of the largest power stations being commissioned during the 1950s, such as Castle Donnington, The 400 kV grid of the 1960s had a capacity of about 1,800 MW.[8]

The generating authority thus had full scope for establishing power stations in any part of the country. Although initially the planning of new power stations was conducted on the basis of locating them in the same region as the load to be met, the longer term trend was to develop to their logical conclusion the criteria for location which Ferranti had first used to establish a site at Deptford. Power stations such as West Burton, at 2,000 MW, could therefore be sited on the Yorkshire coalfield, on relatively cheap land and near to supplies of cooling water.

CAPITAL COSTS AND SIZE OF PLANT

The justification for concentrating electricity supply and building power stations and generating sets on an increasing scale was to improve the efficiency of supply and to reduce capital costs per kW of installed generating capacity.

Scale factors tend to produce lower costs as the size of the power station and generating set increases, because the capital cost of constructing them rises less than proportionately to the increase in the electrical rating of the set.[9] Some of the reduction in capital costs which follows from scaling up power stations can be attributed to the main generating machinery, the boilers, steam turbines and alternators, which may account for about 40 per cent of the total cost of the power station. There are also savings from ancillary machinery, such as coal handling equipment, feed water tanks, pumping gear, fans, etc., which, although comparatively unsophisticated technically, can be used much more efficiently on a large scale than on a small one. Finally there are the building and civil engineering works (which may very well amount to 25—30 per cent of the cost of a whole station), on which costs may be reduced as scale increases.[10]

The potential savings in the capital cost per kilowatt of installed capacity in steam power stations were well known to engineers and designers before the generating industry came under public ownership, but for various reasons were not universally exploited. When the British Electricity Authority began to raise the design output of all new stations during the mid-1950s, very considerable economies were effected. Most power stations planned between 1948 and 1952 had total outputs of between 100 MW and 300 MW, no larger than the leaders of the 1930s, and used generating sets of 30 MW and 60 MW. But larger sets, of 100 MW, began to be designed in 1951 for commissioning some five years later.

The time needed to plan and commission a complete power station was such that the savings represented by a 600 MW station with six 100 MW generators over a 180 MW station with six 30 MW generators did not register upon completed power station construction costs until the late 1950s (Table 3.3).

Table 3.3 *Capital Costs of New Power Stations Commissioned*

Year	Costs (£ per kW)[a]		Year	Costs (£ per kW)[a]	
	Current prices	Constant prices[b]		Current prices	Constant prices[b]
1948	51·5	90·1	1956	58·6	63·0
1949	53·6	88·5	1957	58·3	61·1
1950	58·5	87·3	1958	54·5	54·5
1951	63·6	86·0	1959	54·5	54·5
1952	68·0	82·9	1960	54·7	54·7
1953	67·9	79·9	1961	44·1	43·7
1954	63·3	74·5			
1955	60·7	69·0			

Source: Select Committee on Nationalised Industries, *The Electricity Supply Industry,* HMSO, 1963.
Notes: [a] Capacity measured in terms of maximum output power, rather than installed.
[b] Adjusted to 1958 prices. Estimated constant price levels for 1948 and 1949.

The reduction of about 50 per cent in capital costs (at constant 1958 prices) from 1948 to 1957 could be ascribed in part to some increase in the size of sets, but also to a considerable extent to the efforts of the BEA to produce more standardised and more economical designs for power stations than had existed under the many different generating authorities in the past. The decrease of nearly 25 per cent between 1955 and 1958 was assisted by the arrival of the first 100 MW sets and the phasing out of 30 MW generators in favour of the 60 MW. The further reduction of 24 per cent in 1961 costs over 1960 costs marks the appearance of 200 MW turbo-generator single units and the influence of an increasing number of 120 MW sets.

It was anticipated that construction costs would fall below £35 per kW (£30 per kW at 1958 prices) when the 500 MW stations were commissioned in 1966. Unfortunately, information on a basis comparable with Table 3.3 about the actual costs of construction of the stations envisaged is not available; but the anticipated capital cost gains of the 500 MW and 660 MW sets over the 200 MW and 300 MW sets have not been realised.[11]

In addition to scale factors, lower generating costs are achieved by increasing thermal efficiency. There are some inevitable losses of energy in the process of producing steam in a boiler and electrical output from a turbo-generator. Most of the losses occur in the turbine. Whether the fuel is coal, oil or uranium (for nuclear power stations), the maximum efficiency with which it can be burned (or irradiated) to produce usable steam energy falls within the range of about 75 to 85 per cent. The turbine does well to achieve 35 per cent. Electrical machines are more efficient and over 90 per cent of the energy given by the steam turbine is available as electrical output. The resulting overall thermal efficiency of power stations is between 25 and 35 per cent. Stations commissioned just after the war operated at thermal efficiencies of 25—27 per cent. The 2,000 MW stations of the late 1960s regularly achieve 35 per cent. The best British performance, of nearly 36 per cent, was achieved by West Thurrock in 1965.

Thermal efficiencies of this order are very much higher than were ever achieved by generators driven from reciprocating steam engines, and credit for the high level reached goes to the basic invention of the steam turbo-alternator.[12] It is still the fundamental basis of the generation of electricity in Britain ninety years after first being used. The generation of electricity from nuclear energy is the most outstanding new technique of the twentieth century in the field of power supply and yet a nuclear power station differs from a conventional one only in replacing the source of heat. The nuclear reactor replaces the coal or oil flame, but it is used to produce steam in a boiler (or heat-exchanger) in the same way that a flame does. Nuclear stations still depend upon the efficiency of the turbine as a fundamental determinant of their output efficiency. The other new entrant to the field is gas turbine generation. Its thermal efficiency is lower than in conventional plant, but capital costs are lower too.

The performance of the steam turbo-alternator in terms of thermal efficiency is not directly related to scale. Numerous developments of the basic design contribute to increases in electrical output per unit of fuel input. Design improvements have more than doubled the electrical output from fuel consumed. A ton of coal burnt in 1975 in the average coal-fired power station of the CEGB produced 1,900 kWh; in the most efficient power stations a ton produced 2,200 kWh. During the early 1900s a ton of coal produced rather under 1,000 kWh, and that only at the more efficient turbine-powered stations.

These improvements in efficiency came about because of changes in boiler design and firing methods, because of the successive increases in the temperatures and pressures at which the turbines worked and because of heat-saving methods. The most common firing method used by the 1950s, and regarded as the most efficient for coal-firing, was the burning of pulverised fuel. This overcame most of the problems of boiler stoking and ash removal. It was first used experimentally in 1903 at Acton Lane in London. Cyclone fired boilers followed later. Another improvement in boiler efficiency was gained by using waste steam heat to pre-heat the boiler feed water; this was first adopted in a Parsons plant in Durham in 1916.

The steam pressures and temperatures initially used for turbines were fairly low, but the Newcastle Electric Supply Company, one of the largest in the north east, ordered plant in 1916 for Carville B power station to run at 250 pounds per square inch (lb/sq. in.) and 650°F. Five years later, at North Tees power station, steam pressures of 450 lb/sq. in. and temperatures of 650°F were used, while Hams Hall A in 1929 used similar pressures and temperatures in conjunction with 30 MW sets and 50 MW sets. Advances followed to 600 lb/sq. in. and 800°F at Battersea A station (1933), Dunston B (1933) and Fulham (1936).

Further improvements in turbines came from re-heating the steam after it had passed the first set of turbine blades, while it was still under pressure, and thus getting more work out of it at later turbine stages. Reheat was first used at North Tees in 1921. It was also gradually found that matching one boiler to one turbo-alternator, rather than having a range of boilers to feed several turbines, raised the design efficiency. The most important changes in alternator design were from rotating armature to rotating field (1902) and in the methods used to cool the windings.

All the developments which are described above, in power station size, in the scale of boiler-turbo-alternator sets and in the advancing of generating techniques, took place piecemeal throughout Britain and in an unco-ordinated fashion during the first sixty or seventy years of the industry's history. Three of the foremost power companies before the second world war were the North Eastern Electric Supply Company, which had absorbed the Newcastle company, and two big London groupings, the North Metropolitan and the London Power Supply Company. The North Eastern had a long association with the firms of C. A. Parsons, turbine manufacturers, and with Babcock and Wilcox, boiler constructors. The last major power station they constructed, Dunston B, was one of the most efficient in the country from 1935 right up to the mid-1950s. The London companies had Barking, Battersea and Fulham to their credit and with the Newcastle company had been among the first to use re-heat, had led by installing very large units (105 MW at Battersea) and by ordering a very high pressure turbine at Brimsdown of 1,900 lb/sq. in. and 930°F re-heat, coming into operation shortly before the war. However, other power companies, such as the Shropshire, Worcestershire and Staffordshire and the Kent Electric Power Company, had their own ambitions to advance techniques. There was some rivalry between the different companies involved and there was a tendency for each utility company to have preferred suppliers from the manufacturing side.

In the circumstances, it was not surprising that the range of techniques employed throughout the whole industry was very wide and that as late as 1935 the most efficient station (Battersea A), at 28·6 per cent thermal efficiency, should be more than 40 per cent better than the average for all steam stations, of 20·2 per cent. Nor were matters improved during the war, when much new plant which should have been installed was deferred. The overall thermal efficiency of all steam stations in 1947/8 was still only 20·9 per cent and the most efficient stations were still operating only at about 29 per cent.[13]

TECHNICAL PROGRESS UNDER NATIONALISATION

Since the First World War, different committees and commissions of inquiry had considered the proposal that the generation and distribution of electricity be taken over by public agencies, in order both to increase the minimum area of administration of supply and also to gain the benefits from scale and technical advance. These objectives had been partly achieved by the Central Electricity Board; after the Electricity Bill of 1947 became law, the conditions were established in which concentration, scale change and rapid technical advance could go ahead unhindered.

Electricity demand in Britain was growing at an annual rate of about 6·5 per cent during the 1940s; when the country began to settle back into peacetime conditions, however, demand increases became quite sharp in the latter part of the decade. Between 1936 and 1946 demand had approximately doubled, but generating plant capacity had increased only by 50 per cent, from 8,000 MW in 1936 to 12,000 MW ten years later. Peak demand for electricity was calculated to exceed capacity by 10 per cent to 15 per cent at the time of nationalisation.[14] Consumer demand increased by 9·5 per cent from 1947 to 1948, from 35,000 million to 38,390 million kWh. The British Electricity Authority estimated that 30,000 MW of new and replacement plant would be needed by 1968.[15] In other words, electricity generation was marked out for a period of very rapid growth, which favoured a high rate of advance in techniques, and during the years 1947 to 1950 there was a particularly critical shortage of generating capacity. Adding to the problems of demand growth and the lack of wartime investment, there was great difficulty in getting the annual programmes of plant installation completed as planned in the years immediately after the war. During the three years 1946 to 1948 only 1,200 MW of new capacity came into use, an average of 400 MW per year. Pre-war levels of investment had been running at over 800 MW annually.

It might have been expected that the Authority would respond to this situation by ordering the largest units considered practical at the time. All the experience of power station design from 1900 to the 1930s had underlined the practicality of steady increases in the unit size of boilers and turbo-alternators. Sets of 40 and 50 MW (Barking and Hams Hall) had been pioneered in the 1920s and the 1930s had seen 60 MW turbos used at Fulham (1936), 75 MW sets at Barking B (1933) and 69 MW and 105 MW sets at Battersea A station. These larger sizes of generating unit had also been associated with innovative designs, particularly the raising of steam temperature and pressure at the entry to the turbine and the use of re-heat; some of the larger sets ordered shortly before nationalisation and coming into operation during the 1940s or very early 1950s combined large generating units with high steam temperatures and pressures to become the most efficient stations in the system.[16] At a time of coal shortage the higher thermal efficiencies achieved by more advanced steam conditions and re-heat were an important consideration. Finally, the larger pre-war generating units clearly demonstrated the relationship between size of set and reducing capital cost per kW installed, which was referred to above.

Instead of ordering advanced sets immediately, the Authority found itself more or less bound to put in hand a large programme of construction stretching into the late 1950s based upon two standard sizes, at 30 MW and 60 MW, with steam conditions which were by no means advanced for the time, without re-heat and many of them without unit boilers.[17] The 'standard set' programme put in hand during the years 1947 to 1950 (orders placed as far back as November 1946 were renegotiated to fit the conditions of standard sizes and steam conditions so far as was possible) covered about thirty new stations and ten extensions to existing stations, the major part of the Authority's programme.

The first standard sets of 30 MW were brought into use during 1948, because the size was already an established one; the first 60 MW was commissioned at Staythorpe in 1950. Such was the size of the programme that the standard range of sets still dominated the new plant being commissioned during 1958 and 1959, even though work had started on larger generating units with advanced steam conditions and re-heat during 1950 and 1951. In the new stations, 6,800 MW was installed as standard 30 and 60 MW units between 1948 and 1960. Another 700 MW of capacity in extensions of existing stations was ordered in general conformity to the standard set sizes. Between 1950 and 1958 the standard sets accounted for between 60 and 75 per cent of all generating equipment installed.

The Authority was bound to accept the procedure of ordering these fairly small sizes in quantity between 1948 and 1950 because of an Order of the Ministry of Supply, published in November 1947, before the Electricity Act took effect but after the Organising Committee had begun work on preparing for public ownership. The Order had an important effect upon the thermal efficiency of generating stations in Britain up to about 1960 and upon the apparent level of technical advance in the generating industry.

A report published in 1966, which reviewed the production techniques used in coal-fired electricity generating in Britain, France and the United States, found evidence of comparative technological backwardness in Britain. In 1962 British generating plant produced less than 80 kWh per million Btus (British thermal units) of heat, where French and American plant approached 95 kWh per million Btus. The explanation of this phenomenon favoured by the report was that the average size of British boilers and turbo-alternators was considerably smaller in new plant installed and only caught up with French and American plant in the early 1960s. Similarly, steam temperatures and pressures were less advanced and new installations were not all fitted with re-heat until 1961 (in France 100 per cent re-heat for new plant had been used in 1956 and in America 95 per cent since 1955).

A very large part of the technological backwardness identified may be attributed to the 30 MW and 60 MW generating units upon which the Ministry of Supply decided standardisation should take place in 1947. It was only late in 1956 that the first 100 MW set without re-heat ordered by the Authority came into use at Castle Donnington, and fewer than ten sets of 100 MW were in use in Britain before 1960. Up to 1959 re-heat was employed only in the half-a-dozen power stations where it had been developed as a technique before nationalisation and at the Blyth A and Ferrybridge B power stations ordered by the Authority. Sets larger than 60

MW and with advanced steam conditions were not present in the system in sufficient numbers to have any appreciable effect upon thermal efficiency until after 1960, when Britain started catching up with France and the United States.

Further explanation of the lag in technology which Britain suffered can be found in the age of plant employed for generation, a feature of lack of investment between 1930 and 1945 and an excess of demand in postwar conditions. One-third of the generating sets in use in 1949 were over twenty-five years old, providing about 13 per cent of capacity. Less than 30 per cent of capacity had been installed in the previous ten years and about half of the available machinery and boilers had been installed between 1924 and 1939.

Ten years later, in 1958/9, the proportion of generating capacity over twenty-five years old had risen to 18 per cent.

Although 57 per cent of generating capacity had been commissioned in the previous ten years, the contribution which this more modern equipment had made to improved thermal efficiency was limited by the fact that the standard sizes predominated. The 30 MW and 60 MW sets did not improve thermal efficiency and fuel productivity in Britain very fast, because they were not of an advanced design and represented no major increase in thermal efficiency themselves. The majority of the 30 MW sets in 1946—9 operated at just over 26 per cent. Battersea and Dunston B had achieved 28 per cent in the 1930s. Two or three of the early 60 MW set power stations came into operation from 1950 onwards at about 27 per cent (Staythorpe, Keadby and Littlebrook C) but there were steady improvements in the operating efficiency of this size range, over 30 per cent being reached by Tilbury, South Denes and Marchwood in the late 1950s. The stations which achieved the highest thermal efficiencies during the mid-1950s were those few at which for various reasons experimentation was continuing with higher steam pressures than 900 lb/sq. in., or else where re-heat was being used.[18]

The decision taken by the Ministry of Supply in 1947 appears to have been unnecessarily conservative. It was made necessary by the disorganisation of manufacturing facilities during the war period and represented an attempt to turn out replicate sets. However, the average standard of techniques in generating was held back, possibly for six or seven years, by the 1947 Order; in the United States, for instance, the first high speed generating set of 100 MW to operate at fairly advanced steam conditions (1,250 lb/sq. in. and 1,000°F) with a tandem-compound design on a single shaft was installed in 1947 at the Essex generating station in New Jersey.[19] Operation at these steam conditions did not take place in Britain for another ten years.

On the other hand, this conservatism in design should be seen as part of a chain of events which started during the 1920s. The British generating and supply industry had been highly innovative from the late nineteenth century up to the mid-1930s. Ably assisted by the manufacturers of boilers and generating plant, it had promoted rapid advances in the sizes of turbo-alternators, in steam conditions and in overall thermal efficiency. However the supply industry was fragmented and the range of efficiencies in power plant was wide. Government policy in the interwar years was to concentrate supply on the most efficient stations and to bring the total of capacity installed more into line with demand. Cutting out excess capacity was calculated to provide cheaper electricity.

In 1930 the total capacity of generating stations on the public supply was almost 7,000 MW, whereas SMD (simultaneous maximum demand) amounted to less than 4,000 MW. The objectives of the CEB's National Grid were both to allow the concentration of electricity generation at the most efficient stations and also to bring capacity into a closer relationship with SMD. A figure of 15 per cent reserve capacity for ideal operation was mentioned.[20] The Central Electricity Board was given the power to order generating stations to be operated under its direction, and the Electricity Commissioners gained the power to regulate the annual programmes of installation of power plant by the supply industry. The result was that the construction of the Grid caused a moratorium for several years in power station building. Increased demand of a local nature could, after 1934, be met by transfers through the Grid, instead of by new building. The new plant authorised by the Commissioners, which had been running at annual levels of 500 MW to 600 MW from the end of the war to 1929, dropped to 260 MW per year from the year 1929/30 to 1933/4.

The moratorium effectively meant that during the middle five years of the 1930s there was very little new capacity installed. It is usually the case that major advances in the techniques incorporated in capital equipment are possible only with new installations, and generating equipment is no exception. Although during the early 1930s steam conditions of 600—650 lb/sq. in. and 800—850°F had been used and had come to be expected for important stations, the opportunity for incorporating these standards in new plant was sharply diminished by the lower rate of installation of capital equipment.

The Central Electricity Board had statutory authority to standardise on frequency and voltage throughout Britain, but it carried its duties further during the war, by setting standards for power station design and trying to ensure that new plant conformed at least to the techniques developed in the 1930s. The Electricity Commissioners were charged with the duty to authorise each year's programme of generating plant construction and this authority provided the Central Electricity Board with an effective means of influencing the operating standards of new plant.[21]

Higher pressures and more innovative plant work did continue. Battersea B and Brimsdown A stations both incorporated high pressure units in cross-compound sets, commissioned in 1944 and 1938 respectively, while sets of similar steam conditions were included in plant programmes very soon after the war at Stourport and Portobello (Edinburgh). And the establishment of standards by the CEB at least had the positive effect that new stations built by the independent power companies were unlikely to be very far below the currently accepted practice.

What the encroachment of public authorities upon electricity supply created, however, was a situation in which the pace of technical advance was more determined by the concensus of technical opinion in the industry, constrained by the CEB's and the Commissioners' concepts of the public interest and economic necessity, and in which innovation was less determined by the individual supply company's initiative in specifying more efficient plant and bringing it into existence with the aid of one of the plant manufacturers.[22]

The exigencies of wartime reinforced the control which the Ministry of Supply, the Ministry of Fuel and Power and the public agencies exercised over the industry. Power station building was again cut and major innovations in plant design were not permitted.[23] When the 1947 Order came, a high degree of governmental direction was already accepted within the industry. It did not therefore seem to be much more than a logical continuation of policies begun under the Central Electricity Board. It was in any case a CEB recommendation to the Minister which specified the desired sizes and steam conditions.[24]

The necessity for standardisation in 1947, which affected the plant programmes envisaged for 1946—52 and substantially influenced plant built from 1953 to 1959, was both widely accepted and easily justified at the time. It was expected to result in lower capital costs and a speeding up of manufacture. It was considered that the design effort involved for the turbo-alternator manufacturers in developing and building generating sets could more easily be concentrated if there were only two 'frame sizes' (i.e. the 30 MW and 60 MW). Boiler technology had lagged behind so much that 600 and 900 lb/sq. in. were the only operating pressures which could be built economically and quickly. There was thought to be a shortage of experienced designers and other manpower in the generating plant industry and it was supposed that lower quality coal and the unreliability of boilers would render additions such as re-heat uneconomic. Whether such considerations really required standardisation of plant and whether the policy achieved the desired effects are open to dispute. It is fairly clear that the restrictive nature of the 1947 Order was recognised by the industry.[25] The annual reports of the British Electricity Authority for the years 1948/9 to 1950/1 made mention of the need to order more advanced plant in order to maintain technical progress and the reaction of the Authority in the 1950s was to advance techniques rapidly.

THE ACCELERATION OF TECHNICAL DEVELOPMENT IN THE 1950s

The structure of the BEA as set up in 1948 gave equal emphasis to transmission and to generation as major functions; the Chief Engineer, a former member of the CEB, supervised the three sub-departments of generation transmission and research and also co-ordinated the Generation Divisions. There were twelve of the latter, corresponding to the Area Boards in location, and they were charged with the detailed planning of the power stations needed in each Division, with planning transmission developments and with operation of the Grid and power stations. The emphasis of the CEA's organisation reflected the need to develop the generating side of the industry.

In 1950 the Order which had established the standard frame sizes was revoked, and the way was clear for successive developments of turbo-alternators and boilers up to sizes of 500 MW and 660 MW. There was still a great deal of work to do in setting up an organisation for programme planning and technical development. According to the Herbert Report, there was even five years later a good deal of confusion about the allocation of design and development responsibility between the central organisation and the generating divisions. Although larger generating sets were designed during the period 1950 to 1955, only four were planned for 1956 (one was actually commissioned), five for 1957, four for 1958, ten for 1959 and ten for 1960.[26]

The reasons for this include more factors than merely the organisational delays consequent upon nationalisation. Firstly, there was a degree of technical stagnation. Radiant type, bent tube boilers had not been manufactured in Britain. Boilers for high pressure sets before the war had come from Czechoslovakia. Cyclone-fired boilers, in which a wider range of fuel qualities can be used, were not installed even experimentally until 1957. Although re-heat was used in the north east and London during the 1920s, it was not used by the industry as a whole during the 1930s or the 1940s. Large turbines of 50 MW and above were not generally designed to run at the more efficient speed of 3,000 r.p.m. during the 1930s, but only at 1,500 r.p.m., and the slowness of boiler development had delayed acceptance of set sizes up to 100 MW.[27] Thus many of the boiler and turbine manufacturers were lacking design experience and technical developments of these techniques during the period 1935 to 1950. This meant not only that the senior management and staff of the postwar period were unaccustomed to the latest designs, but that junior and apprentice engineers of the 1930s and 1940s, upon whom much of the design work during the 1950s would devolve, were not being trained in these techniques.

Secondly, the British Electricity Authority had to build up new working relationships with manufacturers of plant. Capacity had become severely restricted because of wartime and pre-war limitations in programmes. The industry was not capable immediately of the effort needed to commission the 1,500 MW per annum planned for the postwar years. The Authority brought new companies into the field.

Responsibility for leadership in design also had to be reconsidered. Under the aegis of the independent power supply companies, there had grown up a close understanding between generating engineers in the industry who planned power stations and the particular manufacturer or manufacturers which their supply authority favoured. These relationships started to break down before nationalisation and were initially replaced by a system in which the Ministry of Fuel and Power took over planning; on the formation of the BEA the system became one of central authority planning and finally a form of partnership was developed between the Central Electricity Generating Board and the manufacturers.[28]

For these reasons, the designs of the 100 MW single shaft, 1,500 lb/ sq. in. 1050°F straight condensing set (i.e. non-re-heat) in 1951 and of the 100 MW re-heat which followed it were, in a sense, experimental. Although the combined design experience of the British Electricity Authority and the manufacturers, assisted by what they knew of the designs used in the United States, was sufficient for a clear understanding of the technical objectives and constraints, the 100 MW and 120 MW sets ordered from 1950 to 1952 were 'development machines', which served the purpose of advancing the state of the art. They were not established designs, in the sense that they had not been refined by experience of installation and use.

The 120 MW re-heat set of 1958 (ordered in 1952) was evolved by using the low-pressure cylinder of the 100 MW straight condensing set and adding a re-heat stage to create a three-cylinder machine, the first cylinder at 1,500 lb/sq. in. and 1,000°F, the second cylinder supplied at intermediate pressure, but also at 1,000°F from re-heat, and the low-pressure cylinder using the exhaust steam from the second stage. Preliminary indications from the first 100 MW straight condensing design (for Castle Donnington power station) had shown that the expected gains from larger capacities and advanced steam conditions would be realised and four power stations were equipped with the 100 MW sets.[29] However, they did not represent a big enough step forward, and design work in connection with them revealed the possibility of building the 120 MW re-heat without exceeding the constraints imposed by boiler size and design or turbine size at their current stage of development.

The 120 MW set was eventually used in a dozen power stations; Blyth A was the most successful station in terms of thermal efficiency. About forty were ordered between 1953 and 1956, and they thus became something of a standard set.[30] But electricity demand continued to increase rapidly during the 1950s. Consumption was rising at about 8·5 per cent per annum during the period 1950—5, and the maximum demand on the system at any one time (SMD) was growing at just over 9 per cent (1951—6). Once technical development of larger sizes was under way it was clear that a large, fully integrated supply system could use the largest size of generating set which could be built within reasonable technical constraints. In 1953 a 200 MW set was considered feasible. As boiler design advanced and higher outputs became available, so research had to be conducted into materials and welding methods for pipework able to withstand much higher pressures than those common in the postwar period. The result of the investigation into materials and welding was that yet more advanced steam conditions became possible. The 200 MW set took pressures up to 2,350 lb/sq. in. at a temperature of 1,050°F. The first machine at this output was ordered for High Marnham in south Yorkshire, a power station which was the largest in Europe at the time it was planned; five 200 MW sets made the total installed capacity up to 1,000 MW. The first 200 MW set was commissioned in October 1959.

Again the 200 MW unit was a development model. Some of the design features were tested on existing units which were being assembled for trial running.[31] Four more 200 MW units were ordered in 1955—6 for two new power stations at West Thurrock (Essex) and Willington B (Derby). Improvements were made in the turbine and alternator design, so that the last four 200 MW units were developed versions of the first.

Table 3.4 provides a resumé of the advances made in the size of generating plant and the steam conditions used between 1950 and 1975. It shows that there was a gap of three years between the ordering of High Marnham's 200 MW turbo-alternator and the next size, of 275 MW. During this time design experimentation continued. Straightforward development of the 200 MW set, by raising the capacity of the boiler from 1,400 klb/hour to 1,950 klb/hour and increasing the turbine flow, was expected to give a potential output to the alternator sufficient to generate 275 MW. Boiler design to suit very high outputs had begun to move faster than the design of turbines and alternators; it was envisaged that constraints imposed by the limitations on transporting by road loads which for the alternator were likely to exceed 150 tons would restrict the size of generator which could be installed. The 275 MW generator seemed to be the largest size of machine which could be specified within the state of the art up to 1956.

However, the increasing of rated outputs was expected to produce further economies in generating costs. Small improvements in thermal efficiency were hoped for from the greater volumetric flow of steam through the turbines, and capital costs per kW installed were expected to fall sharply with increases in unit size. At the time the 275 MW set was being considered, it was known that super-critical steam turbo-generators of that size were being built in the United States and Germany and that they were expected to have a slightly higher thermal efficiency than the sets from which they were developed. But it was decided for the British 275 MW that further economies of size were to be sought by using it as a development model for a 550 MW sub-critical generator of cross-compound design.

While design work on the 275 MW tandem compound turbo-alternator and 550 MW cross-compound set was being undertaken, continued development of the electrical output rating available from existing frame sizes of generator had been going forward. In particular, liquid cooling of the stator (under test on a 30 MW generator at Bold A in Lancashire and on a 60 MW generator at Tilbury) and high-pressure gas cooling of the rotor produced an alternator of 200 MW output, but having its main dimensions only 10 per cent greater than a 60 MW unit and its length about the same. As a consequence, single-line tandem compound turbines driving single alternators of a greater output than 275 MW became feasible, while yet keeping within the constraints of transportability by road.

Table 3.4 *Generating Plant Development, 1950—75 (coal and oil)*

Power station	*Size of unit (MW)*	*Steam pressure (lb/sq. in.)*	*(°F)*	*Steam temperature (Re-heat °F)*	*Year ordered*	*Year commissioned*	*Designed efficiency (%)*	*Operating efficiency (%)*
Castle Donnington	100	1,500	1,050		1950	1956	33·7	32·5
Ferrybridge B	100	1,500	975	950	1951	1957	34·5	32·5
Blyth A	120	1,500	1,000	1,000	1952	1958	35·6	34
High Marnham	200	2,350	1,050	1,000	1953	1959	37·5	34·7
Blyth B[a]	275	2,300	1,050	1,050	1956	1962	n.a.	32·8
Thorpe Marsh[b]	550	2,300	1,050	1,050	1957	1963	n.a.	33·9
West Thurrock	300	2,300	1,050	1,050	1958	1964	37·8	33·5
Drakelow C	350	2,400	1,055	1,055	1959	1966	n.a.	n.a.
Drakelow C[c]	375	3,500	1,100	1,050	1960	1966	39·8	n.a.
West Burton	500	2,300	1,050	1,050	1960	1967	39·2	33·5
Drax[d]	660	2,300	1,050	1,050	1966	1974	n.a.	34·3

[a] Single boiler of capacity 1,050 klb/hour.
[b] Single boiler of capacity 3,900 klb/hour.
[c] Super-critical set.
[d] Single boiler of capacity 4,450 klb/hour.

Consideration was again given to further advances in steam conditions, and this time tentative designs for a super-critical steam turbine were started. Although there was little economic advantage expected from the super-critical set in the immediate future, it was felt by the Authority's engineering department that the development of more advanced materials and manufacturing techniques should be encouraged.

Thus advances had been taking place between 1956 and 1958 in boiler design, turbines and alternators. Research was under way on high pressure pipe materials, welding techniques, blade geometry, cylinder shape and alternator cooling. The situation in 1958 was one in which the potential gains from increased knowledge of techniques appeared to be very well worth pursuing. Techniques were being extended in all directions, and the Authority's engineers thought it only logical to continue extending them as far as they would go. When generator developments indicated that a single-line size of alternator above 275 MW was feasible, the opportunity was taken to undertake a new design of single-line tandem compound set, which would exploit the advances in techniques beyond the sizes under development.

Accordingly, a new size at 300 MW was included in the first programme planned by the new Central Electricity Generating Board during the first half of 1958.[32] The 300 MW set, ordered for West Thurrock power station where the advanced version of the 200 MW set was then being built, was again intended as a development model. If the basic design were established for single-line generation at 300 MW, then improvements in turbine performance, boiler size and generator output could be expected to raise the turbo-alternator's overall capacity well above that of the original design.

It was anticipated that the adaptation of the components from the 300 MW turbine to super-critical steam conditions might allow an increase in alternator output without increasing the size of the whole set significantly. During the latter part of 1958 tenders were invited for two new developments based on the 300 MW design, one to use the existing steam conditions of 2,300 lb/sq. in. and 1,050°F with re-heat to 1,050°F, but to be uprated to 350 MW, and the other to be for a 375 MW super-critical set at 3,500 lb/sq. in., with temperatures of 1,100°F and 1,050°F.

Initial negotiations with the manufacturers suggested that there would be comparatively few problems with the 350 MW sub-critical set and an order for the first turbo-alternator of this size was placed during the early part of 1959. In mid-1959 there were thus five different sizes of generating set on order (the 200 MW, 275 MW, 550 MW, 300 MW and 350 MW), which represented five years of intensive development work, but none of which had yet been commissioned in a power station. A sixth was added some months later when the 375 MW super-critical set was ordered.

THE PLANT CRISIS OF THE 1960s

During 1959 the CEGB had become uneasy about the relationship between planned capacity for the early 1960s and the rate of growth of demand. The Generating Board's predecessor, the British Electricity Authority (which became the Central Electricity Authority in 1955) had been planning for a rate of growth of SMD of 7 per cent for the years 1954 to 1960, but had reduced its plans for plant expansion during the years 1956 to 1962 to a level consistent with SMD growth of just below 6·5 per cent per year.[33] The total output capacity which these plans envisaged for the system is given in Table 3.5.

Table 3.5 *Planned Output Capacity, England and Wales, 1959—63*

Calendar year[a]	*Planned net capacity*[b] *(MW)*	*Implied SMD*[c] *(MW)*	*Actual SMD*[d] *(MW)*
1959	23,900	21,500	32,100
1960	24,800	22,400	24,450
1961	27,200	24,500	27,850
1962	29,500	26,600	32,100
1963	32,000	29,600	30,500

Sources: CEA and BEA, *Annual Reports;* Electricity Council, *Handbook of Electricity Supply Statistics,* 1966.

Notes: [a] End of year.

[b] Planning during 1953 and 1954 included the south of Scotland for 1959 and 1960. The estimated capacity for this area has been removed from the totals.

[c] On the assumption that 90 per cent of plant would be available to meet demand.

[d] Estimated potential demand on the Grid (not all met) during winters of 1959/60, 1960/1, etc.

Table 3.5 represents the situation which would have applied had all plans been adhered to. Some capacity deficiencies would have existed. In the event the total of plant on the system during the winters up to 1962 was maintained at a level between 1,500 MW and 2,000 MW above planned output capacity, by some early commissioning of new generators and by retaining the bulk of the sets which had been designated for retirement. Thus much of the demand was met, and load-shedding or cuts in supply were limited to a few occasions.

Nevertheless, by 1959 there was some reason for alarm. SMD for the winter of 1958/9 had shown a growth of 8 per cent over the previous year and, at nearly 21,000 MW, was very close to the total of plant available. The Board argued with the authorities (the Electricity Council and the Government) that a forecasting basis of 7 per cent growth was much nearer to the long-term trend and began to look for ways of increasing the amount of plant planned for the years from 1964 onwards.

The most immediate result of the perception of the plant shortage was that the Board decided to order another two of the 350 MW sets, one for Blyth B, where the 275 MW development was being installed, and the other for Drakelow C power station, near Burton on Trent, where the first

350 MW set was to go. Ordering two more of the 350 MW turbo-generators so soon was certainly a bold step. It was eighteen months or less since the 300 MW size had been declared viable and had been included in the 1963 commissioning programme. The technical developments on which the 300 MW set was based, in particular the decision that single-line alternators of over 275 MW output could be built, were still at a somewhat tentative stage. So far the larger alternator sizes had been based upon the extrapolated results of test-running new design features of the 200 MW sets on quite small machines of 60 and 100 MW. The boiler size and turbine design of the 300 MW and 350 MW sets were also in the nature of unproven developments.

Confidence was perhaps gained in the success of current developments by the commissioning on schedule of the first 200 MW unit for commercial output at High Marnham in October 1959, and by the performance of the new 120 MW generating units. These 120 MW sets at 1,500 lb/sq. in. and 1,000°F with re-heat had been the first definitive development beyond the 60 MW sets. Half-a-dozen were running at the end of 1959. Nearly two years' experience with the size had shown that a substantial improvement in thermal efficiency had been made. Blyth A station (3 × 120 MW, later 4 × 120 MW) and Agecroft C (2 × 124 MW) were averaging 34 and 33 per cent thermal efficiency respectively on year-round operation.[34]

Confidence in fact was sufficiently high for a decision to be taken in the early months of 1960 that the size of generator unit which would be possible with the new techniques could be substantially raised yet again. Two boilers had already been ordered in 1957 and 1959 at outputs of 3,900 klb/hr each for the 550 MW cross-compound sets at Thorpe Marsh; turbine development had not revealed any immediate size constraints; the research and development programme on the size of alternators had indicated that with suitable cooling of rotor and stator windings higher outputs even than 350 MW should be available. Accordingly, in the spring of 1960 a 500 MW single line tandem compound unit to operate at 2,300 lb/sq. in. and 1,050°F with re-heat was tentatively included in the programme for 1965.[35]

The winter of 1959/60 upheld the basis of the CEGB's worries about the rate of growth of demand. SMD actually rose by 10·5 per cent over the previous year and the long-term trend of demand was beginning to appear to be above 7 per cent and nearer 7·5 per cent per annum. If this was to be a continued rate of increase for the whole of the decade, then the situation which faced the Board was extremely serious. Between the spring and the autumn of the year 1960 the Generating Board had to consider very carefully the two major policy issues:

(a) What level of demand was it likely to face during the next few years?
(b) What were the implications for the plant programme if demand were growing faster than expected?

As soon as the Board decided to act upon the higher forecast of demand growth, they had to find short-term and long-term measures to remedy the low level of plant commissioning.

Three events had combined to cause the expectation of new plant commissioning during the early 1960s to sink to a fairly low level. First there was the decision by the CEA to plan on the basis of a 6·5 per cent growth in SMD from 1955 onwards, affecting the plant programmes of 1961 to 1964. Secondly, the Government had instituted new controls in 1955 over the total amount of generating plant to be installed in ensuing years. The cuts were not large, but they appear to have caused a downward revision of programme plans for plant to come into service during 1958, 1959, 1960 and 1961 by an average of 100 MW per year.[36] Lastly, the programme of nuclear power first announced in 1955 and stepped up to 5,000 MW in 1957 was cut back in the later 1950s, reducing the rate of planned introduction of nuclear plant in the period 1960 to 1968.

The upshot of these events was that, even with the extra two 350 MW sets ordered in 1959 and included as a late item in the 1964 programme, total capacity in 1964 was expected to be below 35,000 MW. If the 1959/60 SMD of 23,100 MW was regarded as being 'on trend' and a growth rate of 7·5 per cent assumed, then the Board was going to have to meet a demand of 33,200 MW in the winter of 1964/5. This level of demand could not be met with existing programmes, even if all the plant under construction were completed on time.[37]

But by 1960 the Board was also aware of the fact that the nuclear power programme was slipping slightly behind schedule, and that there were delays affecting the developed versions of the 200 MW generating sets due to commission in 1961 at West Thurrock and Willington B. During 1961, 1962 and 1963 the rate of commissioning of new plant fell below plan by a small margin due to these delays.[38] A considerable amount of innovative plant was included in these programmes. For instance, the 1961 programme, which was planned for about 2,300 MW, contained the first two nuclear stations at Berkeley (250 MW output) and Bradwell (300 MW output), as well as 3 of the advanced 200 MW sets. In the 1962 programme there was a larger nuclear plant at Hinkley Point (500 MW), further 200 MW sets and the first of the 275 MW sets based upon the 200 MW design. (Table 3.6 contains details of new plant from 1953 to 1970.) To compound the difficulties created by a large amount of novel generating equipment, it was unfortunate that during 1959/60 the Generating Board had both reduced the plant planning cycle to five years and had decided that in conditions of maximum winter peak demand the planning margin of excess plant over SMD could be reduced from 12 per cent to 10.

The disquiet felt during the latter part of 1959 and the early months of 1960 was acted upon in 1960 during the annual discussions with the Ministry of Power and the Treasury. These were usually held during the late summer and early autumn, to settle the forward programmes of investment. The Board's submissions of maximum demand to the Electricity Council were recalculated on a basis of growth at more than 7 per cent per annum.

The new forecasting assumptions were used both to focus attention

Table 3.6 *New Generating Plant 1953—70*

Annual Report	Date of inclusion in programme	Power station	Details of generators	Date of expected commissioning	Date of first commercial operation	Date full output achieved
1953/4	1953	High Marnham	One 200 MW: first ordered, prototype version	1959	Oct. 59	1959
1954/5	1954	High Marnham	Second 200 MW: third and fourth ordered 1955/6	1960	1960	1960
,,	,,	West Thurrock	One 200 MW: advanced development of High Marnham	1961	Oct. 62	1962
1955/6	1955	Willington B	Two 200 MW: developed version, different manufacturer from above	1961	Jun. 62	1962
,,	,,	Berkeley	125 MW first reactor, later revised to 2 × 80 MW each	1961	Jun. 62	1962
,,	,,	Bradwell	125 MW first reactor, later revised to 3 × 52 MW each	1961	Jul. 62	1962
1956/7	1956	West Thurrock	Second 200 MW	1962	1963	1963
,,	,,	Blyth B	One 275 MW: first planned as 200 MW but design stretched	1962	Dec. 62	1963
,,	,,	Hinkley Point	Three 93·5 MW: first reactor	1962	Mar. 65	1965
,,	,,	Trawsfynydd	275 MW first reactor, later revised to 2 × 145 each reactor	1963	Mar. 65	1965
1957/8	1957	Blyth B	Second 275 MW: stretched version of West Thurrock 200 MW	1963	1963	1964
,,	,,	Thorpe Marsh	One 550 MW: cross-compound, two line turbo-alternators at 275 MW	1963	Dec. 63	1964
,,	March 1958	West Thurrock	One 300 MW: prototype for high output alternators[a]	1963	1964	1967
,,	,,	Dungeness A	275 MW first reactor, later revised to 2 × 142·5 each reactor	1964	Oct. 65	1966
1958/9	1959	Drakelow C	One 350 MW: stretched 300 MW, second ordered late 1959	1964	Dec. 65	1973
,,	,,	Thorpe Marsh	Second 550 MW: cross-compound, two line turbo-alternators	1964	1965	[b]

Table 3.6—continued

		Station				
1958/9	1959	West Thurrock	Second 300 MW: third set ordered 1960 for 1965	1964	1965	1969 (280 MW)
1959/60	,,	Blyth B	One 350 MW: similar to Drakelow, second ordered 1960	1964	1965	c
1960/1	1960	Drakelow C	Two 375 MW: super-critical steam, development prototype	1965/6	1967	d
,,	,,	Tilbury B	Two 350 MW: as for Blyth B and Drakelow	1965	Dec. 68	e
,,	,,	West Burton A	One 500 MW: scaled-up 350 MW design	1965	Aug. 67	1968
1961/2	1961	Sizewell A	One 325 MW: first reactor	1965	Mar. 66	f
,,	,,	Tilbury B	Third and fourth 350 MW: last 350 MW sets ordered	1966	1971	e
,,	,,	Eggborough	One 500 MW	1966	Mar. 68	1970 (480 MW)
,,	,,	Ferrybridge C	Two 500 MW	1965	Dec. 66	1967
,,	,,	West Burton A	Second and third 500 MW	1966	Dec. 67	1968
,,	,,	Oldbury	One 287 MW: first reactor, later raised to 2 × 312 MW	1966	Dec. 67	1969
1962/3	1962	Hams Hall A	Experimental 15 MW gas turbine	1962	Dec. 62	1963
,,	,,	Aberthaw B	Two 500 MW	1967	Oct. 71	g
,,	,,	Eggborough	Second and third 500 MW	1967	1970	1971 (480 MW)
,,	,,	Fawley	Two 500 MW	1966	Dec. 69	1970
,,	,,	Ferrybridge C	Third and fourth 500 MW	1967	1967	1969
,,	,,	Fiddler's Ferry	One 500 MW	1967	May 71	1971
,,	,,	Ironbridge B	One 500 MW	1967	Mar. 70	1973–5
,,	,,	Kingsnorth	One 500 MW	1967	Dec. 70	1972
,,	,,	Ratcliffe	One 500 MW	1967	Mar. 68	1969
1962/3	1962	West Burton A	Fourth 500 MW	1967	1968	1969
March 1963	,,	Croydon B	Two 70 MW gas turbines	1964	Mar. 65	1965
,,	,,	Earley	Two 56 MW gas turbines	1964	Dec. 64	1965
,,	,,	Hastings	Two 55 MW gas turbines	1965	Mar. 66	1967
,,	,,	Lister Drive	Two 56 MW gas turbines	1964	Mar. 65	1965
,,	,,	Norwich	Two 55 MW gas turbines	1965	Jan. 66	1966
,,	,,	Rye House	Two 70 MW gas turbines	1964	Mar. 65	1965

Table 3.6—continued

Annual Report	Date of inclusion in programme	Power station	Details of generators	Date of expected commissioning	Eate of first commercial operation	Date full output achieved
1963/4	Autumn 1963	Aberthaw B	Third 500 MW	1968	1972	[g]
,,	,,	Cottam	Two 500 MW[i]	1968	Sept. 69	1973–5
,,	,,	Eggborough	Fourth 500 MW	1968	1971	1972
,,	,,	Fawley	Third 500 MW	1968	1970	1971
,,	,,	Fiddler's Ferry	Second 500 MW	1968	1971	1972
,,	,,	Ironbridge B	Second 500 MW	1968	1971	1973–5
,,	,,	Kingsnorth	Second and third 500 MW	1968	1971	1973
,,	,,	Ratcliffe	Second and third 500 MW	1968	1969	1970
,,	,,	Wylfa	Two 333·6 MW: first reactor, later reduced to 327·5 MW	1968	Nov. 71	[j]
1964/5	Autumn 1964	Cottam	Third and fourth 500 MW	1969	1971	1974–5
,,	,,	Didcot	Two 500 MW[k]	1968	Mar. 72	1972–4
,,	,,	Drax	One 660 MW, prototype at 3,500 lb/sq. in. 1,000°F, with two reheat stages	1970		[l]
,,	,,	Fawley	Fourth 500 MW	1970	1971	1972
1964/5	Autumn 1964	Fiddlers Ferry	Third and fourth 500 MW	1969	1972	1974
,,	,,	Kingsnorth	Fourth 500 MW	1969		
,,	,,	Pembroke	One 500 MW	1969	Dec. 70	1971
,,	,,	Ratcliffe	Fourth 500 MW	1969	1970	1971
,,	,,	Rugeley	Two 500 MW	1969	Dec. 71	1973
,,	,,	Wylfa	Two 327·5 MW: second reactor	1969		[j]
1965/6	Autumn 1965	Didcot	Third and fourth 500 MW	1971	1973/5	
,,	,,	Pembroke	Second and third 500 MW	1970	1971	1972
,,	,,	Ratcliffe	Fourth 500 MW: removed from 1964 programme	1971	1971	1971
,,	,,	Dungeness B	One 660 MW: first reactor of AGR type	1970		[m]

Table 3.6—*continued*

1966/7	Autumn 1966	Dungeness B	Second 660 MW: second reactor	1971		[m]
,,	,,	Drax	One 660 MW: reprogrammed from 1964 plan	1971		[l] 1972
,,	,,	Pembroke	Fourth 500 MW	1972	1972	
1967/8	Autumn 1967	Hinkley Point B	One 660 MW: first reactor AGR	1972		
,,	,,	Drax	Second 660 MW: type now at sub-critical steam	1972		[l]
1968/9	Autumn 1968	Hinkley Point B	Second 660 MW: second reactor AGR	1973		
,,	,,	Hartlepool	One 660 MW: first reactor AGR	1973		
,,	,,	Drax	Third 660 MW	1973		
1969/70	Autumn 1969	Hartlepool	Second 660 MW: second reactor AGR	1974		[l]
1970/1	Autumn 1970	Heysham	One 660 MW: first reactor AGR	1975		
,,	,,	Grain	One 660 MW	1975		

[a] The 3 × 300 MW sets at West Thurrock were finally rated at 280 MW in 1967.
[b] Thorpe Marsh's second 550 MW cross-compound reached 518 MW in the late 1960s, but did not achieve design output.
[c] By late 1975, one of the 350 sets at Blyth was rated at 330 MW, the other at 300 MW.
[d] The 375 MW super-critical sets had not achieved designed output by 1975.
[e] Continuing problems with Tilbury B station left all four sets below 350 MW output.
[f] Sizewell sets reached full rating in 1972, but limitations on Magnox running temperatures kept station output at only 67 per cent of installed capacity.
[g] Aberthaw third set being rebuilt 1973—5.
[h] Kingsnorth station, 4 × 500 MW, not completed until 1975.
[i] Cottam 4 × 500 MW sets not up to rated output 1973.
[j] Rated capacity of Wylfa sets in 1975, 4 × 247·5 MW.
[k] Didcot, 4 × 500 MW, below design output in 1973.
[l] Drax power station delayed, coming into commission during 1974—6.
[m] Dungeness B encountered severe construction difficulties and was reprogrammed for 1976.

upon the immediate emergency and to provide supporting arguments for the level of plant programmes which the Board was by then planning for the years 1965 to 1970. However, the implications of the revision in growth rates were first reflected in the short-term contingency plans made for the years 1962 to 1964.

During the latter part of 1960 it was too late to do anything about the level of plant scheduled for commissioning in 1961 and 1962, but there was a certain amount of manoeuvring room provided by the programme of plant closures. The proportion of old plant in use had risen sharply during the 1950s because of capacity shortages; to reduce the amount of old plant it had been planned to accelerate the retirement of equipment to an average of 400 MW per annum during 1959—64. In 1959/60 the programme had gone ahead as planned, and 315 MW was scrapped.[39] As the likelihood grew that there would again be a capacity shortage, so the rate of scrapping dropped. Only 185 MW followed in 1960/1, and scrapping practically ceased for a few years afterwards.[40] Secondly, the Board took advantage of the joint development by Bristol Siddeley Engines and the South West Electricity Board of peak load gas turbine generation. An experimental 15 MW set was ordered for Hams Hall to operate in 1962. With successful demonstration of the type, 728 MW of gas turbine capacity was ordered in unit sizes of 55 and 70 MW (approximately). The GT plant started to enter the system in 1964. By this means and by re-rating existing old plant above its previous output level, the Board was able to increase the anticipated total of generating plant for 1962, 1963 and 1964 by 650 MW, 1,100 MW and 1,750 MW respectively, without ordering any more new plant (compare columns 3 and 5 of Table 3.7).

It can be seen from the last column of Table 3.7 that the emergency short-term measures, if all scheduled plant had been commissioned, would have proved adequate for the winters of 1963/4 and 1964/5, but inadequate for the winter of 1962/3. However, that particular winter was of such severity compared to the normal winter weather in Britain, that only a completely different planning approach would have ensured that electrical plant was adequate at times of maximum demand.

These short-term measures could only be regarded as a temporary expedient. Not only was there a limit to the amount of extra capacity which could be created by re-rating existing plant and delaying retirement, but it was also a policy which counteracted the efforts to improve thermal efficiency during the 1950s.[41] Thermal efficiency had been held back during the early 1950s by the retention of old plant and the Generating Board was anxious not to repeat the experience. In the long term, therefore, the plant programmes for the year 1965 and for several years following had to be raised considerably above the 2,000 MW per annum which had been planned for 1960—4.

The classically difficult question was by how much the plant programmes had to be raised. In retrospect it can be seen that there were two components to the capacity shortage of the early 1960s. In the first place,

Table 3.7 Changes in Planned Total Capacity, 1958/9—1961/2

Calendar year	Pre-1960 planning basis		Post-1960 planning basis		Actual SMD c (MW)	Derived plant requirement d (MW)
	Plant programme for year a (MW)	Total plant on system b (MW) (Actual at end 1959 = 25,100)	Plant programme for year a (MW)	Total plant on system b (MW)		
1960	1,898	27,100	2,404	29,300	24,445	27,200
1961	2,404	29,350	2,271	31,800	27,856	30,800
1962	2,271	31,150	1,845	33,900	32,100	35,650
1963	1,819	32,800	2,461	36,600	30,488	33,900
1964	1,727	34,850	2,421	39,400	31,779	35,300
1965			4,529	42,900	36,079	40,100
1966					34,530	38,350

a Planned to come into operation during the ensuing winter, e.g. 1960 plant for winter 1960/1.

b These totals take into account plant retirement and are based on expected, rather than planned, commissioning; i.e. they take into account plant delays and early commissioning. 1960 differs from 1959 by more than 1,898 MW, because of the late commissioning of plant planned for earlier years.

c Winter of 1960/1, 1960/2, etc.

d Based on 90 per cent plant availability.

the underlying long-term trend of SMD had been put at 6·5 per cent by the Central Electricity Authority, whereas it would probably have been more appropriate to put it at between 7 per cent and 7·5 per cent, at least during the period 1955 to 1965.[42] But the shortfall in the forecasting basis was discovered at a particularly unfortunate time, 1959 to 1963, during which some special factors were acting to push the rate of growth of SMD well above the long-term trend. So the second component of the capacity crisis was a four-year period, from the winter of 1958/9 to the winter of 1962/3, during which SMD grew at 9 per cent per annum.

Explanations of the 9 per cent trend can be found in the concurrence for a few years of various separately determined variables. The boom in the building of new houses had accelerated demand for electricity as opposed to gas;[43] there was a rapid movement away from domestic consumption of coal during the late 1950s;[44] in addition the winters of 1959/60 and 1961/2 were rather cold, while the winter of 1962/3 was extremely severe.[45] Ideal conditions thus existed for large numbers of people to wish to turn to electricity as a means of heating. Newly designed and relatively cheap electrical heaters, such as fan heaters, were on the market; some easing of restrictions on hire purchase and credit sales meant that the electric fire became the immediate solution to heating problems. However, the forecasting methods used by the supply industry as a whole were such that the effects of an explosion in domestic demand went unnoticed until 1961.[46]

When the real rate of increase in maximum demand during those four years was recognised, it was not apparently realised that the short-term component might be giving a very confusing picture of the long-term trend. Load forecasts and prognostications of the future growth of electricity consumption suggested that new factors might be pushing up the trend above 7 per cent; the 7 per cent long-term trend was quoted consistently as a reliable lower estimate. By 1963 the Generating Board was submitting estimates of load to 1970 based upon 7·9 per cent growth in SMD, and these were being used to settle the 1968 generating plant programme. The plant programme was planned to expand at 9 per cent per year to 1970.[47]

EXPANSION OF PLANT PROGRAMMES

The combined effect of discovering that demand forecasts had been underestimated and that the real growth rate, as well as being higher, was also rising, persuaded the CEGB in 1961 and 1962 that it had to plan for really massive plant programmes in the years 1966 to 1970.

Table 3.8 shows what large plant programmes were planned under the pressures of the early 1960s. In the out-turn, programmes of the size forecast for the late 1960s were not achieved, and neither were they really needed. Generating capacity rose quite slowly, from 25,500 MW in 1960 to 46,900 MW in 1970, a rate of increase of just under 6·5 per cent per

Table 3.8 *Plans and Programmes, 1960—4, New Generating Plant and Total Capacity*

Calendar year	Programme of new plant (MW)	Planned total capacity[a] (MW)	Calendar year	Programme of new plant (MW)	Planned total capacity[a] (MW)
1960	1,898	27,130 (1959)	1965	3,176	39,561 (1962)
1961	2,404	29,350 (1960)	1966	4,556	44,517 (1963)
1962	2,271	31,800 (1961)	1967	5,300	49,100 (1963)
1963	1,845	33,600 (1961)	1968	6,590	56,173 (1964)
1964	2,461	36,600 (1961)			
			1969	7,000[b]	61,000 (1964)
			1970	5,590[b]	66,800 (1964)

Source: Wilson Report (op. cit.) and CEGB, *Annual Reports*.
Notes: [a] The dates in brackets indicate the year in which planned total capacity was proposed at the levels indicated.
[b] Tentative programmes not subsequently confirmed.

annum, while the maximum demand on the system (SMD) increased even more slowly, from 23,100 MW in 1959/60 to 39,700 MW in the winter of 1969/70, an annual rate of increase of just over 5·5 per cent.

THE RECORD OF TECHNICAL CHANGE IN THE 1960s

Nevertheless, the situation at the time looked serious enough to cause the Board to order a number of very large power stations of advanced design, and to order them very quickly. The urgent construction programme, imposed upon the rapid technological and scale developments pursued in the 1950s, played havoc with the supply industry's previous record of successful, if conservative, technical advance. A very high proportion of the plant included in the programmes of 1961 onwards reached its commissioning stage late, some of it was extremely late (see Table 3.6).[48]

The 100 MW and 120 MW units were a generally successful development, and the 200 MW frame size, as modified and developed for installation in West Thurrock, gave excellent service.[49] Similarly, the 275 MW design installed at Blyth B came into service fairly well on time and achieved its rated output, although its thermal efficiency was below that of the 200 MW. The first 550 MW cross-compound for Thorpe March had an equal measure of success, but the second did not reach designed output.

The 300 MW size never achieved more than 280 MW output, and that was four years after the planned introduction. Development work on the design was required during and after installation. Eight 350 MW sets were eventually ordered, the first four for Blyth B and Drakelow C and the other four for Tilbury B. The Drakelow sets achieved operation at a restricted rating only a year late. A number of years of development work was needed after commissioning, before this type approached its design output in the early 1970s. The Blyth and Tilbury versions of the 350 MW had not reached design output by the mid-1970s; neither had the 375 MW super-critical set ordered for Drakelow C as a development prototype.

THE 500 MW TANDEM COMPOUND TURBO-ALTERNATOR

It was only the 500 MW tandem compound turbine, with a hydrogen-cooled alternator and unit boiler of 3,400 klb/hour steam output, which was built in quantity. After the decision was taken in principle that this frame size could be accommodated within the constraints of transportability and using known techniques of boiler, turbine and alternator design, the first unit was ordered for West Burton power station, to be commissioned in 1965. It actually reached service some two years late, in August 1967, being preceded by another 500 MW design at Ferrybridge C (December 1966). The design thermal efficiency was put at 39·2 per cent in 1961, but the achieved efficiency in service was 35 per cent.

The anticipated shortage of capacity caused the 1966 programme to be raised to over 4,500 MW. Plant orders for 1966 included five 500 MW sets, as well as four at 375 and 350 MW; shortly after this orders were placed for another four 500 MW sets. By early 1962 ten 500 MW sets were on order, and the plant programmes included three power stations of 2,000 MW with four 500 MW generating units in each (West Burton, Ferrybridge and Eggborough). During the rest of 1962 and early 1963 another twenty 500 MW units were ordered and the number of power stations planned to include 500 MW sets rose to nine. The 1967 plant programme, finalised during the latter half of 1962, did not include any coal or oil generating sets other than the 500 MW type. Inclusion in the previous year of the 350 MW and 375 MW sizes had not implied a continuing interest in those generators and a decision to standardise on 500 MW sets was probably made early in 1962.

By March 1964 thirty-seven 500 MW sets were on order (forty-seven were eventually ordered) and power station construction programmes included thirty 500 MW sets in ten stations (Table 3.6).

This power station programme first began to run into difficulties because of site problems. Power stations containing four of the 500 MW sets cover a large area, and contain turbine halls, boiler housings and cooling towers which make some cathedrals look small. Extensive foundations are needed, but the coastal and riverside sites which had to be chosen provided the type of ground in which foundation work required a great deal of preparation. Protective works had to be set up and extensive piling was needed. When the buildings started to rise, troubles centred on the boilers, which are the first major plant item to be constructed on the site. The design of boilers of higher output had been setting a lead for generator design in the 1950s, but it had apparently not been followed up by careful development work to consolidate the technical basis for the expansion in boiler size. Some plant was delayed because tests during construction revealed mechanical defects, in other cases boiler failures occurred during early operation. Hairline cracks in welding were a particular source of trouble.

Construction of steam turbines to give approximately three-quarters of a million horsepower also presented difficulties. The CEGB set up research programmes into the incidence of turbine casing cracking due to thermal fatigue, turbine blade erosion caused by the high water content of the large quantities of steam passing through the low-pressure cylinder of very large turbines and other technical problems. These programmes were frequently run in collaboration with the manufacturers. The electrical side of the generating sets was not without its troubles either. When many of the other development problems of the 500 MW sets had been tackled and some twenty of them were in use there was a series of failures in the stators of the alternators.[50]

The wide range of technical and constructional difficulties met by the 500 MW programme and the seriousness of their effects were very much greater than any snags which had affected the earlier programmes of the publicly owned supply industry. The postwar programmes of 30 MW and 60 MW generators had suffered some delays, mostly caused by planning difficulties, shortage of manufacturing capacity and material deficiencies, and these had reached a fairly high level in 1950 and 1951. But these were delays of months rather than over a year. They were delays which had their origin in the postwar economic situation, in restrictions imposed by government and in the adjustments necessary during the transfer to public ownership. They were not caused by technical or design failings. Technical difficulties and design problems did, of course, occur before the 1960s in electrical supply equipment, but the industry worked to development procedures which prevented them from affecting a wide range of generating plant all at once.

Not only were the technical failures of the 500 MW programme unprecedented, but the nature of the capacity shortages which occurred was also quite novel. In the early days of the National Grid, during the life of the Central Electricity Board, the capacity reserve between total available output and SMD had been progressively and deliberately run down. Indeed this 'rationalisation' of generating capacity to a level nearer total demand was one of the two main reasons for the existence of the Grid and the CEB. Increased confidence in the performance of the Grid and of the more advanced generating stations which were the product of developments in the 1930s and 1940s had caused the capacity gap to be narrowed to a point where planned capacity for the late 1950s was only 12 per cent above SMD. In 1960 this was lowered to 10 per cent. The reliability of generating plant and of the Grid had never been higher than in the period 1958—60, when between 92 and 93 per cent of plant was ready to deliver its maximum output during the coldest winter months.

But the technical shortcomings of plant developed from about 1960 imposed quite a different pattern upon the relationship between capacity and SMD. Delays in plant commissioning, the inability of plant to reach its rated output until some considerable time after first commercial operation, and the actual breakdown or enforced shutdown of new plant for fault rectification (particularly the 500 MW sets, since they were in the majority), caused capacity shortages of a new kind in the late 1960s. In spite of the fact that SMD grew at a much lower rate than forecast during the late 1960s and at a lower rate than plant capacity, load shedding still occurred in the winters of 1966/7, 1967/8, 1969/70, 1970/1 and 1971/2.[51]

These load reductions took place, not because of high demand, but because the technical performances of the latest generating equipment had shown a marked deterioration since the beginning of the decade. Plant outage at times of maximum demand grew from typical levels of about 8 per cent in 1960 to 15 or 16 per cent by the middle of the 1960s and had reached averages of over 22 per cent by 1969, 1970 and 1971. In this worsening situation the major reason for outage was mechanical or electrical breakdown.

At the end of the 1960s there were two public investigations into the failures of the 500 MW programme. The first, the Wilson Committee, was set up by the Minister of Power in 1968; its eight members included three prominent industrialists and three civil servants. The Wilson Committee eschewed the task of examining the CEGB's decision procedure in depth and concluded that the major reasons for delay and failure in the 500 programme were the vast increase in workload created by the ordering spate of 1960—4 and the shortage of design and managerial skills in the manufacturing companies and the CEGB respectively. They were critical of the CEGB's handling of site construction and some other aspects of management.[52] The second investigation was made by the Select Committee on Science and Technology in January 1970.[53] It also concluded that design capabilities were lacking, but elicited very little more evidence about the programme's failures than had been provided by the Wilson Committee.

Care was taken by the Wilson Committee to emphasise that remedial measures had already been taken by the CEGB to prevent the recurrence of the delays and technical failures met during the 500 MW programme. Similarly, during the hearing conducted by the Select Committee the submissions of witnesses carried the implication that what had gone wrong was mainly a question of mistakes in detailed design, which could be and had been put right by the supply industry and the manufacturers. Neither inquiry attempted to go deeply into the background of the 500 MW programme, nor to question the way in which technical change in the CEGB came about.

Nor indeed would there have been any reason to probe further, if the 500 MW problems had been merely one isolated outbreak of failures with a single type of turbo-generator in an otherwise successful series of power station developments. But when the programme of the CEGB since 1960 is more closely considered it seems that this is very far from the case. It was not only the 500 MW set which experienced considerable delays and technical failings, but also the sets leading up to it, which, as the

Chairman of the CEGB confirmed, had performances which were as bad as or worse than that of the 500 MW unit.

The measure of the seriousness of technical delays may be best illustrated by considering how the plant programmes for 1960 to 1970 turned out in terms of achieved results. Table 3.9 compares the plant programmes planned with the out-turn.

Table 3.9 *New Plant and Total Capacity, Plans Compared with Results*

Calendar year	Plant programmed[a] (MW)	Plant commissioned (MW)	Planned capacity[b] (MW)	Capacity available (MW)
1960	1,898	1,935	27,130	26,771
1961	2,404	1,859	29,350	28,649
1962	2,271	2,725	31,800	31,403
1963	1,845	1,671	33,600	33,118
1964[c]	2,461	1,158	36,600	33,355
1965	3,176	3,498	39,561	36,670
1966	4,556	2,501	44,517	38,457
1967	5,300	4,938	49,100	41,463
1968	6,590	3,783	56,173	44,343
1969[d]	7,000	2,779	61,000	46,857
1970	5,590	3,535	66,800	49,281

Sources: Wilson Report and *Annual Reports.*
Notes: [a] Plans made for the fifth (and in 1964 for the sixth and seventh) years ahead.
[b] General estimates made by successive CEGB *Annual Reports* of anticipated capacity in future years.
[c] From 1 January 1964 new definitions of 'commissioned plant' were introduced to cater for plant which was synchronised but not fully operational.
[d] The plant programmes for 1969 and 1970 were projected in 1964, but not subsequently confirmed.

Some deficiencies of plant commissioning occurred in the years 1961—3. There was actually a shortfall of 813 MW in commissioned plant over that programmed by 1963, but the total of capacity was only 482 MW behind plan, thanks to the emergency measures taken by the CEGB. From 1964 onwards the achievement fell steadily further behind the plans made earlier, until the anticipated capacity for each year was being reached two or three years later.

It is only fair to note that after 1964 load forecasts began to be revised downwards after the very high estimates made in the early 1960s, and thus the levels of planned capacity originally envisaged for the last two or three years of the decade became notional rather than actual targets. However, delays and difficulties with power stations containing the 350 MW, 500 MW and 660 MW generating units continued to affect plant programmes well into the 1970s.

NUCLEAR GENERATING STATIONS

The British nuclear power programme had its origins in the postwar atomic bomb project. The first generation of power-producing reactors were known as Magnox plants. They used a graphite moderator inside a steel pressure vessel. The fuel was natural uranium contained in magnesium alloy and the heat transfer medium was carbon dioxide. Work on the production of power from nuclear energy began in the late 1940s and decisions to develop the Magnox type followed during the early 1950s.

The considerations which governed the choice of reactor type were those of safety combined with engineering simplicity. Graphite as a moderator was easier to design for than many of the alternatives; carbon dioxide was a safe coolant; natural, rather than enriched, uranium was felt to be more certainly available as a fuel in an unstable political environment.[54] Most materials which might be used for containing the fuel would slow down the reaction of natural uranium undesirably, and for this reason the magnesium alloy was developed which gave the reactor type its name. This feature limited the operating temperature of the reactor to below the melting point of the alloy; in practice the Magnox reactors supplied steam to the turbine at a maximum of 750°F. Steam pressures were typically 700 lb/sq. in. and only in one case as high as 927 lb/sq. in. These operating conditions were rather less advanced even than those of the standard 30 MW and 60 MW sets established by the 1947 Order.

Magnox reactors were very much more expensive than conventional plant in terms of capital cost. The first commercial plants, Berkeley and Bradwell, were expected to cost about £160 per kW, including the fuel charge, and in fact turned out at about 10—15 per cent more. Conventional plant being commissioned at the same time (1962) was of the order of £42 per kW. The Magnox reactor lost out on both the heating side and the generating side. The reactor itself produced less useful heat per £ than other reactor types (which use ordinary water as a coolant and moderator, for instance) and the turbo-alternator was less efficient than for conventional plant, thereby raising its capital cost per kW.[55]

However, by the late 1950s emphasis had unfortunately begun to be laid on nuclear power as a cheap source of electricity. The parties to the choice of Magnox were the engineers and other personnel of the atomic energy project and the government. The electricity supply industry was not really involved. The BEA had some responsibilities for the provision of power supplies on a large scale and helped the project's engineers to place contracts for equipment.[56] Whether the engineers and administrators on the nuclear project anticipated the ratio which would apply between nuclear and conventional generating capital costs by 1962 is not clear, but there is evidence that the forecast that Magnox power stations would compete with coal or oil in overall cost originated in Government circles rather than from the project engineers. Aside from the issue of comparative costs, the actual responsibility for the choice of the Magnox system lay with the project authorities and not with the Electricity Authority.

The Central Authority had virtually no nuclear design or engineering strength as late as 1955, when the first nuclear plant building programme had been announced. It may have questioned the choice of Magnox, but it did not challenge it. The decision to go ahead at that stage of nuclear development has been defended on the grounds that it was justified in terms of safeguarding fuel supplies and providing alternative energy sources, but this explains neither the size of the subsequent programme nor the way it was pursued.[57]

The Central Authority was dissatisfied with the high cost of the Magnox programme and made pointed comparisons in its 1955/6 *Annual Report* Between nuclear and conventional plant. The low steam conditions were also running counter to the major aims of the generating programme, to reduce capital costs and raise thermal efficiency. The Central Authority thus acted to try and reduce nuclear capital costs as much as possible, by exerting pressure to get the plant designs scaled up. In the development of the eight commercial nuclear stations eventually built in England and Wales, successive increases in the scale of Magnox plant took place, from 45 MW per reactor (electrical rating) for the AEA plant at Calder Hall through four or five steps up to a projected output of 590 MW per reactor for the final station at Wylfa.[58] No two of the commercial stations were alike. Each had novel aspects of design and was an attempt to squeeze slightly better performance out of the basic concept.[59] Capital costs were reduced by some 30 per cent per kW at constant prices, but the returns to scale were not as great as for conventional plant, because of the limitations of the reactor design and the lower turbine efficiencies. The running costs of the nuclear stations tended to be only 40 per cent of the average for all coal and oil stations and about 45 per cent of the most efficient stations which they might be regarded as replacing. The determination of their economic value rested heavily on the relative prices of conventional and nuclear fuels, and on the intensity with which the Magnox stations could be used. It was thus a blow to the economics of the nuclear plant when they had to be de-rated because of the corrosive effects of hot carbon dioxide gas on some relatively minor components.

In the case of the Advanced Gas-cooled Reactor (AGR), the choice of system rested with the new generating authority, the CEGB. The AGR also used a graphite moderator and carbon dioxide as the coolant, but the fuel was partially enriched uranium. Enrichment meant that the reaction was not slowed down by the fuel being contained in stainless steel; the overall design allowed a considerably higher gas outlet temperature and steam could be fed to the turbines at the Generating Board's standard steam conditions of 2,300 lb/sq. in. and 1,050°F.

Because of the higher temperatures, a smaller core, increased burn up of the fuel and a quarter the amount of graphite per MW of output compared with Magnox, the AGR was expected to be much lower on capital cost. A plant using the design principles of the AGR was built by the Atomic Energy Authority at Windscale and commissioned in 1962, in order to provide practical experience of the type and to make research tests. In 1964 the CEGB asked the nuclear industry to submit tenders for the second generation of nuclear stations and extended the invitation to submit designs which used American techniques based on water as a coolant.

The Board's decision in favour of the AGR, announced in 1965, took into account capital costs, running costs and plant availability over a twenty-year life. Although the AGR was slightly more expensive on the first, £78 per kW instead of £71 without fuel, the forecasts of running costs and availability swung the balance in its favour. The AGR was expected to generate at 0·457d per kWh as against the boiling water reactor at 0·489 per kWh.[60] The resulting contract was awarded to Atomic Power Constructions for a 1,200 MW station next door to a Magnox plant at Dungeness. Dungeness B was to have two AGR reactors of 600 MW (electrical output), each supplying steam at standard conditions to one of the new 660 MW turbo-alternators.

Three more AGR stations were ordered, at Hinkley Point in 1967, Hartlepool in 1968 and Heysham in 1970. There was some continued development of the design in these stations, but the main parameters were unaltered. The reactor output was raised to 660 MW, and changes were made to the fuel elements and boiler design. Major difficulties were experienced with Dungeness. The steel lining of the pressure vessel distorted and the boiler design had to be rejected. The consortium working on the site was forced into liquidation by the heavy extra costs which were incurred. Instead of being completed in 1971, its planned start-up date was put back to 1976. The other AGR stations were delayed by about two years each by technical problems affecting the performance of fuel elements, the behaviour of the graphite core and the corrosive effects of very hot carbon dioxide upon metal parts. The capital costs of construction rose considerably during the programme, as a result of delay, inflation, technical difficulties and unexpectedly costly aspects of the design. The out-turn costs without fuel were expected to be about £150 per kW in 1973, equivalent to a 1965 price of £108 per kW.

The weakness of the AGR programme was that the basic design concept was not ready for commercial application in 1965, nor for that matter three or four years later. For that reason the very precise costing procedures which the CEGB applied to the comparison of AGR with other systems were inappropriate and provided misleading information. The Windscale AGR reactor was not a demonstration or test of features upon which commercial operation of the AGR would depend. Thus it did not fulfil the function which Calder Hall had performed for the Magnox programme, of proving the design. The Windscale reactor operated at much lower steam temperatures and pressures than the commercial AGR, used a different type of fuel element, which was not suitable for the later plants, and had a steel pressure vessel instead of a steel-lined concrete one. Its overall heat rating was 113 MW, leading to an electrical output of about 30 MW, compared to an intended rating of 1,450 MW for the Dungeness AGR leading to 600 MW output (electrical). The thermal efficiency of Windscale was 28·5 per cent compared to a designed 41·5 per cent from Dungeness. The scale-up of the design was over ten times the output at one jump, compared to the much more gradual steps taken in the Magnox programme. The changes in the techniques made necessary by scaling up and raising the operating temperature were the factors which led to the delay and cost increases.

CONCLUSION

The 500 MW generator programme and the AGR programme contained what can only be described as important mistakes. In both cases underdeveloped plant was ordered and the subsequent difficulties were costly and damaging to the investment programme. They also damaged the reputation of the CEGB and the plant builders and affected the reputation of British technology abroad. Yet it must be recognised that the generating authorities, the CEGB and its predecessors, were boldly innovative in their approach, pushing forward the techniques of generation as far and as fast as possible. It would not be in the public interest that the competence of public authorities such as the CEGB should be too much open to criticism, because an unnecessary conservatism, such as that which afflicted the generating programme in the 1940s, might result.

It is very difficult to determine where responsibility for the mistakes should lie. It is natural for the Generating Board to point to the manufacturers' responsibilities as suppliers of the 500 MW sets and to the BEA's role in the design of the AGR, and to draw attention to the fact that teething troubles with new plant are common in most technical advances and have indeed occurred elsewhere in the world.[61] This does not allay disquiet about the procedure followed in bringing about these technical changes.

In the 500 MW programme there were faults of boiler design; welding techniques and pipework to withstand 2,300 lb/sq. in. and 1,050°F were lacking; turbine shafts did not perform satisfactorily. Had such faults occurred in plant installed in the 1920s and 1930s the manufacturer would naturally have accepted them as his responsibility. But the situation which applied in Britain during the 1950s and 1960s was very different. As the dominant purchaser of plant, the CEGB (and BEA before it) set the standards for techniques and forced the pace of advance. The opportunity for a plant manufacturer to exercise his judgment on what technical advances were desirable was much diminished by the disappearance of any alternative domestic customer to whom he could turn for business if he was doubtful of the specifications requested for plant.

The generating authority showed some recognition of this altered balance by increasing the amount of research it undertook on generating techniques, and also engaged in engineering development, but it did not go far enough in establishing its own competence to determine whether a new technique was ready for introduction, nor did it institutionalise its commercial arrangements with the manufacturers in a way which would ensure that premature advances were not made. The weaknesses of generating research were pointed out by the Herbert Committee in 1956. It took another seven years for the generating industry to expand its research efforts by opening up new laboratories. The Power Engineering Research Steering Committee, representing the supply industry and the plant manufacturers, was only set up in 1966. Both measures post-dated the important technical decisions of the period 1955 to 1960, which they might have been expected to guide. By contrast, the advancing of the techniques used for transmission in Britain was backed by a carefully planned research programme, in the transmission research facilities set up by the CEB and later extended by the BEA and CEGB.

Secondly, there is the question of teething troubles. It is true that most new techniques are accompanied by introductory troubles, and it is for this reason that their introduction is usually accomplished through prototypes, pilot plant and other means. With very large turbo-generators these mechanisms are not so appropriate; the methods of progressing large projects and the load on the generating industry and its suppliers were such that five, six or seven years elapsed between an order for a new frame size and its commissioning in the general investment programme. In the early 1960s the Generating Board was making a jump from the standard sets ordered in the mid-1950s, of 120 MW, to a standard set four times as large at 500 MW, at a time when no operating experience of sets between those sizes had been gained. Since power station construction lead times delay the evaluation of a new size, it would have seemed appropriate to have established a separate development programme aimed at establishing successive sizes of turbo-alternator. The approach actually used confused the aims of a development programme, and its need for considered evaluation, with the urgency of the investment programme, providing more plant to meet demand.

With the AGR, the Generating Board was in an anomalous position. Although experienced in the design of Magnox reactors, the Board had not gained the experience necessary to anticipate the problems which might arise between the building of a small prototype reactor and scaling up by ten times the design and operating conditions. The AEA was the statutory authority for research reactors; the CEGB did its best to acquire enough understanding of nuclear techniques to be able to choose the second generation intelligently. It was, even so, really forced to depend upon the Atomic Energy Authority's judgment. The AEA was not strictly in the position of being able to say in 1965, on the basis of Windscale and other knowledge, whether the full scale commercial design for Dungeness B would work. It undoubtedly expressed an honest opinion, in hoping that it would do so and believing that the AGR was the best bet for development. Nor was the CEGB in a position to reject the AEA's advice. There may have been a suspicion at some levels of both organisations that what was required was an interim size plant to demonstrate the AGR principles at commercial scale and commercial ratings, but again the Board did not distinguish the rather different needs of a development programme from those of the more general programme of investment in plant.

NOTES

[1] Separate arrangements were made for Scotland.

[2] R. H. Parsons, *Early Days of the Power Station Industry*, Cambridge, 1939.

[3] The North Eastern Electricity Supply Company (NESCO) achieved a good deal of integration in north east England.

[4] Joint Select Committee of Parliament ('Cross Committee'), 1898; Electric Lighting Act, 1909; Haldane Committee, 1916; Board of Trade Committee, 1917.

[5] Installed capacity indicates the rating of the generators used, whereas output capacity gives the station's net contribution to the Grid after internal needs are met.

[6] To a power station of the Commonwealth Edison Co. in Chicago.

[7] 'Large orthodox stations or nuclear stations can however seldom be sited near the load centres and must therefore feed into the main transmission network. Thus there must be a substantial and continuous growth in the power movements.' Lecture by Deputy Chairman F. H. S. Brown (CEGB), British Electrical and Allied Manufacturers Association Export Conference, 8 October 1961.

[8] 100 MW is 100 million watts, and one watt is the energy supplied by one volt at one amp. Doubling the voltage raised the power transmitted by a factor of about six, but the current required increased less than three times. Transmission costs tend to be more closely related to the level of current carried, hence the returns to scale.

[9] An article in *Economica* of August 1961 ('Replacement of Obsolescent Plant', by F. H. S. Brown and R. S. Edwards) suggested that power stations face an 80 per cent increase in capital cost per kW for a 100 per cent increase in output.

[10] Ministry of Fuel and Power, *Inquiry into Economy in the Construction of Power Stations*, HMSO, 1953.

[11] In 1961 it was estimated that power stations containing four 500 MW sets would cost £35 per kW, but by 1967 they were being estimated at £54 per kW. At 1961 prices this is £47 per kW, which is approximately the same level of cost as for the 200 MW and 300 MW sets. Ministry of Fuel and Power, *Report of the Committee to study the Electricity Peak Load Problem in Relation to the Non-Industrial Consumer*, Cmd 7464, HMSO, 1948.

[12] A steam turbine was patented in Britain in 1884 by C. A. Parsons and the first turbo-generator was built in the same year by Clarke, Chapman, Parsons at Newcastle.

[13] F. D. R. Buckling & A. J. Surrey, 'An International Comparison of Production Techniques: the Local French Electricity Generating Industry', *National Institute Economic Review*, May 1966.

[14] Ministry of Fuel and Power, Peak Load Committee, Cmd 7464, HMSO, 1948.

[15] British Electricity Authority, *Annual Report*, 1948/9. The actual total of new plant installed to 31 March 1968 was 33,800 MW.

[16] The three most efficient stations in 1952 were: Dunston B II, two 50 MW sets at 600 lb/sq. in. and 849°F, with re-heat and a unit boiler arrangement; Littlebrook B, two 60 MW sets at 1,235 lb/sq. in. and 825°F, with re-heat; Stourport B, two 60 MW sets at 1,250 lb/sq. in. and 950°F. All were ordered before nationalisation but commissioned afterwards.

[17] Steam at 600 lb/sq. in. and 850°F for 30 MW, and 900 lb/sq. in. and 900°F for 60 MW. Similar steam conditions had been used since 1933 and surpassed since 1938.

[18] Portobello HP, Stourport B, Dunston B II, Littlebrook B.

[19] V. A. Pask, 'Power Stations and their Equipment', *Proceedings of the Institute of Electrical Engineers*, 1955, pp. 169—88. High-speed sets (3,600 r.p.m. in the US, 3,000 r.p.m. in Britain) were more difficult to build in large sizes than the 1,800 r.p.m. and 1,500 r.p.m. sets. The Essex design was later up-rated to 125 MW by adding a re-heat stage.

[20] *Report on Electricity Supply*, PEP, London, 1936.

[21] The *Annual Report* of the CEB for 1946 states that for some years in the past the Board had made arrangements with the undertakings to standardise turbo-generator steam conditions at 600 lb/sq. in. and boiler sizes at about 235 klb/hour and 335 klb/hour.

[22] The Herbert Report (*Committee of Inquiry into the Electricity Supply Industry*, Cmd 9672, HMSO, 1955) makes the same contrast, but applies it to the pre-nationalisation and

post-nationalisation situations, rather than seeing it as an earlier trend. The evidence suggests that the slow-down of innovation occurred in the 1930s.

[23] Pask, 'Power Stations and their Equipment', op. cit.

[24] *Electrical Review,* 21 November 1947, p. 766.

[25] The BEAMA lecture (Brown, op. cit.) refers to the Order apologetically, and an article by Donkin and Margen written in 1951 argues for larger units (*Proceedings of the Institute of Electrical Engineers,* 1952).

[26] Two 100 MW sets came into use in 1957/8, three 100 MW and one 120 MW in 1958/9, and four 100 MW, seven 120 MW and one 200 MW in 1959/60.

[27] Pask, 'Power Stations and their Equipment', op. cit.

[28] The CEGB took over the generation function from the CEA in 1958.

[29] Ferrybridge B, Aberthaw, Castle Donnington and Willington A. Only Ferrybridge B and Aberthaw had re-heat stages added.

[30] Some of the 120 MW sets replaced orders made earlier for the 60 MW sets in the 1953—9 programme.

[31] Liquid cooling of the stator of the alternator was adopted after trials on a 30 MW set at Bold A; the internal cooling of conductors was tested at Willington A on the 100 MW set.

[32] The main recommendations of the Herbert Report, that generation should be separated from the main supervisory role of the Authority, had come into effect on 1 January 1958. The 300 MW set seems to have been the first of the Board's sets.

[33] BEA and CEA, *Annual Reports,* 1953/4 to 1957/8. Planned expansion in the earlier years was 50 per cent over each six-year period and in the later years 44 per cent over each six-year period.

[34] As late as 1973 Blyth A was still fifth in the power station 'top twenty' at over 34 per cent.

[35] This 1965 programme was to be settled later in 1960. Although previously a six-year period from ordering to commissioning of plant had been allowed, the CEGB was implementing a recommendation of the Herbert Report by reducing the planning cycle to five years.

[36] Planned programmes of 1,252, 1,759, 2,038 and 2,379 MW were cut to 1,140, 1,647, 1,898 and 2,292 MW.

[37] 35,000 MW of plant, if available in the winter of 1964/5, could in principle have met an SMD of 31,500 MW if 90 per cent of plant were in use. In fact the 10 per cent margin allowed for 'plant outage' was too narrow during times when much innovatory equipment was being used, and the outage margin was later raised to 14 per cent and higher. The SMD forecast for 1964/5 to determine the 1964 plant programme had been put at 30,000 MW in 1959.

[38] The plant programme had been about 600 MW behind plan on average since 1954. The average over 1961/3 was 850 MW (*Report of Committee of Inquiry into Delays in Commissioning CEGB Power Stations* (Wilson Report), Cmnd 3960; HMSO, 1969).

[39] Including Carville B station in the Newcastle district, where Parsons' 5×11 MW units had been installed in 1914.

[40] 7 MW in 1961/2, 11 MW in 1962/3, 23 MW in 1963/4.

[41] Thermal efficiency had risen to 26·5 per cent by 1960, thanks to the use of the 60 MW, 100 MW and 120 MW sets. It reached 27·7 per cent in 1964, with new machines of 34 per cent and above (the 200 MW, 120 MW and 100 MW sets), but dropped back to 27·3 per cent in 1966, because of the use of old plant and delays in commissioning new plant.

[42] Maximum potential demand grew from 18,100 MW in 1955/6 to 36,077 MW in 1965/6, a rate of increase of about 7·3 per cent annually.

[43] Select Committee on Nationalised Industries, *The Gas Industry,* HMSO, 1961.

[44] At least partly attributable to the Clean Air Act of 1956.

[45] The period 23 December 1962 to 6 February 1963 included the most severe cold spell of more than a month's duration for at least eighty-five years.

[46] Select Committee on Nationalised Industries, *The Electricity Supply Industry,* op. cit.

[47] This was to fit in with the 4 per cent growth target set by NEDC and to ease the plant margin, as well as to meet forecast growth.

[48] Wilson Report (op. cit.). In 1968, 7,000 MW of plant was behind schedule; 63 per cent of units ordered were more than six months late and 43 per cent were over twelve months late.

[49] Although both 200s were commissioned about twelve months late, these were the sets which achieved the record thermal efficiency of 35·78 in 1965.

[50] Select Committee on Science and Technology, *Generating Plant Breakdowns, Winter 1969/70*, HMSO, 1970. Six failures had occurred in the period October—December 1961.

[51] Some load shedding in February 1972 was attributable to the miners' strike; in the winter of 1970/1 capacity was affected during December 1970 by a work to rule of power station employees.

[51] Wilson Report, op. cit.

[53] *Generating Plant Breakdowns*, op. cit.

[54] i.e. its supply, from Canada, was apparently preferred to dependence on the United States, which would have been necessary for enriched fuel.

[55] Water cooled and moderated reactors have steam supply temperatures lower than Magnox, but they tend to compensate for this by the low cost of the reactor, giving overall generating costs which in the United States are competitive with conventional costs.

[56] M. Gowing, *Independence and Deterrence*, Vol. 2, Macmillan, London, 1974. Gowing says that Risley did not hold the BEA in high regard and that Harwell thought it had no proper method of progressing large projects.

[57] The original programme in 1955 envisaged more than 2,000 MW. At the time of Suez and fears of an oil crisis this was raised to 7,000 MW. A year later it was cut back to 5,000 MW, but the fuel supply argument had disappeared with the arrival of a coal surplus.

[58] Not attained in practice, being rated at 420 MW per reactor in 1975.

[59] Trawsfynydd (the fourth station) had the highest steam conditions; Dungeness had a thicker reactor pressure vessel; the seventh and eighth stations, Oldbury and Wylfa, had concrete pressure vessels.

[60] 'An appraisal of the technical and economic aspects of Dungeness B nuclear power station', CEGB, July 1965.

[61] The plant manufacturers' reply is that the CEGB, being a near monopoly buyer, was squeezing their margins so much that design, workmanship and delivery were bound to suffer: see G. B. Richardson, 'The Future of the Heavy Electrical Industry', *BEAMA Report*, 1969.

4 The Choice of Automatic Telephone Switching Techniques

Summary

Strowger automatic switching had been the standard technique employed in the British telephone system since the 1920s. By 1946 the Post Office was considering what type of exchange switching should replace it. Its disadvantages in a telephone system which was to become increasingly heavily used were that it had a high maintenance requirement, required a large amount of switch and trunking equipment and was a relatively slow method of switching.

The maintenance requirement was an undesirable feature, because it meant that the engineering costs of running the system were likely to grow as fast as the total traffic carried. The bulky nature of the switching equipment meant that Strowger was expensive to provide and that the exchange buildings which had to be found in crowded city centres needed to be fairly big and to contain provision for expansion. The slowness and inflexibility of switching affected the capacity of the line network and made the addition of new subscriber facilities difficult to achieve.

Agreements existed between the Post Office and its exchange equipment suppliers for the conduct of research on a co-operative basis. A formal procedure for bringing about technical change had been evolved; joint decisions of the Post Office and the five exchange manufacturers were discussed within the British Telephone Technical Development Committee, and the work necessary to develop new equipment was allocated to individual corporate members. The basic structure of the BTTDC was used for the development of the new exchange techniques on which the Post Office had started work in the late 1940s. The committee structure was adapted and a new research agreement was established specifically for the exchange project.

The main functions of the BTTDC were to rationalise and make the best use of research facilities, and to ensure that agreement was reached on common standards and technical specifications for telephone developments. Its method of functioning was to produce a consensus on the nature of marginal improvements to the established Strowger switching methods. It was not suited by its constitution to the resolution of conflicts on issues when real grounds existed for conflicting technical opinions, and where exploratory development and some open-ended research were needed to establish the technical parameters affecting the choice of a wholly new technique.

The indications were that the Post Office had made up its mind on the choice before negotiatons with the manufacturers began. The system the Post Office favoured, time division multiplex, used electronic valve switching. It was a technically elegant solution with a large amount of common equipment and the advantages of reliable components, fast switching and space saving. Its economy in the use of equipment might have produced low capital costs if it had become fully developed. Its disadvantages were that its high degree of technical sophistication made it inflexible and created major difficulties of inter-working with the rest of the system.

Development of time division multiplex under the Joint Electronic Research Agreement did not provide conditions in which a number of experimental solutions to the problem of the choice of a new technique could be evaluated. Work on the alternatives by manufacturers was restrained, being carried on outside the context of official agreements, and it was not until 1960 that other systems were given serious official backing. The result was that, when new types of exchange were needed in the mid 1960s for installation in the larger type of exchange applications, neither time-division multiplex nor the reed-relay system which succeeded it were ready.

To fill the gap the Post Office decided to install crossbar exchanges, a type which had not been included in the development programme. Crossbar switching employed electro-magnetic techniques instead of electronic ones. The types of exchange installed in Britain were adapted from models developed by the manufacturers for other markets. They were not ideally suited to the British system, their main disadvantage being that, having been developed without Post Office participation or the expectation of use in Britain, they did not include the features which the Post Office regarded as desirable.

As a result of the unsuitability of crossbar systems as developed, the Post Office had only a restricted choice available when it came to make a committing decision on techniques in 1972. By that time reed-relay exchanges for large applications were within two or three years of commercial service and the Post Office had to decide whether to make a further commitment to crossbar exchanges or to invest in the further development of the reed-relay system as the major exchange type of the future. Detailed study of the reed-relay and crossbar types available showed the former to be more suitable. Since the Post Office had never sponsored the development of a crossbar exchange *ab initio*, the types available for comparison with reed-relay had features and design philosophies which would have required more fundamental and more costly development to make them suitable for use than was involved for the reed-relay design. It may well have been the case that the technical merits of the reed-relay design were superior to those of the crossbar. Both systems are widely used by foreign telephone administrations. But the choice in the Post Office's decision was determined more by the absence of official sponsorship of a crossbar system than by competitive evaluation of the alternatives.

The Post Office's interest in research on new types of capital equipment can be traced back to the beginning of the century. Having assumed responsibility for the trunk network before 1900, it had promoted the development of new types of cable. Laboratory facilities were built up in central London and in the early 1920s the research station at Dollis Hill was set up. Post Office work on transmission techniques, particularly in connection with under-sea cables, had achieved for it an international reputation. This tradition was well maintained in postwar years and extended into satellite transmission.

There was a strong professional association of Post Office engineers. Its *Journal*, published regularly since 1906, constitutes virtually a complete record of Post Office research down the years. Prior to the electronic exchange, the Post Office had been content to allow manufacturers of exchange equipment to lead in exchange development. The industry had in fact not been well established in Britain until after the First World War and Britain tended to follow technical developments elsewhere, rather than to lead. In the first major decision on automatic exchange types, taken between 1918 and 1924, a policy of testing alternative exchanges in commercial installations from a number of manufacturers had been followed.

What is interesting about the story of the electronic exchange is that the relationship between the Post Office, as the only large domestic customer, and the equipment manufacturers who made up the supplying industry had been developing over a period of thirty years before the joint agreement on electronic development was made. There was early recognition of the dangers of the market structure which existed — that uneven loading of the capacity of the manufacturers might result from the single customer phasing its orders or favouring one supplier to the exclusion of others. The arrangements made for market-sharing also took account of the responsibility of the Post Office for technical development. As the only large domestic customer it would have a determining influence upon what new techniques were adopted and when they were brought into use, while the industry would have the job of developing them and manufacturing new equipment. In recognition of this responsibility, the Post Office undertook to agree with the industry on the technical changes that were desirable and necessary.

It would be obtuse not to recognise here that the BTTDC represented sincere effort of a pioneering nature to deal with a genuine problem. The economic waste to the Post Office and the industry of having different techniques developed by each manufacturer, and then of one being chosen, appeared a serious consideration. Added to that, companies might be forced out of business by competitive development, which could damage the economy. However, the agreements made between the two sides failed to recognise that on some occasions competitive development was the only way to make a valid evaluation of alternative techniques. By cutting out wasteful competition, they almost succeeded in abolishing the analytical procedures needed to make a choice between techniques.

The mechanism for interconnecting callers on a telephone network may be either manual or automatic. Manual mechanisms are relatively labour intensive and have for many years been less economic than automatic ones, except in a relatively few special applications. As a consequence automatic mechanisms predominate in the telephone services of the major industrialised countries.

The basis of automatic mechanisms for connecting telephone users is most commonly a set of switches. For the exchange to fulfil its function, the design of the switches and their interconnecting wiring must be such that when a call is originated an electrical path is set up through the exchange to the required outgoing line. This electrical path is called the speech path. A simply visualised analogy to the design is a complicated railway crossing. Lines feed in from several directions and the crossing (the exchange) must be capable of providing a rail route (speech path) from each of the incoming lines to any required outlet. In this analogy the railway points correspond to the switch of the telephone exchange. Both railway and telephone engineers refer to the function of guiding traffic as switching. But whereas the railway engineer has not recently seen radical changes in switching techniques, the telephone engineering profession has been involved in developing new switching techniques for some decades. This chapter considers how these changes have come about.

The telephone switching process is necessarily more complex than the railway one, because the automatic exchange functions without a human operator, a condition which would be judged to be unacceptably risky in railway systems.

In order to fulfil its task, the automatic switching system must incorporate a sufficient number of electrical paths through the exchange for the traffic it has to carry, it must include sets of switches arranged to set up any required path and there must be a control mechanism which will respond to the subscriber's demands for connection. There are also some ancillary functions which the exchange must fulfil, such as carrying different current conditions to provide a signal to the wanted subscriber, clearing a speech path when the connection has ceased, metering and billing the consumer's use of the service and having some capacity to deal with faults or failed connections in the speech paths.

The earliest type of automatic switch was invented by a Kansas undertaker, Almon B. Strowger, in 1889. It is called, unsurprisingly, the Strowger switch. It was the most widely used in the world up to the 1970s, and within the United Kingdom will be the predominant switching mechanism in the telephone network until about 1990. It has proved adaptable and long-lasting, because it is very simple. A large number of contacts, as many as one or two hundred, are arranged in a co-ordinate array, as potential outlets. A path through one of the outlets is established by the mechanical movement of a connecting arm, which rises to the required contact level (a 100-outlet switch might have ten levels with ten outlets in each level) and then traverses to the required outlet. The control of the system is contained in the switching mechanism. The number of electrical pulses sent to the switch determines the selection of outlet. The movement of the arm is created by electro-magnetic attraction as in an electric bell, or by electric motor drive. With the invention of the telephone dial, which sends timed electrical impulses to the exchange, the Strowger system was well established by 1900.

Where the manual exchange is labour intensive in its use of operators, the Strowger exchange needs a considerable maintenance effort and in

Britain after the second world war this was beginning to be felt by the telephone system as a constraint.[1] There are other disadvantages of this automatic exchange. Its capacity to serve special needs is low. Its capacity for being programmed is strictly limited and its reliability is rather below the present standards required by telephone engineers. In switching calls its speed of operation is slower than is desirable for some of the complex functions of a modern telephone system.

Interest in using electronic devices (a valve can be made to function as an on—off switch) to replace electro-mechanical exchanges began in the 1930s. The advances made in electronic technology during the war triggered off active research into the electronic exchange in Britain as soon as the war ended. An exchange incorporating electronic switching to replace Strowger became a major aim of Post Office technical policy.

The ensuing story has almost dramatic quality. The Post Office's approach was highly innovatory. However, in pursuing an ambitious system which was technically ingenious, the Post Office initially decided against the development of two non-electronic types of switch, the reed-relay and the crossbar, which were coming to the fore alongside electronic devices. Circumstances, particularly the expansion of the British telephone network, then conspired to force acceptance of both these two developments into the network, while the more innovative approach languished. The reasons for these events and their effects on the telephone system are discussed in the main part of this chapter, after an introductory section on the development of the telephone service.

BRITISH TELECOMMUNICATIONS

The telecommunications business, telephones, telegrams, telex and data transmission, is run by the Post Office. In the late 1940s the Post Office's annual turnover was rather below £200 million, of which the posts formed just over 50 per cent and telephones and telegraphs nearly 48 per cent. By 1975 the telecommunications business had grown to become over 60 per cent of the turnover of £1,850 million, the postal side being approximately one-third. Giro and data processing services had been added to the more traditional business, but were still relatively small.

The position of the Post Office up to 1969 was legally that of a revenue-earning civil service department. It was thus rather different from the other public corporations, such as the Gas Council or the Coal Board. Probably the most important differences, from the point of view of the events described below, were that its managerial structure followed the pattern of the civil service and its finances were not under its own control. Indeed, with minor exceptions, up to 1961 and the Post Office Act of that year all income was delivered directly to the Exchequer and expenditure had both to be voted by Parliament and also approved by the Treasury. However, during the 1950s the needs of the Post Office as a business had increasingly been recognised. The 1961 Act established operating conditions in which it could function as a business corporation.

TELEPHONE DEVELOPMENT

Telephones were invented in America by Alexander Bell and Thomas Edison in the mid-1870s. Private companies started services in Britain in 1878 and 1879 and the public telephone network did not come fully under Post Office control until 1912.[2] The basis of Post Office encroachment was the Telegraph Acts of 1863, 1868 and 1869, which established a Crown monopoly of telegraphic communications. In 1880 a court action by the Crown established that this included telephone communication, and companies from that time (and town corporations from the 1890s) operated services only under licence. The Post Office opened its first exchange in 1881, and a planned take-over of the long distance network was completed in 1896. After the 1880 court action the companies having access to Bell's and Edison's patents combined to form the United Telephone Company; later, as the National Telephone Company, this became the only large system operator in the United Kingdom other than the Post Office itself. But the licences issued set a limit on the period of independent operation and in 1912 the Post Office, which already operated the trunk network and a large number of exchanges, took over the remaining independents.

At this time there was about 500,000 subscribers in the United Kingdom (Table 4.2). The manufacture of telephone equipment, even after thirty years of the service, was scarcely established in Britain. There were no automatic exchanges in the National Telephone Company, even though the Strowger system was demonstrated in London as early as 1897. The first automatic exchange was of Strowger design and opened at Epsom in March 1912 with 500 lines. The equipment was manufactured in the United States and imported by a company newly formed to develop automatic telephony in the United Kingdom, the Automatic Telephone Manufacturing Company of Liverpool.

Epsom was essentially an experimental installation, intended to test the working of an automatic exchange and the degree of acceptance it would meet in the system. Similar equipment was installed in the Engineer-in-Chief's office in Post Office headquarters at about the same time. Other systems of automatic switching had been developed after Strowger and in 1914 a Lorrimer Rotary exchange was put into public service at Hereford. The American Western Electric Company gained an order for a service exchange at Darlington. This trial exchange also used a Rotary mechanism. Siemens Brothers (of the UK) entered the field in 1918 with a developed version of Strowger; in 1922 a very early version of an automatic crossbar exchange was installed at Fleetwood, Lancashire.

By the early part of 1924 the Post Office Engineer-in-Chief, Colonel Sir Thomas Purves, had recommended standardisation of automatic switching on the Strowger system. London telephone exchanges were being converted to automatic working and the Automatic Telephone Manufacturing Company (later to become the Automatic Telephone and Electric Co.) had offered a practical solution, to be used with Strowger, to the problem of dialling between exchanges in the densely telephoned area of the capital.[3] The trials of different automatic systems and the decision in favour of Strowger set the scene for a rapid expansion of automatic working, halted only by the war.

At the same time that automatic equipment for exchanges was standardised, arrangements were made for all the existing exchange manufacturing companies (four in number) to be able to produce Strowger-switched exchanges. The agreement made between the four companies and the Post Office covered technical specifications and pricing arrangements for standard components. In 1928 a fifth manufacturer had become established as a supplier of exchange equipment and bulk supply agreements were made. One of the results of the agreements, which provided for the sharing out of orders for exchange equipment between the five and the exclusion of new entrants to the market by competitive tender, was that technical development was co-ordinated by the Post Office. All changes in the switching and other technical systems used by the Post Office were discussed by committees representing the manufacturers and the Post Office. The interworking of telephone switching and signalling systems requires a high degree of reliability and standardisation. The British Telephone Technical Development Committee was a useful instrument for implementing this, and even quite small changes in techniques were subject to scrutiny and had to receive the Engineer-in-Chief's office's approval. Price and quality control were also made possible, by having the companies' costs and working practices open to inspection by the purchaser.

THE BRIDGEMAN REPORT

Although the Post Office did not achieve the full legal status of a public corporation until October 1969, for many years before that date it was fulfilling the role of a public corporation, in that it was providing a commercial service which was run as far as possible in the national interest. To provide a commercial service through a government department which was organised on civil service lines was not an easy task. If there were times when the Post Office appeared dilatory about opening up new services, or seemed to have a slightly old-fashioned attitude to the demands of its customers, these traits could be excused on the grounds that they were caused by its anomalous position rather than by any lack of concern about the standards of the service.

The Post Office was unable to create a commercial structure for the telephone service at the time of nationalisation (1896—1912), but on the other hand the telephone service was certainly not unenterprising in its first thirty years of public ownership. The service provided was re-organised and automatic working was rapidly introduced. The London telephone system, in particular, was radically overhauled in these early years and the 'Director' system of dialling between exchanges in the metropolitan area was introduced during the 1920s.[4]

During the 1930s expansion was rapid and the introduction of automatic exchanges affected about half the system in ten years. This automatic service was not just provided to large urban exchanges, but also to very small rural ones, and the engineering department adopted a pioneering attitude in developing and installing automatic exchanges for every application, down to those serving as few as fifty or even twenty connections. The enthusiasm for technical change and the improvement of standards may perhaps have outstripped conventional commercial prudence and economic calculation.[5] But the risk-taking paid off, and during the 1930s the service expanded, lowered its prices and paid its way.

Nevertheless, the managerial and financial restrictions affecting the postal and telecommunication services did not pass unnoticed. There was a House of Commons inquiry into the telephone service in 1921, and in 1932 an external Committee of Inquiry under Viscount Bridgeman presented its report on whether changes in Post Office organisation would be in the public interest.[6]

Bridgeman tackled head-on the problem of whether the Post Office should be a public corporation. In rejecting the idea, one of his main grounds was that it would remove the services from the 'wholesome operation of public criticism'. It is clear that the Committee developed during their work a respect and admiration for the high standards and regard for the public interest which pervaded the department's work. They were unable however to ignore the signs of weakness in the management system and in the financial arrangements.

With regard to finance, Bridgeman proposed that the Post Office, instead of paying its total receipts to the Exchequer and going cap in hand for running expenses and capital expenditure, should pay a fixed annual sum to the Exchequer, plus 50 per cent of any surplus. The remainder would accrue as a Post Office Fund. These were not radical suggestions, and they were considerably less 'business oriented' than the arrangements which eventually established self-contained finance for the Post Office in 1956 and 1961 (see below, pp. 118—22). They were implemented, however, for only a very short time before the Treasury resumed control at the outbreak of war. On the management side, Bridgeman reported that the Secretariat at headquarters, consisting of twelve members at Secretary or Assistant Secretary level, exercised a very high degree of central control. Recruited like any other entrants to the civil service, they were senior public servants, such as those at the heads of other government departments, whose education, training and experience had done little to acquaint them with the business of running postal, telephone and telegraph services.[7] Below the level of the Secretariat, Controllers were at the head of the functional departments. The country was divided into Districts each with its surveyor, and the surveyor was responsible for all Post Office services in his area.

The engineering function was represented at headquarters by the Engineer-in-Chief and his department, although there was of course no engineering representative of the Secretariat. The engineering department at the District level was entirely separate from the surveyor, who had no authority over it. Orders to the superintending engineer, his assistants, inspectors and workmen could not go direct from surveyor, district telephone manager or Head Postmaster to the District engineering staff. Instructions had to pass upwards to the Secretariat and then pass down again through the Engineer-in-Chief's office to the District engineering sections. The lack of representation of the services functions, or of engineering, at the Secretariat level meant that that body was no place for resolving policy which in any way involved alternative technical strategies and their commercial implications. In practice the engineering department had to go its own way for lack of a co-ordinating function. Bridgeman recognised the department's achievement in these difficult circumstances and noted that engineering experience was too seldom brought into policy making. It is to be doubted whether the integration of commercial, financial and technical objectives within Post Office policy was an activity which was considered in any part of the organisation.

Bridgeman's proposals for re-organisation covered both headquarters and Districts. He suggested that a Board should replace the Secretariat and that the main functions of general operations, supply, engineering, finance, etc., should be represented on it. In the Districts, a Regional Director was to be responsible for carrying out all Board policy decisions. He would have wide authority over his District, and be assisted by staff representing the engineering, financial and personnel functions.

The Bridgeman approach to re-organisation was largely accepted and changes followed over the years leading up to the period where the story of the electronic exchange opens. However, change was not speedy. Only two Districts had been re-constituted as Regions by the outbreak of war. Even in 1950 the Post Office was still digesting the Bridgeman recommendations. Overall, the transition from the Post Office as a department of government to the Post Office as an organisation which reflected the commercial climate in which it operated, and the corporate responsibilities which it carried, was a long-drawn-out affair. Even as late as 1965 the composition of the Board was being reformed. From being an effective but narrow and over-centralising organisation (as the Secretariat, before Bridgeman), it had swung the opposite way, to represent all the line and staff functions at the most senior level. In 1965 its size was reduced from twenty to seven members, in order to make it a more effective instrument in management.

Because the suggestions of the Bridgeman report were not rigorously carried through, and because the transition to a commercial enterprise was a gradual one, some of the failings to which Bridgeman drew attention persisted well into the 1940s and 1950s. The central direction of staff on minutiae was still much in evidence after the war and was sometimes treated as a subject for innocent humour.[8] Relations between headquarters and the Regions involved many of the frustrations of pre-Bridgeman days. For instance, in 1937 a committee had considered the future of operators in conditions of mechanisation expected to make the majority redundant.

Eleven years later its report was still confidential and thus its recommendations were not known to the majority of people it affected. Another instance was that Head Postmasters had considerable authority over the running of the telephone service, even though the telephone manager was really responsible for it.

These characteristics of the telephone service and its organisation inside the Post Office are mostly important for the light which they throw upon the way in which the engineering department worked. It had existed since 1870, in what was recognised both by Bridgeman and the brief historical survey referred to above as a separate organisation within the Post Office. Rather than its functions being integrated with other aspects of the business, the engineering department had been forced to generate its own standards and objectives. Regionalisation according to the Bridgeman proposals indicated an end to the semi-isolation in which the department had worked, but Regionalisation was only slowly accomplished. It seems probable that the new relationships which had to be established in order to integrate engineering and commercial considerations into a process of business policy making took even longer to form.

DEVELOPMENT OF THE ELECTRONIC EXCHANGE, 1945—75

Up to the outbreak of the Second World War, the telephone service in Britain had undergone fairly steady expansion. Technical progress, in terms of the type of equipment available to subscribers, the ease of making calls and the possibilities of long-distance communication, had been satisfactory, if not spectacular, since the Post Office took over the whole system in 1912. As far as mechanisation was concerned rapid progress had been made up to 1939, the number of subscribers on automatic exchanges having exceeded the number on manual exchanges as early as 1938 (Table 4.1).

But for the intervention of the war, it is likely that the exchange system over the whole of Britain would have been converted to automatic working for local calls by the late 1940s. That would have meant that the inhabitants of conurbations such as Birmingham, Glasgow and London would have been able to dial their calls to some hundreds of thousands of other subscribers in the same Director area; within large towns such as Leeds, Bristol and Nottingham some tens of thousands of subscribers would have been linked in the same multi-office area; in the countryside and small towns dialled calls over a range of several miles between linked exchanges would have been possible. The intended date of complete mechanisation might have been 1945. This was considered to be a likely date for completion shortly before the war and substantial progress had been made by 1940. Between 1930 and 1939, 1,600 manual exchanges had been converted to Strowger automatic working and well over 1,000 new Strowger exchanges had been installed, so that the goal of full automation, except for trunk calls, was certainly in sight.[9]

Table 4.1   *The Number of Subscribers on Each Type of Exchange, 1920—75*

at 31 March	On automatic exchanges	On manual exchanges	Total (millions)
1912	...	0·5	0·5
1920	...	0·6	0·6
1925	...	0·8	0·8
1930	0·3	0·9	1·2
1935	0·6	0·9	1·5
1940	1·2	0·9	2·1
1945	1·4	0·8	2·2
1950	2·1	1·0	3·1
1955	3·0	1·0	4·0
1960	3·8	1·0	4·8
1965	5·4	0·6	6·0
1970	8·5	0·1	8·6
1975	12·7	...	12·7

Sources: Telecommunications Statistics, Post Office, 1974, and *Annual Reports.*
Notes:
Figures are given to nearest 100,000.
Only a few thousand subscribers were connected to the first (experimental) automatic exchanges installed from 1912 to 1924.
Subscribers are recorded as separate exchange lines up to 1930; thereafter as exchange connections.
Nine thousand subscribers on thirteen manual exchanges remained in 1975.

As it happened, when the war ended hardly any further progress had been made towards mechanising the system. It might therefore be expected that the first priority after the war would have been to return to this task and get it finished, albeit later than anticipated. However the war itself and certain postwar conditions of life in Britain conspired to prevent the Post Office from taking up where it had left off in 1939. So far from eliminating the 800,000 subscribers and 2,240 exchanges which still operated on manual methods, the telephone service was actually forced to increase the number of subscribers who had access to a manual service only and could dial none of their calls. (Table 4.1.)

MECHANISATION DELAYED . . .

What had happened was as follows. The exchange equipment programme was naturally considerably slowed down by the war. Some outstanding contracts were fulfilled during late 1939 and in 1940, but the level of ordering dropped almost immediately from over £5 million per annum to less than £1 million; expenditure on exchanges to be installed averaged only about £1 million per annum from 1941 to 1946, whereas the planned levels were five or ten times that amount. Expenditure on local lines also fell drastically. These local lines from the exchanges to strategic points in the locality represent the spare capacity of the system, and when not regularly provided in advance their absence prevents a reasonable rate of expansion in the number of subscribers.

When exchange equipment could be purchased again in 1946, Post Office orders rose very rapidly, but the telephone manufacturers were not immediately able to respond, because of material, labour and fuel shortages. Prices had risen so much that the 1938 level of ordering (£5 million per annum) bought only half as much equipment.

Coupled with all these troubles, the Post Office had once more to contend with Treasury control of finance. Bridgeman had suggested that the Post Office surplus on commercial account should be retained, instead of going wholly to the Treasury (the principle of self-contained finance). Greater freedom to invest on the basis of a trading surplus had stimulated the capital expenditure programme before the war, but full Treasury control of the surplus was re-established during the war.[10] In 1947 the telecommunications manufacturing industry was ordered by the Government to divert as much capacity to fulfilling export orders as it could and by 1950 the total capital programme of the telephone service was being restricted to £29 million annually, which at pre-war prices was less than the amounts available in 1937.[11]

At the same time, something very strange had happened to the demand for telephone services. In 1935 it had been expected that, without the intervention of war or restrictions, telephone penetration of the UK market would saturate at about 4 million exchange lines after twenty years of continuous development. Although some brief surge of extra demand after the war was thought likely, while the back-log of people wanting to be connected was cleared, both its size and its persistence were severely underestimated. The level of demand for connection to the service approached 700,000 applications by 1947. (It had before the war averaged just over 200,000, of which a little under half were met by existing subscribers giving up their telephones, making a net addition to the system of a little more than 100,000 per year.) Little increase occurred in the number of lines given up annually and the waiting list thus reached 500,000 in the late 1940s, in spite of the Post Office connecting a net total of some 700,000 new subscribers by 1950. And at these extraordinary levels the waiting list remained for nearly ten years, defying the best efforts of the Post Office to eliminate it.

During the 1950s the waiting list was very gradually reduced to more manageable proportions. By the end of the decade it had shrunk to around 200,000, largely because the Post Office had been able to maintain an annual rate of installations in the region of 400,000. However some of the reduction in demand may be attributed to a sharp increase in connection charges, rentals and tariffs from 1956 onwards. The structure of charges up to 1956 closely reflected that of the 1930s, at which period the telephone service was attempting to stimulate business by cutting rates. From 1956 onwards a series of alterations in charges gradually brought the service to a point where prices reflected costs more closely. It is interesting that in the first few years of this policy the number of people giving up their telephones annually increased sharply; there is thus some evidence that the extraordinary level of demand after the war was a result of under-pricing the service.

. . . BUT TECHNICAL DEVELOPMENT CONTINUES UNCHECKED

Whatever the cause, the telephone service was under severe pressure to expand the number of exchange connections available for some ten to fifteen years after the war had finished. If the demand for service and the capacity available to meet it had grown in an orderly fashion, there would perhaps have been very few manual exchanges left in the system by 1950. The time would then have been ripe for considering the most recent trends in telephone switching.[12] As things were, conversion of manual continued at the rate of some 90 exchanges per year (Table 4.2), mostly of the smaller type, but paradoxically the total number of exchange connections on manual exchanges started to rise again, peaking at 1,050,000 in 1956. This was because, in the situation of shortage, some of the demand from new subscribers was met by manual connections.

Table 4.2   *Exchanges in the Telephone Service, 1920—75*

at 31 March	Automatic	Manual	Auto-manual and trunk	Total
1920	13	3,262	n.a.	3,275
1925	26	3,751	n.a.	3,800
1930	307	4,323	n.a.	4,647
1935	1,627	3,815	n.a.	5,463
1940	3,213	2,510	202	5,925
1945	3,534	2,240	221	5,995
1950	4,091	1,775	238	6,104
1955	4,576	1,351	261	6,188
1960	5,088	921	304	6,313
1965	5,592	437	337	6,366
1970	6,033	105	375	6,513
1975	6,241	13	373	6,627

Sources: as for Table 4.1.
Note: Auto-manual exchanges are switchboards associated with automatic exchanges for the purpose of providing operator services to the automatic exchange. Trunk exchanges do not have any subscriber lines, but handle trunk calls only.

While postwar shortages made impossible the achievement of a fully automatic system, wartime developments opened up new horizons for methods of switching traffic. In particular, telephone engineers throughout the world were becoming keenly aware of the potential of the electronic valve as a fast and versatile type of switch. Apart from operating some thousands of times faster than the electro-mechanical Strowger equipment, the valve had a capability of allowing one set of connections in an exchange, one speech path, to be used by a large number of separate callers all at the same time. The technique was to divide the time available on the speech path into millionths of a second and sample each of up to one hundred conversations at intervals of one hundred millionths of a second. Each conversation would thus be sampled 10,000 times per second, and for a period of about a half-millionth of a second on each occasion. Whatever voice frequency was sampled at each hundred millionth would be sustained by the equipment for the remaining ninety-nine millionths, until the next sample was taken. Since voice frequencies do not change significantly in such short periods the speech transmitted on this basis would be perfectly intelligible.[13]

This method of valve-switching was called 'time division multiplex'. Work on electronic switching of this kind was probably begun by the Post Office a few months after the war. Responsibility for technical development had become a highly centralised function, the Research Section being a branch of the Engineer-in-Chief's office. In April 1946 the Research Section contained sixty-three qualified engineers and fifteen qualified scientists. Its work programme was described at the time as being formulated on the basis of requests from the other engineering branches, but it was also responsible for initiating work to advance techniques. The research staff were distributed among the circuit laboratory, with one or two testing stations for exchange apparatus, the Radio (Experimental) Branch, with its associated stations for transmitting and receiving tests, and, finally, the main building of Dollis Hill laboratory in north-west London, where work on transmission and telephone development was concentrated. Dollis Hill had been the headquarters of Post Office research since the 1920s, and a small team here originated the work on time division multiplex switching (t.d.m.) during 1946. An article on engineering developments written some two years later by the Engineer-in-Chief records that a team of research personnel had been formed for 'uninterrupted work' on the 'all-electric exchange'.[14] But at this early stage no indication is given in published documents of what direction work was taking, nor whether other types of exchange development, such as crossbar switching, were also the subject of research. The inquiry by the Select Committee on the Estimates into the Post Office in 1950, for instance, was told only that an electronic exchange which avoided maintenance difficulties was being developed as a high priority.[15]

One early application of electronics to the telephone system was the electronic traffic machine. Assessing the performance standards of an automatic telephone network is extremely complex, since demands for calls originate from widespread and unrelated sources (the subscribers) and the capacity of a given number of exchange equipments to deal with different levels of traffic requirements is very hard to measure in practice. One of the great telephone engineers who developed statistical theory to cope with the problem of how much trunking and switch provision to make for a given volume of traffic was the Dane, Erlang, after whom the basic unit of telephone traffic measurement is named. But much of the theory developed about call congestion in automatic exchanges was very difficult to test and during the thirty years after Erlang, machines were built of which the purpose was to originate a large number of calls randomly and test their failure rate in the exchanges. In 1947 the Post Office designed an electronic version which came into use in 1949; it was judged to be a big improvement on its two mechanical predecessors.

The next development was to replace the 'Director' equipment at a London telephone exchange (Richmond) by an electronic version. Directors function in Britain to store the number dialled by the originating caller, in a large urban network of many exchanges, while a route is established from the caller's exchange to the exchange of the required subscriber. The Director then sends the number to the selectors of the distant exchange. Since the Director equipment receives heavy use and may handle thousands of calls per day, it formed an ideal test-bed for many of the electronic components being developed for telephone applications.

THE POST OFFICE'S DECISION

In the year before the electronic director was installed, that is to say in 1950, a series of articles began to appear in the official journal of the Post Office engineers covering the theory and early technical development of electronic exchanges.[16] From the amount of detail and the descriptions given of the technical solutions adopted to some of the problems encountered, it is clear that a number of fundamental decisions relating to the direction of exchange development in the Post Office were already at least half-formed in the minds of influential engineers in the Research Branch. The decisions were: that the next major change in switching techniques for the Post Office was going to be to electronic exchanges; secondly, that the principle of t.d.m. switching was the most promising to develop; thirdly, that the time was ripe for pressing ahead with this new venture. By way of confirmation, a small experimental prototype exchange on t.d.m. principles was built as early as 1951 in order to demonstrate to a study group of the switching division of the Research Branch whether these ideas were practicable.

The implication of the research and development work on electronic exchanges is that other types of exchange development, particularly crossbar, had been excluded from the same pattern of prototype development, and that electronic t.d.m. switching had been chosen in preference to other types of electronic switching. In fact Flowers' first article, of July 1950, devotes several paragraphs to basic switching comparisons, concluding that it would be difficult for a crossbar exchange to compete on economic grounds with Strowger or t.d.m. switching, and this appears to be the reasoning behind the decision to reject crossbar.

OTHER DEVELOPMENTS

Outside the Post Office in the late 1940s and early 1950s there was a correspondingly keen interest in electronic switching, as well as in other switching developments. The Swedish telephone system, which was larger than Britain's in terms of the number of exchanges (6,700 in 1946), but smaller in its number of exchange connections (probably under 1 million), was developing the use of crossbar switching. Being at a stage of mechanisation very close to that reached in Britain, the Swedish telephone administration was expecting to install crossbar for both very large exchanges and comparatively small 200-subscriber units. Experimental electronic exchanges were undergoing development in Germany and the United States. In Germany it was the telephone equipment manufacturing companies which were leading the development of the new techniques. Siemens and Standard Electrik Lorenz (SEL) were designing experimental electronic systems. In America, Bell Telephone Laboratories had started during the 1940s to design a fully electronic exchange, which incorporated many new concepts of telephone service to the subscriber. The Bell network used crossbar switching for the large exchanges in big cities, where the British system used the Director, and development of crossbar techniques was comparatively advanced by the time that Britain started on the electronic exchange.

Closer to home, as far as the Post Office was concerned, was the work of the British companies which manufactured telephone exchange equipment and associated line, subscriber, cable and transmission apparatus, under market-sharing agreements for the UK.[17] Although all five were involved in the utilisation of new techniques, and Ericsson and Standard Telephones and Cables were later to take a lead in electronic exchanges, it was Automatic Telephone and Electric and the General Electric Company which appeared most innovative after the war. GEC played a major part in developing t.d.m. systems with the Post Office. AT & E maintained an interest in crossbar and its research subsidiary, British Telecommunications Research (BTR), developed ideas for electronic control of exchanges.

In the 1940s and 1950s BTR, under G. T. Baker, developed a number of telecommunications applications of electronic techniques. It was provided with facilities by the Post Office in 1957 to test a Director equipment based on a magnetic drum as the registering device. The magnetic drum was also applied to exchange control functions. BTR, like Bell in the United States, was experimenting with space division electronic exchanges, but by 1957 Bell Telephone Laboratories were already building a medium-size space division electronic exchange for commercial testing.[18] This was to go into service at Morris, Illinois, in 1960. GEC's contribution was to undertake exploratory development of t.d.m. techniques and it was successful in solving a number of the initial technical difficulties. Opinion in the industry on the relative merits of time division and space division was far from uniform. The Post Office's t.d.m. system was to carry up to 100 calls on each metallic speech path, and this represented an enormous potential saving on common equipment (i.e., equipment which could be used by any subscriber to set up a call) which had to be installed in the exchange. The Morris, Illinois, system was designed to provide completely new telephone services, such as automatic booking and re-routing of telephone calls and, as such, was a very sophisticated effort. BTR saw the potential of electronics mainly in being able to achieve existing exchange functions in a different way, without necessarily designing a new exchange to this end. GEC's approach was to try to achieve a workable time division system at the earliest date, foreseeing the technical benefits and the extension of services which could follow.

The Post Office Research Branch had designed a demonstration model of the t.d.m. exchange. The systems development department of AT & E had followed this with an electronically controlled space-division model, having nevertheless electro-mechanical switches to establish a speech path through the exchange; it was probably under test during 1953. GEC had set out to solve some of the traffic handling problems of time division. Post Office work was then extended by designing a private branch t.d.m. exchange to serve fifty extensions at the Research Station. This came into operation late in 1955 or early in 1956 and an improved version was working at Dollis Hill in 1959.

The Post Office had begun to study the problems of introducing an electronic exchange into the public network as early as 1951. Expressed simply, these problems centred round the need for exchanges to function ruggedly and reliably within a telephone system that included many departures from the norm and many aspects of working which were less than ideal technically. Telephone systems are very complex and can well be upset by misuse from subscribers, accidental overloading, the receipt of unusual or distorted signals from related equipment and a considerable number of other hazards. But the complete failure or erratic behaviour of a public exchange is totally unacceptable for a telephone service. Strowger equipment was extremely well adapted to the conditions of telephone working, in that it represented a 'carthorse concept', able to plough on through mud, bad weather or the eccentric behaviour of its human controllers. The t.d.m. system invented at Dollis Hill was more like a racehorse. In the hands of skilled users and over a chosen course it performed with a speed and efficiency which made Strowger look old-fashioned, but when presented with misuse or unusual conditions, the equipment could be temperamental and refuse to function. Even space-division electronic systems had this characteristic, which caused the Morris, Illinois, exchange to be built with a capacity for clearing faults which were liable to develop in service.

At an early stage the Post Office had decided that the design and production problems were such that the telephone equipment manufacturers would be needed to help with the programme of t.d.m. development. Obviously such a course of action required that the agreement of the companies be obtained in choosing t.d.m. as the best technique, an awkward task, since they were likely to be enamoured of the systems which they had been developing themselves. However, a means of achieving this purpose was to be found by building upon the arrangements which already existed for agreeing technical developments to equipment in service.

THE BTTDC

The British Telephone Technical Development Committee (BTTDC) had come into existence as a co-ordinating body for technical change in the Post Office in 1933. Under the chairmanship of one of the Assistant Engineers-in-Chief of the Post Office, and with representation from the five companies which supplied exchange equipment, the BTTDC co-ordinated such developments in the 1930s as the new 2,000-type step-by-step selector, one of the main items of equipment in a Strowger exchange. When a new piece of equipment was required, the Post Office presented the need to the Committee, and this allowed an interchange of technical ideas. When a specification was agreed by all six parties, development was allocated to one of the companies by the Manufacturers' Technical Development Committee (MTDC) and if other companies wanted to contribute ideas, the MTDC provided a forum for the interchange of proposals.[19]

The origins of the BTTDC are to be found in the market-sharing agreements for telephone equipment and exchange apparatus which were made between the Post Office and eight companies in the industry (three did not make exchanges) in 1928. Bulk contracts for telephone and exchange equipment were placed with the Bulk Contracts Committee (BCC) of the telephone manufacturers, at prices agreed by non-competitive means, and the work so made available was distributed between the member companies according to their manufacturing capacity at the time and on other criteria.

Because of the liaison provided by these committees (the BTTDC, MTDC and BCC), technical contacts between the Post Office and the manufacturers were well developed. The main discussions took place over the letting and fulfilment of contracts under the Bulk Supply Agreements, but within the BTTDC there were nine sub-committees with responsibility for different aspects of technical change. There were thus well-developed relationships between engineers in the Post Office and in the manufacturing companies. The BTTDC, however, had not previously been used for a major programme of exploratory development.

THE POST OFFICE RESEARCH BOARD

As mentioned above, the engineering function of the Post Office had been highly centralised. The main engineering activities were line installation, the building of exchanges and equipping or extending them, as well as local maintenance and fault finding. Much of this work was co-ordinated by the Engineer-in-Chief's office through the Regional Director, but there was scope for engineers to gain a variety of experience. Within the body of engineers identical grades existed up to 1948 between different branches and transfer between telephone development, research, transmission and other branches was both facilitated and encouraged by this means as part of career development.

Research had been a fairly small branch of the Engineer-in-Chief's office during the inter-war period. Although very active in trunk line techniques and radio, it had not been involved in the development of the major automatic switching techniques of 1889—1945. Technical developments of Strowger techniques (particularly in 1922 — the Director mechanism) and rural mechanisation of small exchanges had been subjects on which the Engineer-in-Chief's office set the requirements and the manufacturing companies produced the equipment. On the other hand, by 1945 there was a telephone switching division in the Research Branch, and it was staffed by engineers some of whom had experience of designing, installing and improving Strowger equipment during their earlier careers in the Post Office.

In the late 1940s the Research Branch began to grow.[20] It already had considerable expertise in electronics, gained from radio research and the use of electronic transmission techniques. A wartime team had developed one application of t.d.m. for military use and the further application of this technique to telephone switching was foreseen in 1946. Reduced maintenance was seen as the benefit. There were two aspects to electronics work. On the engineering research side, research teams were applying electronic theory to switching, long-line transmission (trunks), telegraphy and even postal mechanisation. There were also scientific groups where basic electronics and thermionics were studied.

THE JOINT ELECTRONIC RESEARCH AGREEMENT

When the Post Office decided in the early 1950s that the job of developing electronic exchanges would have to be undertaken by the industry and the telephone service in partnership, a fairly long period of negotiation followed before an agreement on a joint research programme was reached in 1956. The agreement was called the Joint Electronic Research Agreement (JERA). It provided for the programme to be handled by a Joint Electronic Research Committee (JERC) under the chairmanship of the Engineer-in-Chief of the Post Office. The form of joint representation which the BTTDC contained was unsuitable for directing a research programme, because the BTTDC function was to promote technical development on a customer-to-contractor basis, but the evidence suggests that the model for the functioning of JERC was indeed that of the technical sub-committees of the BTTDC.

The precise terms of JERA have not been published, nor the membership of the actual committee. The Engineer-in-Chief was its chairman, and it might be guessed that the companies were represented by personnel at the level of engineering director. Probably, however, most of the tasks involved in directing and controlling the project work were performed by sub-committees. JERC's first priority was to design, construct and test a fully electronic t.d.m. exchange for the public network, to go into operation at Highgate Wood in north London as soon as possible. The intended date of installation was to be an early one but the time-scale was subsequently considerably extended; the technical problems encountered were far more severe than anticipated. At first mention, Highgate Wood was expected in service by the end of 1958. By 31 July 1957 the target date had been moved to the spring of 1960. The *Post Office Electrical Engineers' Journal* warned in 1958 that the Highgate Wood equipment was essentially experimental and was likely to prove uneconomic compared to Strowger. The year was not out before the date of introduction had been changed to 1961.[21] By January 1960 the discussion of t.d.m. exchanges had taken on a new emphasis. Electronically controlled but electro-magnetically operated (or mechanical) systems were again being considered and Highgate Wood was being regarded as a 'frontier-of-knowledge' project which would serve merely to define the applicability of particular electronic techniques. Policy changes had by then begun to take place. A large-scale prototype t.d.m. exchange using a modified switching technique was being considered.[22]

Highgate Wood time-division multiplex electronic exchange was finally handed over to the Postmaster General by the Chairman of STC (for the group of manufacturers) in December 1962. It is not clear to what degree the exchange was a straightforward technical failure. An appraisal four years later emphasises that the practical design experience provided was invaluable. But the exchange was not used very much in public service, and live traffic was not handled after a few months. For another two years the equipment was kept on test with artificial traffic and provided useful data. Particular faults which made public use of the t.d.m. system impracticable were excessive power requirements, the presence of noise and crosstalk on speech paths and the inherent gain introduced into transmission by fully electronic circuits.[23]

What went wrong at Highgate Wood was not simply a technical malfunction. The Highgate Wood exchange was the product of development projects by no fewer than twelve different teams, of the manufacturers and the Post Office, located at geographically separate places. Liaison and technical control were difficult to achieve. The exchange had a diversity of techniques which were a major disadvantage; the system was unnecessarily complex. What the venture taught the Post Office engineering teams involved was that the ruggedness of a design, its ability to survive unexpected inputs and its simplicity were of much greater importance than they had previously recognised.

It would be simply contentious to say that t.d.m. was the wrong system to use. In many ways it was an attractive route to faster switching, higher reliability, less maintenance and saving on exchange equipment. But it certainly was not the only way of achieving those objectives. The t.d.m. system was an attempt to apply electronic techniques simultaneously to three major exchange functions, switching, speech path transmission and exchange control, and as such it multiplied the problems of introducing each one. These multiple problems were undoubtedly added to by the JERC method of technical development. A single company, if it had been given a contract to develop t.d.m., might not have been able to achieve a more successful result. But, being in sole control, it would have been able to recognise the problems and change direction more easily.

CHANGES IN POST OFFICE ORGANISATION

While the experimental exchange at Highgate Wood was being developed and built, changes had begun to take place in the Post Office which affected both its financial position and the way it was managed.

The war period had reversed the Bridgeman proposals. Thus, instead of being free to operate on a self-contained budget, the telephone services, the post and the telegraphs were again restricted by being in the position of a revenue department; Treasury control of capital spending restricted investment. For the greater part of the 1950s the service was handicapped by financial control. It was unable to reduce the waiting list for telephone connections and, instead of completing the mechanisation programme begun in the 1930s, it was increasing the number of subscribers on manual exchanges for short-term reasons. By 1955 the problems of the telephone service had become clearly enough recognised for a change in Government policy.

A White Paper on the Post Office was published in October 1955.[24] It accepted that the waiting list of nearly 400,000 applications was too high, but it argued that continued restraint of capital expenditure was necessary. Thus the level of capital expenditure, which had grown from £30 million in 1950 to £92 million in 1955 (current prices), was to be pegged for three years at approximately £100 million annually, of which about 95 per cent would go to the telephone service. At the same time a return to the principle of self-contained finance was proposed, which basically meant that any surplus earned by the Post Office in one year would be available for Post Office use in the next year, rather than being absorbed into government revenues. This not only acted as an inducement to reconsider tariff levels (major changes followed in January 1956), but also signalled a new approach to business and technical planning.

A second problem for the telephone service during the 1950s was presented by the comparatively low use made of the equipment by subscribers connected to the service. In spite of the extraordinary level of demand for connection, there was little evidence that demand for the facilities offered was increasing at a corresponding rate. During most of the 1950s the number of calls made per year from each telephone connection was decreasing (see Table 4.3). Having been about 1,050 in 1950, it had dropped below 900 by 1958.[25]

The reasons for this trend are very hard to identify with any certainty. Coupled with the high level of demand for connections, the picture presented is almost paradoxical. It suggests that a large number of the

Table 4.3   *Telephone Use, 1945—75*

Year ended 31 March	Total exchange connections	Local calls (million)	Trunk calls (million)	Calling rate per exchange connection	
				Local	Trunk
(1945)	(2,228,568)	(2,039)	(189)	(911)	(85)
1950	3,032,114	2,940	235	971	78
1952	3,462,980	3,230	261	934	76
1954	3,769,610	3,370	278	894	74
1956	4,265,150	3,865	333	904	78
1958	4,499,637	3,671	327	816	73
1960	4,784,005	3,900	387	816	81
1962	5,209,574	4,500	477	864	93
1964	5,619,933	5,100	624	907	111
1966	6,534,529	6,050	841	926	129
1968	7,387,225	6,880	1,064	931	144
1970	8,550,806	8,270	1,333	968	156
1972	10,028,158	10,330	1,699	1,003	170
1974	11,904,000	12,707	2,138	1,168	180
1975	12,698,000	13,523	2,313	1,166	182

Sources: As for Table 4.1.

people who were anxious to become subscribers were only marginal users, and made less use of the telephone than existing users. Such an explanation is consistent with the forecast made by the Post Office before the war, of 'telephone saturation' being reached in the UK at a level of about 4 million exchange connections. But it is hardly consistent with later developments, when the calling rate increased sharply.

On the other hand, it might be argued that such a pattern was produced by new telephone users, in a country gradually becoming better off, being generally unaccustomed to the telephone, through not having grown up with it in their parental homes. Although anxious to acquire a telephone at home, they learned to make full use of it only by degrees. This explanation gains some support from the fact that, of the total growth in connections between 1950 and 1960 (Table 4.4), almost 73 per cent were new domestic subscribers and only 24 per cent were business rate connections.

Yet a third argument concerns the rental and tariff charges which were

Table 4.4   *Business and Residence Telephone Connections*

	Total connections	Business rate	Residence rate
1950	3,139,510	1,455,329	1,588,120
1960	4,784,005	1,854,537	2,792,448
Increase	1,644,495	399,208	1,204,328

Source: Post Office Telecommunications Statistics.

current during the 1950s. Rentals increased slowly during the 1950s, from about £8 per year[26] to £12 per year.[27] The cost of local calls increased from 1½d in 1951 to between 2d and 2½d by 1960,[28] while longer distance calls varied between about 1s and 4s for three minutes, depending on the distance and time of day, without much alteration for most of the period. Connection charges, on the other hand, which were only 15s at most per exchange line in 1950, went up to £1.10s in July 1962, £3 in January 1956 and £5 in October 1957. By July 1961 the connection charge had risen to £10.

The tariff structure in the early 1950s was one in which the service did not directly recover the costs of expansion of the system, only gradually re-couped the subscriber's equipment cost through rentals, and loaded the larger part of capital and running costs on to the call charges. Consumers were thus only acting in a rational manner by demanding a telephone installation which could be acquired at what appears to have been well below its cost, but then not choosing to use the service heavily. As the decade closed this tariff structure had begun to be reversed. Fixed charges had increased faster than call charges, and the relative stability of the telephone call tariff encouraged both new and existing users to increase their calling rate.

Whatever the reason for the low level of telephone use in Britain and its fall during the 1950s, the phenomenon focuses attention on the type of facilities offered by the Post Office telephone service, and this in turn brings the discussion back to technical policy. In the mid-1950s there were about 4 million telephone connections. Of this total, 25 per cent were connected to manual exchanges where the subscriber was unable to obtain any call directly by himself and a further 42 per cent were connected to non-Director or small automatic exchanges. The subscriber on a small automatic exchange had access to very few others, outside the two or three hundred on his own exchange, by direct dialling. A non-Director exchange might include anything from 2,000 to 15,000 subscribers who could dial to each other, but who had to revert to operator service for all other calls. Some 33 per cent of the connections were on automatic Director exchanges in the large conurbations. Only in these Director areas did the average subscriber have access by direct dialling to a large number of other subscribers whom he might wish to call.[29] With manual trunk working, most calls beyond the local distance required the assistance of one or two and very occasionally three operators. Although demand trunk working (the facility to make a trunk call on demand rather than by booking) had existed since 1934, congestion and delay could still occur, and the process of making a call was demanding of both the subscriber's and the operator's time.

On the engineering side of the Post Office, these characteristics of the system were felt to be undesirable and the interruption to the mechanisation programme was much regretted. Between 1947 and 1949 a technical committee, the Trunk Mechanisation Steering Committee, worked at the main proposals for the automatic working of long distance calls. Two stages were planned, first the automatic working of trunk calls through the control of a single operator and then the extension of the automatic system so that subscribers could also dial long distance. The two stages were known as Operator Trunk Dialling (OTD) and Subscriber Trunk Dialling (STD).

Restrictions on capital spending acted as a brake on this kind of proposal. The management of Post Office affairs through a functional Board was not so well established as a system that the conflicting needs for more exchange connections, for more exchanges, for a higher rate of conversion from manual and for trunk dialling equipment could all be reconciled. The effect of continued control of finance by the Treasury was to make more difficult the task of relating different technical policies to their costs and the economic benefits which might be expected.

Completing the transfer from manual to automatic working received lower priority in these conditions of restraint than fulfilling the demands for new connections. Plans for the OTD and STD systems, however, as well as for the development of the electronic exchange, became firm during the years 1954 to 1956. Coinciding with the beginning of the five-year experimental period of self-contained finance (1956—61), the new policies of the telephone service were set out in two White Papers published in 1957 and 1958, entitled *Telephone Policy* and *Full Automation*. The telephone service was to become increasingly oriented towards the consumer, STD services were to commence in January 1959 at Bristol and all manual exchanges were to be phased out by 1970.[30]

One of the main items of new equipment required for OTD and STD services is a controlling register translator. Its function is to receive the digits of the distant subscriber's exchange and number, set up a signalling and speech path to the distant controlling exchange in the required exchange's group and then repeat the required subscriber's number when the distant controlling exchange has provided a signalling and speech path to the subscriber's exchange.

Development of three different types of register translator was carried out successfully under the auspices of the British Telephone Technical Development Committee. The Automatic Telephone and Electric Company used the technology it had developed for the Lee Green exchange equipment (see n. 18, p. 138) to produce a magnetic drum equipment; it also developed an electro-mechanical type for use in Director areas. General Electric produced the electro-mechanical non-Director register translator and a fully electronic type (actually used at Bristol) based upon cold cathode valves. Ericsson Telephones developed the equipment at group centre controlling exchanges to receive and process the signals sent from register translators.[31] The development work which was necessary to introduce OTD and STD was quite different from that required for the electronic exchange and demonstrated the BTTDC arrangements at their best. The nature of the equipment to be built was determined by discussion and each manufacturer was able to follow its own specialism to some extent.

The performance standards and methods of working were defined by the existing exchange network of Strowger equipment, which all the parties knew very well. The relationships between Post Office personnel and those of the manufacturers were well established from previous Strowger developments. The interface between the new equipment and the existing was clear-cut. Each new piece of equipment made relatively modest changes in the technology, changes which in any case had been under test in public service for a year or two before the STD equipment was finalised.

ELECTRONIC EXCHANGES ENTER THE SYSTEM, 1965—75

In 1961, the establishment of the Post Office and its finances as a commercial enterprise separate from the Government was embodied in legislation by the Post Office Act. In the previous five years, which were of an experimental nature, tariff revisions, combined with a number of changes in the service designed to stimulate business, had contributed to a total surplus of over £50 million on an annual income averaging just over £400 million. But the legal and constitutional status of the Post Office as a department of Government, subject to the day-to-day financial and administrative authority of Parliament, had not changed. It was not until October 1969 that the Post Office became a fully fledged public corporation.

After the changes in the 1950s capital spending increased rapidly during the 1960s, from about £100 million at the beginning of the decade to £200 million by 1966 and £450 million by 1970. The number of new subscribers connected annually began to grow much faster by the middle of the decade (Table 4.1) and the progress made in providing STD facilities was such that nearly three-quarters of all trunk calls made were dialled within ten years of the service starting. Telecommunications was becoming a growth sector of the economy. The amount of traffic handled had grown fairly slowly between 1945 and 1960 (Table 4.5), at just over 4 per cent annually. In the 1960s this growth accelerated to 7 per cent.

Because of the rapid expansion of the system, the disappointing progress made toward the fully electronic exchange by the t.d.m. route was a fairly serious blow. It was not just a question of delay with a system which would be ready for service in the mid-1960s or a little later. The experimental exchange at Highgate Wood provided evidence that the fully electronic exchange might still be ten years away, or even more. In 1956 the Joint Electronic Research Committee, setting their objective as an experimental t.d.m. exchange, to be followed by further prototypes, had given themselves a fairly long time scale. By the beginning of the 1960s engineers in the telephone exchange systems development branch of the Engineer-in-Chief's office were uncertain whether the telephone service could afford to wait. With planned expansion going ahead at an increasing rate and with the success of STD, the need for exchange equipment was multiplying. Much telephone capital equipment, because it has to be

Table 4.5   *Telephone Traffic, 1920—75*

Year ending 31 March	Local calls (million)	Trunk calls (million)	International calls (million)	Proportion of trunk calls dialled (%)
1920	795	54	...	...
1925	852	77	...	...
1930	1,205	117	...	...
1935	1,595	85	...	...
1940	2,098	117	...	...
1945	2,039	189	...	...
1950	2,940	235	1	...
1955	3,615	306	2	...
1960	3,900	387	3	...
1965	5,600	736	6	41
1970	8,270	1,333	16	73
1975	13,523	2,313	73	87

Sources: As for Table 4.1.
Note:
The definitions distinguising a local from a trunk call altered as follows.
In 1922, trunk calls were defined as over 7½ miles,
In 1934, trunk calls were defined as over 12½ miles,
In 1936, trunk calls were defined as over 15 miles,
In 1958, trunk calls were defined as any call beyond the home or adjacent charging group.
Thus the annual figures for each call group are not strictly comparable.

ultra-reliable, is built to a quality and performance standard which demands that it is kept in service a long time. Many items of the switching network may be expected to have lives of thirty-five years. If the expansion of the 1960s was to take place with Strowger equipment, then the system would still contain a great many electro-mechanical, step-by-step exchanges at the end of the century. Because of the necessity for equipments in a telephone service to interwork, the existence of a great deal of machinery using older techniques could inhibit the introduction of new subscriber facilities and newer switching methods at a later stage.

When the Post Office adopted the initial objective of developing the electronic exchange, it may have been too early to foresee the big expansion in the provision of telephone services during the 1960s. On the other hand, by 1956, when JERC began the development phase, there was ample evidence in the form of the persistent demand for 4—500,000 new exchange connections each year. Furthermore, the work of preparing for STD was well advanced under the aegis of the Trunk Mechanisation Steering Committee and the BTTDC; the member companies of JERC were themselves working on new equipment for STD. In addition the manufacturer representatives on JERC were well aware of the demand for new equipment, which was arising from the programme of completing conversion of the remaining 1,200 manual exchanges to automatic working, and this policy was under discussion when JERC was formed.

What was really required during the 1950s was an exchange development programme leading to production versions of exchanges that could replace Strowger in the early 1960s.

If the function of JERC had been to make a co-operative technical decision on future exchange policy, then it is inconceivable that such issues as these would not have been resolved by the parties to the agreement. There is no indication, however, that in its original terms the Joint Electronic Research Agreement contained any provision for the alternative development of space-division or crossbar systems, to provide equipment to fall back on should the t.d.m. system by delayed.

In retrospect, it is difficult to escape the conclusion that a conflict existed between the Post Office and various manufacturers. AT & E had produced the magnetic drum register controller outside the institutional arrangements of the BTTDC; it was independently licensing a crossbar electro-magnetic switch of advanced design from the Swedish government, in spite of lack of interest from the Post Office. Articles in the AT & E *Journal* express a strong view to the effect that new techniques would be better introduced into the exchange network by piecemeal development of electronic equipments to replace separate sub-systems of the exchange function, rather than by designing a complete electronic exchange at once.[32]

There were other developments of equal significance 'under the counter'. Siemens-Edison-Swan had started to undertake work on the trunking principles of a space-division electronic exchange and before 1960 Ericsson Telephones had begun the development of a small exchange based upon space division principles and using reed-relay cross points. The Siemens work was later incorporated into the TXE-1 and TXE-3 experimental exchanges, while Ericsson's design was developed to produce the TXE-2. GEC had built a model electronic exchange in 1956.

However, the relationship which had been built up over the years on the technical side between the Post Office and the manufacturing companies, embracing both the market-sharing agreement and the co-operative development structure, was an extremely close one. No public disputes or open conflicts of policy broke out during the years following the Joint Agreement. It appears that JERC worked in a special way. One might imagine that the Committee would be a forum for resolving the conflicts presented in the mid-1950s, or that it would be a powerful central body for carrying out Post Office policy. Instead, it acted as an organisation in which differences of technical opinion could be forgotten, not resolved. Once the Post Office had communicated to the manufacturers its desire to build a t.d.m. exchange, there was no room for a thoroughgoing evaluation of the alternatives. The decision had been taken by the Post Office and, whatever misgivings may have existed within the research departments of the companies or elsewhere, they were prepared to co-operate in the development.

But, as the end of the 1950s drew near, the conflict avoidance approach began to display an unexpected virtue, flexibility. Having been a one-way channel of communication from the Post Office to the manufacturers, JERC became two-way. The private venture research conducted by the companies began to influence the Post Office, and truly co-operative development work was pursued in the 1960s. The views of the manufacturers were followed up by design studies of alternative t.d.m. systems. Private venture work by the companies continued and by 1960 the way was open for alternative developments to t.d.m. Highgate Wood was by that date behind schedule and no longer commanded as much confidence from the Joint Committee as in 1956. Detailed appraisal in 1960 of paper studies and private work by companies resulted in a decision to continue with t.d.m. hardware development, but also to include the development of experimental exchange equipment towards a space-division reed-relay system, based on the earlier work by Siemens.

ELECTRONIC SWITCHING, PHASE TWO

With the eclipse of the Highgate Wood exchange, the Post Office was obliged to reconsider its technical policy. The Joint Electronic Research Agreement and the experimental t.d.m. exchange had reflected a policy with two distinct aspects. On the one hand, there was the decision not to take electro-mechanical exchanges further than the Strowger system, that is to go straight for electronic exchanges. On the other hand, there was the commitment to the high speed 100-channel time division multiplex exchange, which Highgate Wood was intended to test. It was this second decision which had to be reviewed.

The Post Office research effort which had begun in the 1940s, and which had the general objectives of saving maintenance and exchange equipment and improving switching and reliability, as outlined above, had concentrated upon the one line of development. T.d.m. was an attractive solution because it appeared to make the best use of the benefits which electronic techniques conferred on the engineer. The expensive part of Strowger mechanisms was the selector and trunking equipment, that is the uniselectors and two motion selectors, arranged in banks to process a call through the exchange, and the associated wiring, which provided speech paths through the exchange for the subscribers' conversations. T.d.m. techniques could carry 100 conversations on one metallic path through the exchange; they appeared to offer savings by being economical in their use of the switching or selecting devices which set up the calls. But it was common knowledge among telephone engineers that electronic alternatives to t.d.m. were available, particularly space division multiplex. In this system the speech paths through the exchange are physically separate and many more switching elements, or cross-points, are required.

Otherwise space division had much the same attractions that time division offered.

In November 1960 the Institution of Electrical Engineers held a three-day conference on electronic exchanges. It was attended by six other nations developing electronic systems, apart from Britain, and here the proponents of time division and the proponents of space division were able to argue the merits of their respective cases in full session. A Post Office engineer, reporting on the conference, summarised and evaluated the arguments in favour of each system. The operational problems of space division systems seemed to be nearer solution and the first experimental exchange of Bell Laboratories was already working at Morris, Illinois. But it was recognised that the costs of a valve operated space division system would be high. Providing a valve as a switch at every cross-point (that is, at every point where switching might be necessary, at subscriber terminals, in trunking circuits and in junction circuits) was expected to be expensive, because of the cost of individual valve components. It was on these grounds, that the Post Office research effort had originally been directed at time division multiplex. In the absence of a much cheaper valve or a valve substitute, space division appeared workable but uneconomic. The time division multiplex system, on the other hand, was designed to be economical in its use of crosspoints and trunking in the exchange. A few hundred cross-points with appropriate switching devices could replace some thousands of valves or semi-conductors needed for space division multiplexing. The problems with t.d.m. was that, although the devices and techniques required were known by 1960, the demonstration of these techniques in a public service exchange presented greater practical difficulties than for space division. Highgate Wood was the world's first public t.d.m. exchange and its introduction was still some two years off. As we have already seen, that experimental exchange failed to achieve its major objective.

The argument can be seen as one between the simplicity, but high cost, of the spatial array of cross points and the technical elegance and economy of the shared speech path approach, which had its penalties in tempera-mentality and low fault tolerance. It was a Gordian knot, which could be cut by the replacement of the valve or semi-conductor as a cross-point with a very simple and much cheaper device, called the reed-relay. A relay is an electrical device, such that when a particular current flows the relay causes a circuit to be completed. The reed-relay is simply a pair of metal contacts, overlapping inside a sealed glass-tube but not quite touching. When a magnetic field operates from a coil surrounding the tube, the contacts close, making a simple switch. Some delegates at the conference indicating the direction of future development by describing the reed-relay as the ideal cross-point for electronic exchanges. Two experimental reed-relay electronic exchanges were nearly complete in Germany and Bell Laboratories were also trying out this type of switching unit.

Reed-relays to replace valves as crosspoints would favour space division systems. They offered no advantages to time division multiplex, which used the valve to perform complex functions. Reed-relays were not 'electronic', because the function of the valve as an electronic switch was replaced by an electro-magnetic action. To electronic switching engineers who were admirers of the elegant t.d.m. solution to switching problems, the 'non-electronic' action of the reed-relay almost seemed to discredit reed-relay systems. A certain amount of rivalry existed between the national systems and the Post Office *rapporteur* gently chided the delegates at the conference who talked about reed-relays as if they were electronic devices.

Nevertheless, very soon after the IEE conference, the Post Office engineering department decided upon a major change of policy. Two further t.d.m. exchanges planned for Pembury (Kent) and Goring (Oxon.) were abandoned; development of t.d.m. equipment was suspended and the concept of shared speech-paths for public exchanges, which the Post Office had pursued for some eighteen years, was referred back for further research.

This redirection of technical policy was accompanied by some tightening up of the management system for controlling development. The Joint Electronic Research Committee had been set up on the same co-operative lines as the BTTDC. Although a top-level organisation on the engineering side, JERC had not aimed at a high degree of executive control of electronic developments. Within the general direction provided by the Post Office's decision to go for t.d.m., the detailed management of the various projects had been under separate control in each company. As Highgate Wood had shown, under this method of organisation there was really no agency with effective overall management responsibility. The deficiency was rectified in 1964 by creating the Reed Electronic Project Executive Board, to which all major decisions on reed-relay exchanges were referred. Under the Board, a project operating panel undertook the task of management control.

REED-RELAY SYSTEMS

The Reed Electronic Project then started upon an intensive programme of developing, testing and installing reed-relay exchanges. During the years 1961 to 1975 three basic systems were being built up. First there was the smallest of the electronic exchanges, which was initially intended to serve large rural applications and small towns. The planned size for these exchanges ranged between 200 and 2,000 exchange lines, but later adaptations were proposed by the manufacturers for an extension of the unit to cater for about three times that number of lines. This type of exchange was designated by the Post Office as TXE-2 (Telephone Exchange Electronic Type 2); the manufacturer's commercial name for it was 'Pentex'. The TXE-2 was inaugurated into the system in December 1966 at Ambergate, and about 750 of the type were in operation by 1975.

The second type of reed-relay exchange was aimed at the larger applications in the British telephone service, exchanges of up to 40,000 lines located in the larger cities and conurbations, very often within a local Director network. Whereas the traffic capacity of the TXE-2 exchange was not intended to go much beyond 220 Erlang, the larger exchange system was expected to be capable of catering for traffic flows up to and in excess of 5,000 Erlang. Starting with a laboratory model, TXE-1, the large exchange progressed through a public service version which was tested at Leighton Buzzard and through a further test model, to the production concept, TXE-4. Tests upon the TXE-4 design were held at Tudor exchange in north London before the first production version was ordered in the early 1970s.

Finally, some development effort was put into an electronic exchange project which was aimed at providing for extensions to the electro-mechanical Strowger exchanges. The equipment involved was intended to be used to enlarge the older type of exchange with electronic units that could be progressively extended, so that the whole exchange was gradually converted to electronic reed-relay working. The designation of this project was TXE-6.

The TXE-2 exchange type was based upon the private venture work done by the manufacturers, but was developed in co-operation with the Post Office. Laboratory models were ready for trial by 1963, one of them designed by Ericssons and the other by GEC. In 1965 these two designs were put into public service to handle part of the live traffic at Peterborough (Ericsson) and Leamington (GEC). The first production electronic exchange to be installed in the UK was switched into service at Ambergate in December 1966. The Ambergate exchange was the product of designs developed jointly by the Post Office and Ericsson. Although the credit for earlier work must go to the company, development from 1963 onwards had been managed by the project operating panel of the Reed Project Board. Instead of committee co-ordinated work by several independent teams, a firm project management structure had become the effective controlling body, headed by the Project Board, while JERC ceased to be the main decision making body. The TXE-2 was the first success of this new system.[33]

The larger type of reed-relay exchange was also based upon independent work by the manufacturers. When the decision was made in the early 1960s to widen the scope of the exchange systems which were under exploratory development, a laboratory model of the Siemens space division exchange was built at the company's laboratory at Blackheath.[34] A public service version of this exchange was installed for testing and evaluation at Leighton Buzzard in about 1963, the design being known as TXE-1. Although it provided useful data for trial purposes, it was unsuitable for a production system. This fact was recognised well before the installation at Leighton Buzzard and a redesigned version was already being built. The second pilot model was put on test at the Post Office circuit laboratory in central London. However, some further development work was necessary before the design, which became known as the TXE-3, was ready for public test in 1967. One of the major differences between

TXE-1 and TXE-3 lay in the system of control.[35] The t.d.m. project had tended to place emphasis upon the speech paths and switches, but the method of instructing an exchange to perform its operations is perhaps of greater importance.

The control of automatic telephone exchanges can be understood more easily through the analogy of a manual exchange. The problem for the automatic is how to set the guiding principles upon which the exchange completes connections (the logic) and how to instruct the exchange's electronic control equipment to apply those principles (the programme). In a manual exchange the logic is contained in the trunking (the way that subscribers' lines are fed into the exchange and presented on the board so that each operator has access to them). The programme is the training given to the operator. It can be changed by retraining or merely varying standard procedures. Changing the logic is a much more complex task, which involves the rebuilding of the exchange. The logic must in any case be designed with the performance and limitations of the control system (the operator-plus-training) in mind. Logic must be designed so that a change of service is within the capability of the control. If the logic were such as to require the control function to perform too complex a task for some new service, so that a rather low success rate were achieved, it would be the logic, rather than the control, the programme or the operator, which was at fault.

The first automatic telephone exchange (the Strowger) sought to copy the actions of the human operator.[36] Abstract problems of theory and design, such as the above, were side-stepped by the simplicity of the concept. System control is dependent upon correct selector responses to the impulses dialled by the caller. The programme of the exchange is set by decisions about which numerical level in each selector switch corresponds to each type of service. The logic of Strowger is 'wired logic'. That is to say, the principles of guiding calls through the exchange are contained in the trunking pattern and the connections between successive banks of switches.

With more advanced exchanges both the control function and the programme can be divorced from the circuit network of switches, so that common equipment provides both control and programme for the switching of the whole exchange. One of the advantages of common control is that more complex exchange functions can be provided. Determining how the exchange should respond to calls then becomes similar to writing a programme for a computer. The differences between TXE-1 and TXE-3 were in the logic of the design of the switch layout and in the provision of computer programme features for the main exchange control.

DELAYS IN DEVELOPMENT

However, the development of these features for TXE-3 had not started early enough for there to be any possibility that the large electronic exchange would be available to replace Strowger in the 1960s. Economic studies indicated that TXE-3 would be too expensive in production to compete with Strowger. Therefore work began on setting the performance specifications and defining the system principles for a further prototype, the TXE-4, which would be able to provide the extended facilities and increased reliability of electronic techniques at a lower cost.

The original parties to the TXE-4 system definition exercise were those of JERC under the management of the Reed Project Board. In September 1969, when the Post Office became a public corporation, the Joint Electronic Research Agreement lapsed, and with it the BTTDC and the market-sharing agreement. Standard Telephones and Cables then took up the contract for a cost-reduced version of TXE-3, and installed a trial exchange at Tudor (north London) in conjunction with the Post Office. On the basis of the Tudor trial the Post Office placed a contract in 1971 with STC for a production version of TXE-4, to be installed at Rectory exchange in Birmingham. The opening date for Rectory was expected to be 1975.

In spite of the much more successful reed-relay electronic exchange developments, the dilemma which had faced the Post Office in 1960 was not resolved during the period 1960—70. The number of subscribers in the telephone service was continuing to expand very fast, the STD service had nearly reached the point where 90 per cent of all long distance calls could be dialled, and the annual rate of growth in the number of calls was approaching 8 or 9 per cent by the end of the decade. Trunk calls increased during the period 1970—4 at nearly 15 per cent per annum. In the absence of large electronic exchanges, a great deal of the new equipment made necessary by this expansion would have to be Strowger, particularly in the larger towns and in the trunk switching network. New investment in Strowger continuing on this scale during the 1970s would only increase the problems of introducing more advanced switching, delay its penetration into the system and perpetuate the high levels of maintenance necessary for the older type of equipment.

HOW TO GET RID OF STROWGER

It will be remembered that there were two aspects of the policy pursued through JERC (see above, p. 125). Time division multiplex had given way to reed-relays and space division, but the commitment to replace Strowger by electronic switching still existed. The delays experienced with the larger type of electronic exchange made this difficult to maintain. TXE-2 exchanges entered service in increasing numbers from 1966, but they were not suitable for all applications. Their small size and limited range of functions made them unsuitable for larger local exchanges and for trunk switching applications.

It was not easy, however, for the Post Office to reconsider the commitment to electronics, both because of the strength of the stand which had been taken and because no contingency plans had been laid for the situation which arose in the mid-1960s.

In the early years, non-electronic systems had been rejected and the substantial development effort on electronics represented by JERA had been welcomed by the Post Office and the industry alike. The Telephone Equipment Manufacturers Association wrote in their *Report* for 1956/7:

'Electronic Telephone Exchanges
The use of electronic methods for telephone switching has been in the thoughts of telephone engineers for many years. When it is realised that between 400 and 500 separate electrical contacts may need to be made in the present type of automatic exchange in order to set up one call and that a fault in any one of these contacts may give rise to trouble, it can be seen that a system which eliminates these contacts might mean a big step forward in the telephone switching problem. For complete success it is not only necessary that a much greater reliability should be achieved, but also that the system should be more economical in operation. The design of such a system, therefore, presents a most difficult but interesting problem for the telephone engineer to solve. A big advance was made during the year when the Post Office entered into an agreement with its five exchange equipment contractors for the pooling of ideas and close co-operation with the object of designing the best possible electronic switching system for use in the British Post Office. A research committee was set up under this agreement under the Chairmanship of the Engineer-in-Chief of the Post Office and this committee has now begun its work in earnest.

This joint research and development arrangement is a matter of considerable satisfaction to the Industry and they would like to place on record their appreciation of the strong and statesmanlike attitude taken by the Post Office at this time. When there is so much ill-informed talk about things which are or are not in the public interest, it is good to see a demonstration of a very natural arrangement for co-operation between the Post Office and its contractors, who have worked together for some 30 years to produce the highly efficient communication system which this country enjoys. It would, indeed, be difficult to imagine an arrangement which was more in the public interest.

It is also natural that the manufacturers at present supplying electro-mechanical equipment are, in their general business of telecommunications, based on a very wide field of activity. Their resources for research, and for the development of the new components which will be required, are more than adequate to provide for the particular application of electronic switching.

Further than this, it is quite clear that the standard of reliability and life required of the basic components for public exchange service will be much greater than that necessary in some of the other fields in which semi-conductors and allied components are used.'

In 1962 the Postmaster-General reiterated at the TEMA annual dinner, reported in TEMA *Annual Report* 1961/2, the determination of the Post Office to convert the exchange system directly from Strowger equipment to electronic.

'Later this year we shall be opening the electronic telephone exchange at Highgate Wood; this will be the first all electronic public exchange to be tested on live traffic in Europe. It is the product of a fine co-operative effort between the Post Office and five of our biggest British manufacturers, and it marks the most important mile-stone in the history of telephony in this country. But this is only a beginning, and already work is very well advanced on new and greatly improved systems. Indeed, so confident are we in these developments that we have recently reaffirmed the policy that the Post Office should plan to move straightaway from the existing Strowger systems, which have served us and many overseas countries so well for so long, to full electronic exchanges. The Post Office and the manufacturers working in unison are already giving high priority to the development of the new electronic system, and this momentum, Gentlemen, has got to be maintained; indeed, it has got to be increased so that the tests and the trials can be completed and decisions taken about production models at the earliest possible date. We believe that we are just as well advanced in this work as the United States of America, and well ahead of most other countries. Together we can, and indeed we must, keep this lead so that the industry has the best and most modern equipment to offer in overseas markets, and we have the best and most modern system for use here at home.'

The Post Office *Annual Report* which appeared in July 1963 stated once again that the Strowger electro-mechanical system would be replaced by 'fully electronic' types of exchange without any intermediate switching development. And this policy was never publicly retracted, although in the following year the *Annual Report* recorded the difficulties experienced with the fully electronic t.d.m. exchange at Highgate Wood and the consequent change of direction.

'Further progress was made jointly by the Post Office and five of the leading British telecommunications equipment manufacturers on research into and development of electronic exchanges. Until recently, research and development work has been carried out on three types of electronic exchanges: one using space-division and two using time-division systems. By the end of 1963 it was possible to decide first that the early potential of the time-division system did not for the present justify more than continued research. On the other hand the space-division system offered excellent prospects for quick progress towards development with a view to production in quantity. The development resources of the Post Office and the industry will, therefore, be concentrated on the space-division system in the immediate future. One application of this system will be tried out at a new exchange of about 3,000 lines at Leighton Buzzard which opens in 1965, and further work on the development of these larger space-division exchanges is also well under way. Another application for small exchanges of up to 1,000 lines will be tried out at Leamington and Peterborough later in 1964 and early in 1965.'

But the need to replace Strowger equipment, particularly at medium size exchanges, was becoming more urgent as each year went by. During 1966 it was recognised that to wait for the TXE-4 to fulfil all new large exchange requirements would be unacceptable.

In a policy announcement placed in the *Post Office Electrical Engineers' Journal*, the Post Office announced the success of the TXE-2, but also hinted at the dilemma which surrounded the choice of electronic or other systems for the second generation of exchange equipment.

'After successful trials . . . the Post Office had decided to order all exchanges in the smaller and medium-size ranges in electronic form . . . The advantages include greater reliability, faster connexions, additional subscriber services, lower maintenance costs and smaller space requirements.

Two other major electronic developments (TXE-3 and TXE-6) . . . should be completed in time for the Post Office to decide to order these types of equipment where it best meets its requirements . . . the Post Office is planning its largest ever programme of expansion. Over the next four years it needs more than £350 million of exchange equipment — three times what was bought in the previous four years.

Most of this . . . will be of the well-tried Strowger type . . . But the Post Office has also decided to meet part of its rapidly increasing requirements by taking some exchanges in the British designed 5005 crossbar system (of AT & E) . . . The scope for 5005 crossbar equipment is small in relation to total needs, but it is needed to provide new exchanges in areas that would otherwise have to wait longer for service.'[37]

AT & E, one of the companies which had maintained an interest in crossbar systems, had been given the opportunity by the Post Office to test a new crossbar exchange, developed for the export market. The test exchange was installed at Broughton, in Lancashire, in 1964 and produced good results. Although this particular example was of 1,200 lines only, the design was capable of extension. It was this type which was ordered by the Post Office in 1966. The need was initially felt to be small in relation to the total of exchange equipment, but crossbar purchases became an increasingly important part of the total capital equipment programme during the late 1960s and early 1970s. Plans announced in 1973 for expenditure on exchanges in the seven years to 1980 included £350 million of crossbar equipment and more than £180 million of TXE-4 large electronic exchanges. Total provision for TXE-2 equipment in the same period was rather less than £100 million. Thus the exchange system which had been excluded from Post Office plans between the late 1940s and mid-1960s had become a major element in capital equipment embodying new techniques by the middle of the 1970s.[38]

The next six years (1966—72) saw intensive activity on the technical front to develop the TXE-4 to the stage where it could be ordered. Little discussion of policy issues appeared in print, but it is clear that the telephone service was under severe pressure. The amount of exchange and line equipment in service was well below the demands made on it by subscribers. Quality of service standards suffered. In July 1971 the *Annual Report* stated categorically that rapid replacement of the Strowger system was essential if an adequate service was to be provided.

By the summer of 1972 the decision process over TXE-4 and modernisation was approaching its conclusion. The policy problem was referred to briefly by the *Annual Report*, and by this time it was felt that the choice to be made lay between the reed-relay electronic exchange (TXE-4) and an advanced type of crossbar design.

'In 1971 the Post Office entered into a 3 year contract with one of its principal manufacturers for the supply of £15m. of electronic switching equipment for large local exchanges (TXE-4). The Board will be reviewing progress with TXE-4 at the end of 1972 and will then conclude whether this system should be used for modernising the local switching network.

Modernisation by the replacement of the existing electro-mechanical (Strowger) system is essential if Britain is to have the fast, fault free, and flexible telephone service that modern technology is making possible and that other advanced countries will certainly have in the 1980s.

There is no dispute about this. But there is a view that the objective could best be achieved by the use, not of TXE-4, but of an improved version of an electro-mechanical (Crossbar) system that is already being used for some purposes by the Post Office.

The Board is not committed to any particular solution in advance of the end-of-year review. Meanwhile the differing points of view were thoroughly explored in discussions with the manufacturers during the latter half of 1971—72. The issues are of great complexity and importance to the Post Office, to industry and to the customer; and the Board has fully accepted the need for the manufacturers to be involved in the evaluation processes leading up to the review. When decisions have been taken they will be reported to the Government because of the scale, nature and importance of the consequences. If premature replacement were decided upon, the immediate effect would be an increase in the annual charges for depreciation.'

Thus the possibility arose of totally reversing the earlier decisions in the 1972 review.

CROSSBAR DEVELOPMENT

By the time the Post Office came to review its technical policy in 1972, crossbar exchanges of one type or another had been in use for over fifty years. A Post Office team had reported on their use in Sweden after a visit in 1947 and two years later a small crossbar equipment had been imported for test and evaluation. It was installed in a minor department of the Passport Office. In spite of the continuing interest of one or two manufacturers, however, no development work was put in hand by the Post Office until after the 1966 decision to order the 5005 type from AT & E.

The first crossbar exchange ordered by the Post Office (as opposed to the Broughton trial exchange) was installed in 1967, soon after the first TXE-2. The 5005, by this time manufactured by Plessey, since the latter's acquisition of AT & E in 1966, was given the Post Office name TXK-1. With Post Office acceptance of crossbar, Standard Telephones and Cables (STC) was encouraged to present an exchange using the same technique and the company anglicised an exchange originally designed by International Telephones and Telegraphs (ITT).[39] The Pentaconta design, on which STC's exchange was based, became known as TXK-3 after being approved for local exchanges.

Local exchanges alone did not account for the predominance of crossbar equipment in the purchasing plans for 1973—80. Crossbar developments began to find applications in the network for switching long distance calls soon after the first local crossbar exchanges were installed. The enormous growth in trunk traffic throughout the 1960s and its expected continuation into the 1970s had made necessary major extensions to the switching network. Transit switching centres for handling long distance traffic began to be added to the system in 1963; by 1969 a plan had been formed to divert much of the peripheral traffic around the London area to sector switching centres. Both these types and the existing trunk exchanges were able to employ crossbar systems. GEC adapted the AT & E 5005 design to produce a trunk exchange and a development of the ITT Pentaconta came into service in the transit switching centres.

STANDARDISATION ON TXE-4

The 1972 review of exchange policy by the Post Office resulted in TXE-4 being chosen as the standard for all large local exchange installations. In addition to crossbar and TXE-4, a foreign designed system had been evaluated, but for a number of reasons the TXE-4 was preferred. Examination of the system designed abroad showed that the amount of redesigning and development needed to allow it to work in the UK environment was too great to make it a viable choice. TXK-1 was a design which could not be used in director systems and was unsuitable for large exchanges above 25,000 connections. TXK-3 might have been acceptable for all applications in large local exchanges, but its space requirements were higher than either TXE-4 or Strowger. In many city centres, where the large exchanges are located, this would have created extra cost and accommodation problems.

TXE-4 offered both the flexibility and the space saving features which were desired, as well as being suitable for director or non-director systems. Its control system, programmable logic, was produced for the TXE-3 in the early 1960s. Programmable logic can be adapted for the provision of new features to the service offered by the exchange and has a high security rating; that is, it can be expected to function with extreme reliability. It is also fault-tolerant in the system devised for TXE-4, because there are sectional control units for speech path selection. If faulty equipment is located by the call-setting processor it can be isolated and bypassed. New features or services can be added by some rewiring of the ferrite core array in the main processor.

Production versions of TXE-4 were planned in 1974 and the Post Office intended to order at least forty large exchanges of this type to reach service before 1980. It is probable that the number of exchange connections on crossbar exchanges will outnumber those on electronic exchanges for about ten years from the 1972 decision, but effectively that decision was intended to mark the progressive phasing out of crossbar from local exchanges, just as Strowger was also to disappear.

CONCLUSION

The issues raised by exchange development are fundamentally those of how technical development should be planned in order that an informed decision, based upon operating data rather than forecasts, may be made at the time that new investment is to be made. The absence of contingency planning in the Post Office's early decisions in the 1950s led to a situation in which crossbar equipment became a necessary but not a planned adjunct to the system in 1966. Regardless of the question of whether crossbar or electronic switching was a more appropriate technique for the Post Office to use in the 1960s' expansion of the system, the Post Office was constrained to adopt crossbar by the fact that the electronic equipment was not ready. Consequently the inclusion of crossbar equipment in the telephone service represented an unplanned step which was already being reversed by the 1970s.

The crossbar exchange designs which were adopted were found by Post Office engineers to have some operational disadvantages which were attributable to the absence of Post Office involvement at the earlier stages of design. As a result, it was not really the case in the 1972 decision that an opportunity existed to choose between three options, TXE-4, crossbar or a foreign system. The last two, which had been designed without British applications in mind, did not 'fit the tracks' of the telephone network and the Post Office judged that adaptation and development to allow them to do so would have been more costly and time consuming than was acceptable.

In order for the Post Office to have been able to maintain the opportunity either in 1966 or in 1972 to exercise a real choice between different types of electronic or crossbar switching techniques, it would have had to take steps at a much earlier stage to encourage at least exploratory development of a number of systems.

The most interesting feature of such a long-drawn-out story of development and decision is the way in which the vital questions of the early stages diminish in importance, the protagonists adjust their positions, the learning process sets in and, rather like in a detective novel, we realise that we should have been watching the actions of a character quite different from the main suspect. When electronic development started, it appeared that a faster and more easily maintained switching system than Strowger must be found. The choice seemed to lie between that of a more developed electro-mechanical system and the 'all electric' exchange with no moving parts, which Sir Archibald Gill, the Engineer-in-Chief, referred to in 1949. In the eyes of Post Office engineers at Dollis Hill, an electro-mechanical switch of high enough reliability and faster speed would be too expensive, and the prospects for economy and reliability of a shared speech path with a very few high performance electronic switches meant that the time division system had to be the first choice for development.

Paradoxically, the cost of the switching element, a critical feature in the economic success of electronic systems, was nevertheless the wrong element to base a decision upon. In the long run both space division (reed-relay) and time division electronic exchanges, and even crossbar exchanges, could be manufactured with cheap enough crosspoint devices or switching elements. All three could be expected to require less maintenance than Strowger, and all three were faster in operation. The crucial exercise in the decision was to recognise which system had an optimum balance of the totality of limiting performance parameters, control flexibility, interworking compatibility, fault tolerance, power consumption, traffic handling, maintainability, etc. Some of the difficulties faced by the Post Office in electronic development could be seen as arising from the failure to set up a strategy of development which allowed it to examine a variety of systems on these aspects.

NOTES

[1] B. L. Barnett, 'Postwar Telephone Developments', *Post Office Electrical Engineers' Journal* (*POEEJ*), January 1948. Subscriber Trunk Dialling.

[2] Hull and the Channel Islands currently operate independent systems. Portsmouth and Hull retained the right to run their own services in 1912, but Portsmouth gave it up in 1913. The Channel Islands started a service in 1923. An early account of general historical value is J. H. Robertson, *The Story of the Telephone*, Pitman, London, 1947.

[3] The decision very nearly went the other way, in favour of the Panel switching developed for New York (see Robertson, *The Story of the Telephone*, op. cit.).

[4] Early technical developments in the Post Office are referred to in Robertson's book quoted above, and are neatly summarised in 'History of the Engineering Department' by E. C. Baker, published as *GPO Green Paper No. 46*, May 1939.

[5] Criteria evolved during the 1920s for the conditions in which automatic working was economic were not adhered to in later capital equipment programmes: 'Killing the Goose', *Traffic*, Oct.–Dec. 1956.

[6] *Inquiry on the Post Office*, Cmd 4140, HMSO, 1932.

[7] Bridgeman said they were described as 'aloof' and indifferent to the public's demands.

[8] Detailed instruction from headquarters extended to such matters as where to display notices (e.g. concerning infectious diseases) and a 1948 directive noted that the tops of

supervisors' desks should be clear 'except perhaps for a vase of flowers', giving rise to the following ver'se:

> No 'Funnies' on the Super's desk
> Nor Ancient Notices on ours
> Nothing to distract or cheer
> Except perhaps a vase of flowers.
>
> Our switchroom now is orderly
> Nothing to speed the passing hours
> Not an item out of place
> Except perhaps a vase of flowers.
>
> Oh Mighty Men in places high
> We thank thee that with all your powers
> There's place amidst officialdom
> For just perhaps some tiny flowers.
>
> Blossoms we amid the Plan
> Save our tears which fall like showers!
> Would you shelve us with the rest?
> Oh spare your blooming little flowers!

The reference in the last verse is to the trunk mechanisation plan which was thought to be a threat to the future of operators (*Traffic,* July 1948).

[9] These are approximate figures; the picture is blurred by the presence of trunk exchanges in the total.

[10] Surpluses were approximately £11 million in 1936, £15 million in 1937, £18 million in 1938.

[11] The 1950 figure represented £12·6 million at 1937 prices.

[12] An article appearing in the *Post Office Telecommunications Journal* in August 1950 was written by a member of the Engineer in Chief's staff with very much this intention. (J. A. Lawrence, 'Contemporary Telephone Mechanisation Abroad and Possible Future Trends', *POTJ*, Aug. 1950, pp. 154—61.) Lawrence surveys the three main types of electro-mechanical exchange, which were at the time Strowger or step-by-step, rotary driven selectors and crossbar selector systems. He concludes that Strowger is the most economical type for mixed urban and rural use, but notes that competitive claims have been made for the new and developing types of crossbar equipment.

[13] J. A. Lawrence, 'Problems of Electronic Exchanges', *POTJ*, Spring 1961, pp. 91—6.

[14] A. J. Gill, 'Engineering Developments', *POTJ,* Feb. 1949. The words 'all electric' to describe a valve-operated exchange indicate that for the engineers the attraction of the electronic exchange was that it had no mechanical moving parts, unlike a Strowger exchange, which was a mass of jerking and chattering switches and arms, and that the electric exchange used electronics, not magnetism, to perform the actual switching.

[15] Select Committee on Estimates, *The Post Office,* HMSO, 1950.

[16] T. H. Flowers, 'Introduction to Electronic Automatic Telephone Exchanges', *POEEJ,* July 1950, January 1951 and April 1951.

[17] There were five at the time (Automatic Telephone and Electric; Ericsson Telephones; General Electric Company; Siemens Brothers; Standard Telephones and Cables) which exclusively supplied exchange equipment.

[18] BTR developments are reported fully in the journals: D. Halton and J. F. Greenaway, 'Principles of a Magnetic Drum Register Translater', *ATE Journal,* April 1956; K. G. Marwing, 'Lee Green Magnetic Drum Register Translator', *POEEJ*, July, 1958; T. H. Clark, 'Electronically Controlled Crossbar Exchange', *ATE Journal,* Jan. 1957 (the principle was stated to be equally applicable to Strowger switching, but crossbar was better because quicker); L. J. Allen and R. L. Hobbs, '100-line Private Electronic Exchange', *ATE Journal,* Oct. 1957.

[19] R. W. Palmer and W. L. Brimmer, 'The BTTDC', *POEEJ,* Jan. 1949.

[20] Qualified engineers in 1946 were fewer than 80, but this number grew to over 150 by 1954. Scientist grades were introduced in 1948. Total numbers, including support staff, grew from about 300 in 1946 to 800 in the mid-1950s.

[21] Announcement in the House of Commons by the Postmaster General, July 1957.

[22] *POEEJ*, January 1960. Highgate Wood was intended as a demonstration equipment, backed up by a Strowger for live traffic.

[23] L. R. F. Harris, 'Electronic Telephone Exchanges', *POEEJ*, Oct. 1966. On the other hand one of the Post Office engineers who pioneered t.d.m. work argued ten years after Highgate Wood (when the alternative systems were facing their own problems) that the only fault of t.d.m. was that engineering development stopped too early.

[24] *Post Office Development and Finance*, Cmd 9576, HMSO, 1955.

[25] Corresponding rates of calling for foreign countries should be interpreted with caution, because of differences in statistics and telephone distribution. However, the British rate does appear low even in the 1970s, as the following table shows.

Calling rate per year

Number of calls per telephone in use (not per connection)

Japan	1,880	Italy	1,130	Canada	1,660
Fed. Rep. Germany	780	United States	1,360	United Kingdom	750
Sweden	1,150	France	500		

Source: POTJ, Spring 1972, p. 34.

The number of telephones may exceed the number of telephone connections by 30 or 40 per cent in most countries, but the calling rates would move closer together when adjusted for this distortion only if the systems in Britain (and in France and Germany) had a greater number of instruments on each line than elsewhere.

[26] Residence connection rate in London, 1 July 1952.

[27] Residence connection rate anywhere in UK to October 1961.

[28] But the limitation on 'local' calls, 5 miles up to 1958, was then extended to any telephone in the same or adjacent 'charging group' (a term which related to STD provisions); thus the local call became one of up to 15 miles.

[29] This analysis of the services available is simplified for the sake of brevity.

[30] Cmnd 303, HMSO, 1957 and Cmnd 436, HMSO, 1958.

[31] *POEEJ*, January 1959.

[32] *ATE Journal*, 1956 and 1957, particularly articles by Threadgold (Jan. 56), Baker (Oct. 56), Clark (Jan. 57), Baker (Jan. 57) and Davison (July 57). The second article by Baker has a memorable opening paragraph:

> There are two theories as to how man arrived on this earth. According to one he was created unchangeable and complete on a certain day in April in the year 4004 BC. According to the other he evolved by slow and gradual stages from the primordial ooze.

It goes on to show how the Strowger system can be adapted to accept electronic techniques (the theory of evolution) and the reader is left to judge what systems may be likened to the first theory.

[33] Hillen, Long and Porritt, 'Field Trial of Two Small Electronic Exchanges', *POEEJ*, April 65.

J. A. Lawrence, 'First Production Electronic Telephone Exchange', *POEEJ*, Jan. 1967.

[34] Siemens had meanwhile been absorbed into Associated Electrical Industries. Ericsson and AT & E were acquired by Plessey in the mid-1960s.

[35] S. H. Sheppard, 'Leighton Buzzard Electronic Telephone Exchange', *POEEJ*, Jan. 1967; Harris, 'Electronic Telephone Exchanges', op. cit.; May, 'Electronic Exchanges', *POEEJ*, Oct. 1972.

[36] Robert Vincent, 'The Girl-less Cuss-less Telephone', *Traffic*, 1968. Alvin Strowger is said to have watched exchange operators pick up a plug and search the rows of sockets, first vertically then horizontally, for the right number. His selector does the same.

[37] 'Policy Statement', *POEEJ*, July 1966.

[38] It was expected by the Post Office that more TXE-4 equipment would eventually be included in the 1973—80 programme.

[39] ITT is the parent company of STC.

5 Process Innovation and Growth in the Gas Industry

Summary

The nature of the cost problem in the gas industry was not difficult to identify. The carbonisation process had become fairly well developed by the twentieth century and was no longer labour intensive. Its costs were, however, almost wholly determined by the price of coal of an increasingly scarce type. The effect of doubling the price of gas coals during the 1950s was to raise gas making costs by more than 50 per cent and this was inevitably registered as a price increase. Increasing efficiency elsewhere could not, as with electricity, serve to mitigate significantly the effect of coal prices, because capital efficiency could not be improved and thermal efficiency was as high as it could be expected to reach.

An alternative to carbonisation as a gas-making process was therefore the only way of avoiding price increases, which were eroding the industry's competitive position in the fuel market. But, although the nature of the problem was easy to agree, the direction in which the solution lay was problematic. The strength which the industry displayed was in the way it went about deciding on a development programme to change gas making techniques.

Underpinning the developments of the 1950s there was a background of research on the nature of the transformation of feedstock into gas; this research had been initiated in the 1930s as a result of the industry's ties with the department of chemistry at Leeds University. Following up the early research, an institute had been set up by the industry as a whole some years before nationalisation to experiment with gas making techniques.

The development of new techniques was not, however, regarded as the preserve only of the research function. The industry before nationalisation was fortunate in having a number of relatively large companies, even though it was otherwise fragmented. The larger companies were forward looking enough to have technical programmes of their own. These threw up new techniques which continued to be pursued after nationalisation, and their existence gave the regional Boards of the gas industry an independent and authoritative standpoint from which to assess the other new techniques being put forward during the 1950s and 1960s.

The arrangements which were made for the administration of research under public ownership reflected the federal structure of the industry. The Research Committee of the Gas Council included a small number of academically qualified people, some Council members, the directors of the research stations and technically qualified senior personnel from the Area Boards. Thus there was a balance of the more theoretical approach, the practical gas engineering consideration and the commercial and financial constraints of operating gas undertakings.

Decisions about which processes to pursue did not prove easy to make, and work went on simultaneously in a number of directions. The industry did not make the mistake of determining a single direction at an early stage and failing to evaluate alternatives. In the earlier work new coal processes were favoured for base-load plant while oil-based techniques appeared to offer the best prospects of providing peak-load plant. But the economics of the complete gasification of coal were somewhat uncertain. Fortunately, the industry was not faced by growing demand pressure and so it was able to delay large-scale commitment to new processes. Experimentation, pilot plant installation and commercial test continued of a range of processes which emanated from the Area Boards, from sources abroad and from the research programme itself. In this research programme the choice of projects was subtly determined by a consensus established between the Research Committee, the research stations and representation from the production side of the Area Boards. The openness displayed by the industry to possible lines of development may be attributed to its federal structure and the method of administering the development programme. The strength of the professional association, the Institute of Gas Engineers, may also be regarded as useful in providing a forum for the disinterested and independent discussion of technical problems.

Most of the Boards in the industry firmly resisted the idea of building large coal gasification plants (of Lurgi design) for supply through a distribution grid; their grounds for not supporting the scheme were primarily economic. On the other hand, more than half agreed to participate in the methane importation plan. Its advantages were the low delivered cost of heat and the value of having the rich gas as a source of enrichment for other gas supplies.

When the oil-based continuous reforming processes became available from ICI and from the industry's own research programme, the Gas Boards invested in them very rapidly. The main reasons for this were that demand for gas had started to grow and the oil-based processes were several times more efficient than carbonisation in terms of capital costs and labour costs, while the feedstock cost was marginally lower. The process was also independent of the market for by-products. Much credit is due to the industry for having developed the gas recycle hydrogenator (GRH) and catalytic rich gas (CRG) processes, in a classical demonstration of applying research to industrial problems. Additionally, credit must be given for the way the decisions were made. Decisions to invest were soundly based upon reliable cost information and the techniques involved were thoroughly tested, being based both upon pilot plant and commercial demonstration plant. There was therefore no uncomfortable dawning of disillusionment when the promises held out for new techniques failed to materialise. The industry experimented with a wide range of new processes for gas making and therefore was not lacking in alternative lines of development when setbacks were experienced with the coal gasification projects. Finally, the federal structure of the industry ensured that there was room for more than one view on technical and economic problems, making it necessary that experimentation with processes and evaluation of costs were used as a means to resolve potential conflicts about the direction in which technical policy should go.

Gas manufacturing plant is not a subject to which much glamour attaches. On the contrary, the gas works was to many generations between the Victorian age and the postwar world a subject for music-hall humour. The slightly grotesque complex of steel constructions which formed the gas works, announcing its presence through an unmistakable smell in the less salubrious part of town, was scarcely regarded with the reverence reserved for the wonders of technology. Yet gas technology has been one of the most successful postwar British innovations.

When nationalisation came in 1949, the industry was battling with a severe problem, the supply and cost of its basic feedstock, coal. Organisational improvements resulting from nationalisation did not solve the basic problem, and the industry went through a period of twelve years (to 1961/2) in which sales rose by only about 1 per cent per year; in that time, indeed, sales to the major market, the domestic consumer, actually receded by a small amount. The decline in domestic sales to 1960 was quite marked, from 1,392m. therms in 1950/1 (the first full year of nationalisation) to 1,268m. therms by 1959/60. The effect was large enough to cause overall sales (domestic, business and public lighting) also to dip in the late 1950s. The most obvious cause was the relative change in prices of fuels in the postwar period (Table 5.1).

Table 5.1   *Prices of Gas, Electricity and Kerosene to Domestic Consumers 1950 and 1960 (index nos)*

	Gas	Electricity	Paraffin
1950	100	100	100
1960	173	123	141

Source: Select Committee on Nationalised Industries, *Report on Gas Industry*, HMSO, 1961.

However, industry witnesses to the Select Committee[1] which investigated gas in 1960 stressed the effects of urban redevelopment.[2] Older housing areas, which were already served by gas mains, were being demolished. The new housing areas had to be supplied with electricity in any event for lighting and, so it was claimed, electricity boards were willing to install a network for heating as well at little extra cost. By contrast, a gas main was a heavy capital outlay which the housing developer was not always able to afford. The 'all electric' house was advertised in the 1950s as an advantageous feature. The reasons for decline were probably more complex than either of these simple causes, but they all serve to reinforce the picture of an industry with little prospect of expansion and rapidly increasing costs, unable to afford favourable terms for the attraction of new business.

That there was even a small upward movement in gas sales during the first twelve years of nationalisation was entirely due to increased demand from the industrial and commercial market. The movement in industrial prices in favour of alternative fuels was, however, only slightly less marked than in the domestic market (Table 5.2).

On the other hand, prices for industrial customers of the gas industry were as much as 40 per cent below domestic prices, and it can be seen that they rose less fast than the latter between 1950 and 1960. In addition, there were process industries where gas heat had special advantages; in the largest of gas's commercial sectors, catering, represented by hotels, schools, canteens and restaurants, gas was almost universally used, electricity not being regarded as a close substitute. Industrial and commercial gas sales grew at about the same rate as the index of industrial production during the 1950s, but its competitors, electricity and oil, grew at twice and three times that rate respectively.

Table 5.2 *Prices of Gas, Electricity and Oil to Industrial Consumers 1950 and 1960 (index nos)*

	Gas	Electricity	Oil
1950	100	100	100
1960	161	133	140

Source: As Table 5.1.

Throughout this first period of public ownership of the gas industry, a determined search was being made for new gas feedstocks and new gas-making processes. The traditional gas process is called carbonisation and the fuel it starts from is a special quality of coal, known generally as coking coal. For various reasons the difficulties of the gas industry could be laid at the door of dependence upon this special type of coal. It was because carbonisation was fairly efficient in terms of heat conversion and could be developed little further that the opportunities for increasing the productivity of the gas making aspect of carbonisation were only marginal in 1949. The industry was doing well to improve thermal efficiency overall from 71 per cent in 1949 to 75 per cent by 1953/4. The effect that this order of improvement had upon the efficiency of gas production, however, was only about 1 per cent, since gas products formed only a quarter of the thermal output of the carbonisation process. Increases in coking coal prices far outstripped the best efforts of the industry to improve its efficiency. Between May 1949 and September 1960 the coals used for gas making increased in price by 108 per cent, inevitably producing gas price increases.

Thus it can be seen that the carbonisation works, while not deserving to be treated with the ribaldry frequently directed at it, was at best in the position of a rather ancient servant; the techniques it embodied had been developed about as far as they could go, and changed economic circumstances made their continued employment a slight embarrassment to the gas industry.

But the efforts of the industry had begun to produce new supplies of gas in the late 1950s and new consumer appliances had been developed. Sales began to increase steadily from 1960/1. Although the increase was not at first very dramatic, it became quite remarkable in the late 1960s. The quantity of gas sold almost exactly doubled between 1960 and 1970. From 1970 to 1975 it increased by two and a half times (Table 5.3).

Table 5.3   *Gas Sales, 1949—75 (million therms)*

Years	Domestic	Industrial	Commercial	Total
1949/50	n.a.	n.a.	n.a.	2,315 [a]
1950/1	1,392	590	420	2,402
1954/5	1,379	720	474	2,573
1959/60	1,268	819	454	2,541
1964/5	1,727	915	528	3,170
1969/70	3,362	1,159	714	5,235
1974/5	5,710	5,921	1,301	12,932

Source: Gas Council, *Annual Reports.*
Note: [a] Adjusted to twelve months from total for eleven months.

The boom in gas sales was led by the domestic market. Demand doubled in that sector in the first seven years of the 1960s, and sales of boilers, warm air units and space heaters show that higher standards of comfort in the home were of great assistance to gas sales. In the second period industrial sales led the boom. Having grown slowly to 1,159m. therms by 1969/70, industrial sales increased by nearly five times to 1975.

What were the reasons for the success of gas in the 1960s and 1970s, when it had been such an undistinguished performer in previous years? It is interesting that the faster rate of growth in gas sales was started by the domestic sector, when one remembers that it was this sector which had most handicapped the expansion of the industry in the 1950s. The most satisfactory explanation of this phenomenon is that a major change in the heating habits of the society took place in the space of a very few years.[3] Domestic consumption of coal first began to fall in the late 1950s; the trend became much sharper in the decade 1960/9, amounting to a decrease of 40 per cent of sales. The alternative sources of heating were electricity, oil (or paraffin) and gas. Statistics suggest that gas was not widely used for heating in the 1950s. The gas industry's 12·2 million domestic customers in 1957/8 used only about 109 therms each per year, only sufficient to indicate, at the most, the presence of one gas cooker for every domestic customer and one gas fire for every third customer. When the coal fire as a major source of domestic heating began to go out of use, however, people found gas at least as attractive an alternative as electricity. The figures in Table 5.4 show how domestic gas sales climbed in the 1960s at twice the rate of domestic sales of electricity. The table slightly understates the performance of gas, because up to the critical year of 1960, sales continued to decline, reaching a low point at 1,267m. therms in 1959/60. Thus the actual growth in the three years 1959/60 to 1962/3 was 18 per cent.

Table 5.4 *Consumption of Electricity and Gas by Domestic Consumers, 1957—73*

Year to April/March of	1957/8		1962/3		1967/8		1972/3
Domestic sales of electricity (kwh)	22,108		43,569		56,376		76,752
5 year increase %		97%		29%		36%	
Domestic sales of gas (therms)	1,326		1,493		2,652		4,603
5 year increase %		13%		77%		74%	

Source: Gas Council, *Annual Reports,* and Electricity Council, *Annual Reports.*

Gas was increasingly being used for space heating and central heating. Average consumption per domestic customer increased from 109 therms per year in 1957/8 to 211 therms per year ten years later and to 357 therms per year by 1972/3. Electricity sales per domestic customer increased rather faster up to 1962, but by 1972/3 were still only about two and half times the 1957/8 figure.

It is arguable that gas would never have had this impact upon the domestic heating market if its price relative to electricity or oil had continued to increase in the same way after 1960 as it had before. Table 5.1 shows the extent to which gas was losing ground in price terms, but even by 1960 it had not been priced out of the market. Comparisons made in 1960 of the best gas systems for water heating, space heating and central heating on domestic premises showed that gas could perform at lower costs than the standard installations which used coal, electricity or oil.[4] That gas was able to develop the market for domestic consumption in what were relatively new fields of application is a tribute to the effectiveness and foresight of the research undertaken on utilisation. Convector room heaters and instant water heaters offered the consumer a standard of comfort and convenience which other fuels could not easily match, and the new appliances were available in time to meet the new sources of demand. Much of the advantage would, however, have been lost if there had not been rapid change in the feedstocks and processes used in gas manufacturing during the 1960s.

As long as the industry depended upon coking coal, and could achieve only marginal changes in the coal to gas conversion rate, its prices were closely tied to the prices charged by the National Coal Board. During the 1950s a number of Gas Boards had installed peak load processes which converted oil into a very close substitute for the standard gas. There had also been a trend towards buying gas from coke ovens, run by the steel industry or the Coal Board, and using 'tail gas' from the final stage of the petroleum refining process. Both policies had helped to control costs, but they could not provide a way of meeting the base-load demand for gas at lower overall costs.

During the late 1950s a number of processes had been developed by the Gas Council and the Boards for reforming lean gases to rich, by cyclical and continuous reforming, and for using light distillate feedstock (LDF) from refineries as a feedstock for gas manufacture. Two events then sparked off the exploitation of these discoveries. The first was the completion of satisfactory trials of the scheme to import liquid natural gas (LNG), a high calorific value gas which could be used for enrichment, from Algeria by ship. The second was the development by ICI of a new method of making lean gas from LDF,[5] and its successful use with a Gas Council enriching process.

The sudden availability of new processes, new feedstocks and new sources of supply gave the industry tremendous confidence. Orders for new plants were placed so rapidly that the capacity of plant using oil-based processes exceeded that of carbonisation plant by 1966, only four years after those processes had first become available to the industry. The industry was able to avoid further large price increases and even to reduce some prices from the early 1960s onwards. Its position in competition with electricity and oil improved very remarkably (Table 5.5).

Table 5.5   *Prices of Gas, Electricity and Oil, 1962—72 (index numbers)*

| | Gas | | Electricity | | Oil |
	(domestic)	*(industrial)*	*(domestic)*	*(industrial)*	*industrial*
1962/3	100	100	100	100	100
1967/8	92	99	121	115	101
1972/3	100	45	139	133	164 (1972)

Source: Gas Council and Electricity Council, *Annual Reports.* Oil prices are industrial fuel oil representative prices published by the Department of Trade and Industry.

In the first five years of the period shown in the table, the price stability of gas supplies was due to two major factors: the purchases of ready made gas and LNG for reforming into town gas and the invention of the processes based on oil. After 1967 North Sea gas was available for use and this source amounted to as much as 20 per cent of supplies available by late 1968.

Once the pipelines from the Leman Bank and West Sole fields were laid to the shore terminals on the east coast, supplies built up very quickly, and exceeded those from manufactured sources before the end of 1971.

The exploration companies in the North Sea wasted no time in bringing the gas ashore, but the time needed to exploit the new source was very much shortened by the fact that a distribution grid already existed. During the mid-1950s the North Thames Gas Board had pioneered the scheme to import natural gas in liquid form from Algeria to Canvey Island, east of London on the Thames. To deliver this gas to the eight Area Boards taking part in the scheme, a distribution main had been laid for about 200 miles to Leeds, connecting with the main points of supply.[6] With the installation of several hundred miles of high pressure main, North Sea gas could be used in town gas manufacture.

The methane grid distribution system allowed a rapid distribution of North Sea gas; the existence of the large capacity of continuous reforming plant capable of taking natural gas as a feedstock enabled rapid assimilation. The methane scheme also provided a supply of gas on which the experience of conversion in advance of North Sea gas could be obtained.

Gas consumption more than doubled in the years 1968 to 1973. Although the domestic market expanded, it was in the industrial sector that the bulk of the growth took place. Industrial sales grew to about five times their earlier level and accounted for 75 per cent of the total growth of the industry. Having negotiated fairly low prices for the early supplies of North Sea gas, the industry was able to gain very large industrial contracts.

For most people, the success of the gas industry in the 1960s was directly associated with the discovery of natural gas in the North Sea and with the conversion of the supply system to make use of it without treatment. Many people were probably unaware of the technical revolution which preceded this discovery and which laid the foundation of the gas industry's growth. The fact that there were two revolutions in supply, first a change to oil and then to natural gas, meant that the earlier one was eclipsed. It has never received the kind of publicity accorded to Britain's developments in nuclear energy for generating electricity.[7]

And yet there are two reasons why the Gas Council's search for alternative technologies in the 1950s is a story worth telling. The first is that the reserves of natural gas within easy reach of Britain are finite and will become increasingly expensive to exploit. As prices for primary fuels and the convenience of their supply sources vary during the 1980s and 1990s, it is going to be important to maintain an option to manufacture gas which can be used in a natural gas system from a variety of feedstocks. Secondly, the technical programme which the Gas Council followed can be seen in retrospect to have combined enthusiasm for innovation with a shrewd judgment of its commercial value, in a way which merits closer examination.

THE NATURE OF THE GAS INDUSTRY BEFORE 1949

In the first year after the war (1946) the gas industry made and produced about 470 billion cubic feet of gas. Converted at the rate of 450 British Thermal Units to the cubic foot, this amounted to over 2,100 million therms.[8] Its annual output was therefore not far short of that for the industry in the 1950s (2,300m. to 2,600m. therms) but its system of organisation was very different. There were 1,046 undertakings, each one of them a distinct and separate supplier of gas, although many of the undertakings located in the south of England were associated with larger companies through holding companies. In the multitude of suppliers the gas industry resembled the coal mining industry, but it was different in the size of company. Very few coal companies owned more than a handful of collieries, and even the larger companies accounted for only a small proportion of output. The gas industry had a much greater variation in size of company.

Eleven undertakings out of the thousand and more making up the industry sold 38 per cent of the gas, an average of about 80 million therms each per year. The addition of another seventeen undertakings raised the amount to 52 per cent of gas sold. One company, the Gas Light and Coke Company, which supplied large parts of north London and beyond, was big enough to rival in size the Area Boards which took over production and supply in 1949. These twelve Area Boards were to average about 200 million therms each in the earlier years. At the other end of the scale were nearly 700 undertakings supplying less than 6 per cent of the total.

It is interesting to note how the gas industry had already, before 1949, responded to technical changes and to the challenge of the electricity industry. Starting around 1810, town gas had originally fulfilled a lighting function. The invention of the filament electric lamp by Edison and Swan towards the end of the nineteenth century foreshadowed the eventual demise of gas lighting, and the invention of the incandescent gas mantle, an improved gas light, only partly assisted the industry since it reduced the quantity of gas needed for lighting by up to eight times.

However, just as it did again in the twentieth century, in the late nineteenth century, the industry resisted the challenge of electricity by developing new applications of gas. The gas cooker became the mainstay of the industry's growth; early forms of room heater were developed after the First World War. The mass market of the poorer consumers was opened up by the adoption of the pre-payment meter. In 1919 the Fuel Research Board was to pronounce:

'the sheet anchor of the Gas Industry in the future must necessarily be its possession of the cheapest known means of distributing potential heat energy in a convenient form. For lighting and power production the electricity supply of the future may seriously contest the field with the producers of gas, but for the supply of heat, gaseous fuel ought to remain supreme if its production and use are developed on sound lines'

thereby neatly predicting the events of the 1960s.

In the inter-war period the industry was the subject of many official reports, culminating in that of the Heyworth Committee of 1944.[9] While recommending that increased integration of the industry should be achieved by compulsory purchases, the Committee did not go so far as to suggest nationalisation. The advantages of amalgamation were recognised even by the supporters of an independent gas industry. Linking the areas in which customers were reasonably concentrated could result in many small and uneconomic production units being closed down. The National Grid in the electricity industry was being built to link large power stations in the 1930s in order to save extra costs from surplus capacity and inefficient generation at smaller and older power stations. Many gas plants in 1949 were below the minimum size for the highest efficiency of carbonisation, because there had been very little movement toward the integration of supply.

The economics of gas supply were complicated by the dependence on by-products. The carbonisation products from each ton of coal in a typical works of the larger size just after the war might amount to 80 therms of gas, 11 cwt of coke, 200 lb of tar and small quantities of benzole and ammonias. The sales of gas, coke, tar and benzole all formed major sources of revenue for the gas company. The significance of this dependence on by-products was that any economic or technical advantages which might be expected from the centralisation of gas making plant had to be set off against the problem of marketing coke and tar. They were bulky or difficult to transport over more than short distances. Gas manufacture and supply often fitted closely into a localised balance of industrial and domestic demand for coke and gas. A gas company which planned to centralise manufacture had to be sure that its access to coke markets, with the costs incurred in transport, would not adversely affect the economics of the operation. One major exception was in the area of London north of the Thames. Here the Gas Light and Coke Company had achieved close control of coke supply and, with a near-monopoly of gas supply in the area, the company had a wide distribution network supplied through a few large plants.[10]

As far as research and technical policy development were concerned, the industry was by the 1940s rather more advanced than industries such as coal and electricity. Policy co-ordination had led it to set up the Gas Research Board at Poole, with good laboratory facilities and a mandate to examine new gas-making processes, the problems of combustion and other projects. The larger companies had their own research facilities.

In a survey of scientific personnel conducted for the new Gas Council by the Secretary of the Institution of Gas Engineers in August 1949, it was estimated that over 1,300 people were engaged on research, development, testing and control. Of these, 400 had professional qualifications as scientists or engineers. The majority were engaged on routine technical support work, only about 340 being classed as conducting investigations meriting the title of research and development. The Gas Research Board at Poole had thirty-eight research and development personnel, who were to form the nucleus of the Gas Council's Midland Research Station three years later. An important part of their work even before nationalisation was the study of gasification processes under Dr F. J. Dent, the Assistant

Director. Dr Dent had already established a reputation for his work at Leeds University on the hydrogenation of coal (adding hydrogen to the coal substance) to produce methane, and also on producing methane by the synthesis of carbon monoxide and hydrogen.

Many of the remaining research and development personnel had been employed by the Gas Light and Coke Company. At the time of the survey, 146 research and development personnel were working in the North Thames Area, and another 200 on routine testing. The Company had two main laboratories, the Fulham laboratory, concentrating on production, and Watson House, the utilisation centre. Both these laboratories, although integrated into the Gas Council's research programme, remained under the day-to-day control of the North Thames Board, many of whose personnel had remained from the former Gas Light and Coke Company. Fulham was later to house the Gas Council's basic research facility, while Watson House was the centre for the very important work, first on new types of domestic appliances in the 1950s and then on the utilisation of natural gas in the late 1960s. Apart from the area of the Gas Light and Coke Company, there had been small teams of qualified people at laboratories in Manchester, Liverpool, Bristol, the Nechells works in Birmingham and the Central laboratories of the South Metropolitan Gas Company (Old Kent Road, London). None of these groups was larger than fifteen or twenty in number.

Thus an overall picture emerges of the gas industry immediately before nationalisation. It was certainly an old industry, at least by comparison with its competitors. The technology it used was as old as the industry itself, and had been thoroughly developed, to the point where significant improvements in efficiency were not to be expected. But although old, the industry was by no means technically backward. On the contrary, it had a range of technical assets for the new Gas Council and Area Boards to acquire, and it was merely a question of how these latter bodies chose to deploy them.

THE EARLY YEARS OF PUBLIC OWNERSHIP

The industry's weakest point was its structure, which militated against any process of system integration around larger works. But this weakness was the one to which nationalisation was most appropriate, and the first few years of public ownership saw considerable rationalisation. The industry's other problem was the carbonisation process itself, the delicate balance of several markets for by-products and the developing shortage and increasing cost of the coal needed for the process.

When the gas industry was nationalised, the 1,046 separate under-takings were reduced to twelve. Each of the new Boards for gas production and supply was established in an area which was felt to be a unit in the geographical sense. Thus the Eastern Gas Board was made up of an area of East Anglia centred on Cambridge, and the North Eastern was centred on York, with most of North Yorkshire as its Area. Wales was a separate

Area. But in some cases the divisions were rather arbitrary. The four northern counties of Northumberland, Westmorland, Cumberland and Durham, having little geographical unity, were under the Northern Gas Board because as separate units they might not be viable. Complete centralisation was ruled out on the grounds that the problems and needs of gas supply differed in different areas, and a national grid was impracticable.

There were 1,050 plants in operation at vesting day, producing a total of about 2,300 million therms per annum. Most of them were below the level of 1·5 million therms per year which was judged to be the minimum size for efficient carbonisation and were thus due to be closed down. Indeed, in the North Thames Area, where gas supply was most concentrated, it was planned to replace the output of plants up to 5 million cubic feet per day by grid extensions.

Concentration of plant started at once. After five years 180 plants had been closed, and by March 1962, when the first revolution in gas processes was about to break, there were only 341 gas works left in production. Gas supply had by then been centralised upon the most efficient plants. Out of the 341, 74 plants were of a size which could make more than 10 million therms each per year and together accounted for 2,000 million therms out of the 2,736 million therms produced in 1961/2. That there were still 151 fairly small plants, mostly below the average size of 1949, was due to the need to supply isolated outlying areas which could not easily be connected to a main.

The process of plant concentration was accomplished by taking those steps which under a fragmented system of ownership were most difficult to achieve, rationalisation of the coke market and the markets for other by-products, centralisation of gas making at the larger plants nearest to the points of cheap coal supply and the laying down of new distribution and transmission mains, to connect those districts which had previously been supplied by separate undertakings.

The industry was thus poised to take best advantage of the boom in the demand for domestic heating which was about to lift it from its stagnation of the 1950s. In many Areas about half-a-dozen large gas works were supplying the bulk of the demand, the various distribution systems had been integrated and high pressure transmission mains were in use over distances of 30 and 40 miles. However, the process of integration and concentration had been carried out against a background of considerable economic difficulty.

In the appearance which the gas industry presented to the outside world, the problems of the 1950s were fairly straightforward. It seemed to be an old-fashioned industry, which was unlikely to be able to compete with electricity. Weak domestic demand combined with an absence of widespread industrial sales only served to confirm this view of the industry's future. The underlying strengths of the fuel, that it was a convenient form of heat, that it was ideal for many industrial processes, that the energy conversion rate was high and that it contributed to cleaner air, were hardly visible to the general public. The Select Committee on Nationalised Industries viewed the industry as one which was trying hard to compete without the advantage of competitive prices.[11]

However, while the Select Committee was prepared to point to uncompetitive prices as the root cause of the gas industry's malaise, the underlying reasons were by no means clear-cut. The price of manufactured gas was determined by three factors, the price of coal, the efficiency of the carbonisation process and the price obtained by the gas industry for the by-products of carbonisation. Only one of these was within the power of the Area Boards to determine and these Boards thought that a great deal had been done by the industry to make carbonisation as efficient as possible. Largely as a result of the schemes of concentration and the elimination of inefficient plant, the thermal yield of both carbonisation and water-gas making had risen from 71 per cent in 1949 to about 77 per cent ten years later. Various efforts had been made to allow the gas industry to control more directly the selling price of its main by-product, coke. Coke Associations had been established between the two wars, the first being the London and Counties Coke Association of 1931. Their objectives were to regulate marketing, quality and price, and their work was continued under public ownership. The desirability of having the coke-producing ovens of the National Coal Board under the Gas Boards' control was also canvassed.[12] But the market for coke did not turn out well for the industry. In the early years, to 1955, there was a situation of chronic shortage, so that supplies to domestic consumers had to be restricted or rationed in two separate periods. But almost as soon as productive capacity for coke output had caught up with the potential demand indicated in the early 1950s, the rapidly increasing use for heating of fuel oils from petroleum refining caused a surplus and an excess of productive capacity.

Thus the Gas Boards, which had conducted a programme of rebuilding carbonisation plant and increasing carbonisation capacity up to 1956, found themselves in the winters of 1956 to 1958 with 5 or 10 per cent of the year's coke production unsold.[13] The surplus coincided with the completion of the Coal Board's programme for modernising and replacing its own coke oven capacity. Six new plants with a capacity of over a million tons per year came into operation during 1954—8; four other modernised plants, completed during the same period and also producing about a million tons per year, pushed coke production by the NCB up from 5·9m. tons in 1947 to 7·2m. tons in 1956. With considerable increases taking place in petroleum refining capacity in Britain, an enormous expansion was taking place in the use of all grades of fuel oil. Inland deliveries increased from 5·4m. tons in 1955 to 17·4m. tons by 1960. Of course not all of this increase affected the traditional market for coke, but, while coke prices had more than doubled between 1950 and 1960, fuel oils had generally gone up by only about 40 per cent and inevitably space heating consumers were moving away from coke use. Finally, to make matters worse, improvements in the techniques of blast furnace operation had considerably reduced the demand for coke from the iron and steel industry.[14]

The upshot of these events was that the Gas Boards were obliged to increase gas prices step by step with the price increases made by the Coal Board. The margin afforded by improvements in efficiency was very small. On some occasions the Boards were able to absorb increases in the price of fuel, but were then forced to raise prices when freight charges went up. Many of the Boards sought to counteract this trend in the delivered price of fuel by increasing their purchases of coke oven gas. Others were able to buy waste gases from refineries. Most of the Boards tried out new processes of a range of types, based both on coal and oil.[15] In spite of these measures, the price charged for gas had to be increased, with the effect that average revenue per therm sold was 13d in 1950, 17·5d in 1955 and 21·3d in 1960.

Nor was cost the only problem connected with coal. During the years when the Gas Boards were trying to consolidate and expand carbonisation plant as the source of base load supply (1949—56), coal of most types was in short supply. The shortage appeared to affect the gas industry particularly, so that from 1950 to 1954 the plans made by the industry for supplying gas from carbonisation were curtailed, year after year, at the request of the Minister of Fuel and Power. This meant that the amount of coal gas made each year did not rise either as fast as the Area Boards planned, or by as much as they had expanded carbonisation plant to produce it. The peak year for coal gas production was 1955/6, when restrictions on carbonisation were at last relaxed and 2,084m. therms were made.

In order for coal to be suitable for carbonisation, it must contain enough volatile hydrocarbons to produce a good yield of gas. The carbonisation process requires that the coal be heated to 1,000°C. in a closed container, at which temperature about 25 per cent of the thermal value of a coking coal will be given off as gas. Anyone who has seen good quality coal being burnt on an open fire will recall that unburnt lumps on top of the fire frequently hiss and emit a plume of gas or smoke, which will burn if ignited. This is an illustration of the carbonisation process. However, the coals used have to be of that quality which will give a good yield of gas and which will leave behind a solid residue, which is in fact the coke. If there is an insufficient yield of gas, or if the coal leaves a residue which disintegrates instead of 'caking', then the economics of the process are upset.

The highly volatile quality of coal needed originally came from the coalfields of Northumberland and Durham, and by the 1940s it could be found in most of the Coal Board's eight Divisions. The problem was that it was in short supply, since it was required for a wide variety of applications. The Gas Council had occasion to comment more than once in the early 1950s on the problems and frustration of short supplies. The quality of coal supplied was sometimes too low; ash contents of 14 to 18 per cent were regarded as unacceptable. The North Thames Gas Board curtailed the extension of their carbonisation plants because of the shortage of suitable coal.

The traditional answer to shortages of coking coals had been water and carburetted water gas. The processes depend on the action of steam or steam and gas oil on a bed of red-hot coke. The disadvantage in the early 1950s was that it used much needed stocks of coke at a time when the coke market was fairly strong. As one result of the shortage of carbonising coals, Area Boards were unable to increase their supplies of coke and thus were reluctant to develop coke markets, a factor which only increased the demand for oil as a heating fuel. Although the Boards expanded their water gas plant throughout the 1950s, so that water gas as a proportion of total supply reached 15 per cent in 1954/5, the quantity produced declined sharply after that year. From 1955 onwards the Area Boards turned increasingly to new processes and to buying gas from outside the industry.

The traditional source of bought gases was the coke ovens run by the iron and steel industry and the coal industry. The steel industry used coke ovens both for coke production as an ingredient in steel making and for gas supply, to heat the furnaces, while the coal industry merely carbonised coal for the coke market, having only a few ancillary uses for the gas. As a result, the coal industry was the more reliable source of supply.

Coke oven gas was extremely cheap. The Select Committee was told that the average price paid to the coal board and the steel industry was about 6·5d per therm in 1960.[16] The gas required purifying but this added less than 0·5d to the cost. Table 5.6 shows the importance of coke oven gas as

Table 5.6   *Coke Oven Gas Production, 1950—61*

	NCB (m. therms)	Total coke oven gas (m. therms)	Total gas bought and made (m. therms)	Coke oven (%)
1950/1	181	320	2,670	12·1
1955/6	222	410	2,902	14·2
1960/1	266	509	2,890	17·6

Source: Select Committee, *Report on Gas Industry,* op. cit., and Gas Council, *Annual Reports.*

a source of new supply between 1950 and 1960. Of the total increase in supply of 220m. therms, 189m. therms came from coke ovens. In some Areas it became the predominant source of supply (Table 5.7); it was not available in all Areas, only where the coal industry located coke ovens (near the pit-heads) or where there were steel works.

Table 5.7   *Coke Oven Gas in Three Areas*

	Wales		Northern		East Midlands	
	m. therms	*% of total gas available*	*m. therms*	*% of total gas available*	*m. therms*	*% of total gas available*
1950/1	39	49	83	53	131	48
1960/1	95	81	120	66	199	56

Sources: Gas Council and Area Board *Annual Reports* 1950/1 and 1960/1.

The condition of the coke market made coke oven supplies uncertain in the long term. The other source of bought gases, particularly for the Boards which did not have access to coke ovens, was the tail gas from refineries. The North Western Board pioneered the use of refinery gas in 1950, but significant supplies had to await the construction of more refining capacity during the 1950s. By 1960 the North Thames was taking 62m. therms annually, most of it reformed at Romford, the Southern received 30m. therms from Fawley and the North Western 20m. therms from refineries near Liverpool and Manchester. But in 1960 these sources formed only 5—15 per cent of supply for those Boards, and refinery gas was still less than 4 per cent of national supplies.

RESEARCH

In addition to the measures reviewed above, research and technical development were used by the industry to develop new feedstocks, reduce the dependence on carbonisation and thus bring down the cost of gas. Research in this direction had actually begun before the war.

When the industry became nationalised in 1949, the Gas Council was made responsible for the co-ordination of a research programme. Its duties were to consult the Minister of Power every year on the composition of the programme and to arrange for the projects to be carried out. It was understood from the start that any of the bodies in the industry's federal structure could be charged with the conduct of research. Thus the Area Gas Boards received a mandate to participate in the programme, which was not the special preserve of the Council. The arrangements reflected a characteristic of the industry before nationalisation, in that research was conducted both by individual gas undertakings and co-operatively through institutions which represented the industry. The Institution of Gas Engineers (IGE) had founded a Research Fellowship at Leeds University in 1907 and from this beginning had arisen an increasing amount of work with the University. From the Leeds programme had sprung the Gas Research Board, located at Poole, in 1944, where pilot plant studies of pressure gasification and methane production were started under Dr Dent. The role of the larger gas companies based upon London and the municipal gas organisations of Manchester and Birmingham has already been mentioned.

For the direction of research the Gas Council appointed a Research Committee. Its composition is interesting. First there were to be the Directors of the Gas Council's Research Stations, although the stations had not at the time (1950) been established. The scientific world was represented by three Professors of Chemistry, the Livesey Professor of Coal Gas at Leeds and the President of the IGE. Finally there were five Gas Council members, the Chairman, his Deputy and three others. In 1951 it was decided to include the Area Chairmen of the Boards in whose districts the Research stations were to be set, an arrangement which reflected the administrative convenience of having the research stations managed by the local Area Boards.

There was as a result balance of the research and scientifically oriented members, research directors and professors, against practical 'gas men'. This was because the Gas Council was composed of the Chairman, his Deputy and the twelve Area Board Chairmen; the latter were required by the Gas Act to be people who had experience and ability in gas supply. Thus it came about that eight of the Research Committee members who came from the Council or from the Boards where Research Stations were established had qualifications in gas engineering.

It would be hard to say where the actual choice of research projects was determined, but it is tempting to suggest that the composition of the Research Committee would have ensured that any excessive enthusiasm from the 'research' members for a gas process which did not promise to produce cheap gas would be damped by the 'Council' members, who had a responsibility to ensure that their Boards did not make losses.

During 1951 and 1952 the Gas Council determined on three research stations for the industry. Up to that time work had been supported at the Gas Research Board as before, at the two former laboratories of the Gas Light and Coke Company and at Nechells laboratories, formerly of the Birmingham municipal undertaking. The Utilisation Station was set up at Watson House; Watson House Centre was established to provide a service to all Area Boards on the development, testing and approval of new types of gas appliance, including prototype manufacture, and the Research Centre formed an adjunct to these activities. The London Research Station was established at Fulham to work mainly on new methods of making gas in low pressure processes. The Midlands Research Station was formed mainly with personnel from the Gas Research Board at Poole, including Dr Dent and his team. They moved first to temporary accommodation at Nechells, Birmingham and then in 1954 to Solihull, in the West Midland Board's area.

Utilisation is a subject in its own right and will not be dealt with here, but the Watson House work undoubtedly made a large contribution to consumer acceptance of gas as a major heating fuel in the 1960s. Watson House laid down standards of gas quality and investigated the effects of different qualities of gas upon the performance of appliances. Its work led to the understanding that town gas was essentially a mixture of three components, hydrogen, an enriching gas and a ballast, and that changing the proportions could provide a wide range of interchangeable gases.

Research on new gas processes was directed at total gasification of coal or oil.[17] The first major objective was to convert the whole of the feedstock into gas, 'complete gasification', and thus to eliminate residues. Then the output of gas from the process would have a thermal value which approached the thermal value of the fuel input, instead of being only 25 per cent, as in carbonisation. The second objective was to find a process which would be capable of development in such a way as to reduce the industry's total costs per therm in making gas. It was realised that this aim might be fulfilled not only by complete gasification of coal, but also possibly by finding an alternative feedstock for which capital, labour and material costs might be cheaper than those for carbonisation and also cheaper than other coal-based processes.

It was not only at the research stations that new processes were developed. The South Eastern Gas Board had taken over the laboratories of the South Metropolitan Gas Company, in which a method of gasifying heavy fuel oil at low pressure in steam over a catalyst of lime was being developed. A pilot plant was completed in 1951 and the process was given the name Segas. The first plant came into operation in Sydenham in February 1953; the Power Gas Corporation which installed the plant was given a licence to manufacture it for sale elsewhere.

A year later the West Midlands Gas Board installed a small plant for the gasification of heavy fuel oil based upon a similar catalytic process, licensed from continental Europe and called Onia-Gegi. They had come upon the process as a result of experiments to convert a carburetted water gas plant to convert heavy fuel oil as well as gas oil. The North Thames Gas Board was not far behind these two others and by 31 March 1954 had completed plans to install two units each of the Segas and Onia-Gegi plant on an experimental basis. At the same time the North Thames Board ordered a plant for an Italian process known as Gaz Integrale.

The South Western Gas Board was also experimenting with oil-based processes. It had inherited plants for making carbon-black at Gloucester and Cheltenham, which had a large output of oil gas as a joint product. Through co-operative research with the plant construction company they managed to improve this, the Jones gas process, and extended their plant at Gloucester to incorporate the advance. The Jones process came from the Pacific coast of America; in 1954 the South West Board licensed a second American process, the Hall process, to gasify heavy fuel oils. Their fourth experimental plant was another of the Gaz Integrale process similar to that of the North Thames. The North Western Board developed its own low pressure catalytic process known as HTR. It was made available rather later than the others, but became widely used for peak load during the mid-1960s.

In July 1954 the North Eastern Gas Board started up a plant at York to produce 1 million cubic feet per day of oil gas from the Segas process. They had licensed the process from the South East Board in order to gain operating experience of catalytic oil cracking plant. In continuous operation its capacity was about 800,000 therms per year, which was a commercial size output. Meanwhile the Gas Council began to exercise its co-ordinating role and the suggestion was made during 1954/5 that each of the twelve Area Boards should construct a plant based upon the Segas process or the Onia-Gegi process, in order that experimental data and operational experience should be built up quickly from a variety of sources. By 1958 twenty-five oil gasification plants were in operation and a further fourteen were under construction. Their total capactiy was to be 120m. cubic feet per day; this should be compared with installed capacity for 1957/8 of approximately 1,500m. cubic feet per day for coal gas and 900m. cubic feet per day for water gas. Four Area Boards, the Scottish, North Western, Northern and Wales Boards, did not take part in the construction programme for catalytic oil plants at this early stage.[18] The most ambitious of these low pressure catalytic oil plants was constructed by the South East Board between 1956 and 1958 at the Isle of Grain. The Segas plant, at low pressure, was built alongside a new high pressure process developed by Shell; the whole installation was to have output of 74m. cubic feet per day. The Micro-Simplex process, developed outside the industry, was tried out by some Boards. The Wales Gas Board developed its own catalytic oil plant.

The significance of these experiments in low-pressure oil gasification is that they gave a number of Area Boards the experience of operating a catalytic process which could be used either for gasifying heavy fuel oils or for reforming refinery gas. The amount of gas they produced was still only 132m. therms annually, 4 per cent of supplies, in 1962/3. The low pressure processes were also cyclical; a process run of the plant, to produce the necessary conditions for gas making, had to be alternated with a gas producing run. However, by providing experience of oil plant, the experiments gave the Area Boards a basis from which to judge the technical merits and commercial prospects of the high pressure processes when they became available.

The main programme of research into new methods at the Gas Council's laboratories showed an early bias towards coal gasification. The Research Committee did not seek at an early date to re-direct the work which the research stations were pursuing at the time of nationalisation. The London Research Station at the outset was closely geared to the practical needs of daily gas production, and its programme included investigation of the means of removing by-products and impurities, the improvement of carbonisation plant, as well as one project to make gas from oil and steam.

The main work at Beckenham had been on the ultilisation of gas, and a team working on industrial utilisation was soon built up in the Midlands. The Midlands Research Station centred its work around experimental developments which had been originated by Dr Dent, who became Director of the Station in 1951.

Dr Dent's work at Leeds for the Joint Research Committee of the gas industry had led him to discover in 1937 that gasifying coal at high pressure in steam and oxygen led to the production of methane by the direct action of hydrogen on the coal. He had also developed a way of producing synthetic natural gas by the use of a catalyst. Both discoveries were to figure prominently in the work of the research stations during the late 1950s and 1960s, but more immediately the object of the Gas Council's programme was the complete gasification of coal in a Lurgi plant.

The Lurgi process of coal gasification was invented in Germany. In order to provide a pilot scale test of Dr Dent's discovery of coal hydrogenation, the Gas Research Board had ordered a pilot type Lurgi gasifier, but it was not installed until after the transfer to Birmingham. In the meantime the research team, with representatives from two Area boards and the National Coal Board, went to Holten in Germany where samples of British coals were gasified in the Lurgi company's pressure gasification pilot plant. The object was to discover whether non-caking and weakly caking coals from Britain, which were not acceptable for carbonisation, could be gasified successfully. Not having had a Lurgi gasifier at work in this country, the Gas Research Board had been unable to find out previously whether the process was suitable for British coals, which are of different composition from German hard coals and lignite. The tests which were conducted in 1952 showed that a gas yield of 220 to 240 therms per ton of coal could be obtained.

This compared very favourably with carbonisation. The total thermal content of a ton of carbonisation coal is about 310 therms and the traditional gas-making methods were able to extract little more than 80 therms of this as gas. The Lurgi process had a net thermal gas output estimated by Dent to be about 190 therms per ton of coal under commercial conditions, because the heat input in the form of steam and oxygen had to be subtracted. Even so, Lurgi promised a way of increasing gas output and freeing the gas industry from the coke market.

The Gas Research Board's Lurgi pressure gasification pilot plant had been bought in order to test Dent's ideas about the production of methane from coal. It was commonly supposed that methane production from coal was occasioned by the release of gaseous hydrocarbons contained in the coal (methane is a gas formed of hydrogen and carbon), or else that it occurred from the interaction of carbon monoxide and hydrogen. Dent's observations at Leeds had suggested that it was the direct action of hydrogen upon the coal and upon the carbon substance of partially decomposed coal when steam was blown through it which produced up to one-third of the normal methane output from coal gasification. The experiments at Holten tended to confirm his discovery. Since the Lurgi gas produced tended to be 'lean', that is, with a calorific value around 300 Btu/cu. ft. instead of the 475 Btu/cu. ft. which was more normal for town gas, it had to be enriched. One route to enrichment was by methane synthesis, for which Dent had also developed a process at Leeds and tested it in a pilot plant.

But the Birmingham Research Station was concerned with the economics of gas making, as well as the chemistry. Basically the Lurgi process involves introducing coal at the top of a closed cylindrical pressure vessel and blowing high pressure steam and oxygen through the coal from the bottom at temperatures of about 1,200—1,300°C. If Dent's observation of the hydrogen to coal reaction were correct, then the Lurgi generator might be adaptable to producing extra methane from the coal or the coke carbon, leading directly to a gas of acceptable calorific value. The attempt to raise the methane output was one of the main lines of experimental work at the Nechells Laboratories and later at Solihull. The other major gasification work by the Birmingham Research Station was concerned with the direct production of methane from coal, in processes where powdered coal was used, and in the development of a fluidised bed gasifier.

Work on the complete gasification of coal was only at the pilot plant stage in 1953, and results on a commercial scale could not really be expected before the end of the decade. In the meantime plans for large-scale gas production by the standard Lurgi process, as tested at Holten, were being considered. A joint committee of the National Coal Board and Gas Council was formed to consider large-scale coal gasification in 1952; the West Midlands Gas Board and Scottish Gas Board each made proposals for a Lurgi plant, the sites finally settled upon being at Coleshill, east of Birmingham and at Westfield in Fife.

When the results of the tests at Holten appeared favourable to large-scale Lurgi manufacture, and two Area Boards were ready to go ahead with plant construction, the Gas Council set up a study group to consider whether there existed a good case for a national grid. Their general conclusions were that high pressure coal gasification at the coal-fields, oil gasification processes and methane reforming were all likely to have operating economies which would make a grid advantageous. In a detailed study the group estimated that a Midland Lurgi plant of 109m. cubic feet per day and an oil gasification plant of unspecified size at Southampton could together deliver gas to the Area Boards through a grid at about 10d per therm.

However, it was at the North Thames Gas Board that work had begun which eventually made grid construction practicable. During 1955 the Board had made contact with an American company (in fact a joint subsidiary of Continental Oil and Union Stockyard of Chicago, thus named Constock) to discuss the prospect of importing methane. By 1957 plans had been agreed to import a trial load of natural gas (methane) liquefied at —260°F, and by 1961 a full-scale operation was planned to supply over 300m. therms per year to seven Area Boards through a grid pipeline. Methane gas, the main constituent of natural gas, is a compound of carbon and hydrogen which has the high calorific value of 1,018 Btu/cu. ft. Methane delivered by pipeline made a grid economic, even though the gas was unsuitable at the time for direct distribution to consumers.[19]

According to Sir Henry Jones, Chairman of the Gas Council, it was in 1955 that the industry turned its thoughts away from expansion mainly based on coal and began to look seriously at other sources of gas production. It will be remembered that the Segas and Onia-Gegi programme was promoted in that year. The supply of carbonisation coal was still well below requirements and overall forecasting predicted an energy gap for Britain over the next five years. Although coal-based research was to continue for a number of years, it no longer had priority.

The Annual Report for 1954/5 announced that a programme of work had been started on producing gas by the interaction of highly superheated steam with petroleum oils. The North Thames Gas Board was reported to be constructing a pilot plant to test this process in 1957. The availability and lower price of fuel oils made oil processes more attractive than coal-based ones. The programme of work at the Midlands Research Station, which had scarcely touched on the use of oil during the early 1950s, was becoming increasingly biased towards oil by 1956.

The years 1954 to 1957 at the Research Station were very active ones. New pilot plants for testing processes were being constructed, partly because of the move from Nechells to Solihull, and considerable progress was made on the complete gasification of coal and oil. For a short period oil gasification work was running parallel to coal gasification, with a good deal of cross-fertilisation between the two streams of development. In a very interesting way the evolution of successful base-load oil plant benefitted considerably from the early work done on coal; one of the main oil process developments was achieved through the use of oil in a gasification plant originally designed for use on coal.

The gasification processes for coal which were known in the immediate postwar period, such as the Lurgi generator, the manufacture of producer gas or even the use of coke to make water gas, all had the disadvantage that they produced a lean gas. The reason for this was that the constituents of the coal were converted for the most part into gases of low calorific value, such as hydrogen and carbon monoxide, or into inert gas, such as nitrogen. Too little of the coal was converted to gaseous hydrocarbons, compounds of carbon and hydrogen such as methane (CH_4). The chemical route to the creation of richer gases was to cause hydrogen to react with the carbon in the coal, a process called hydrogenation. Hydrogenation of coal to produce liquid hydrocarbons, such as motor and aviation spirit, had been developed by the German company IG Farben and by ICI in Britain between the wars. Dent, in his work on the gaseous hydrogenation of coal at Poole, had constructed a pilot plant using the technique of blowing a hydrogen-rich gas through a fluidised bed of powdered coal.

When work started on producing gaseous hydrocarbons from oil, the team used the same technique, but supplied hydrogen-rich gas and oil to the bottom of a fluidised bed of coke. The process was conducted under pressures of 20 to 50 atmospheres, with the oil molecules breaking down and receiving hydrogen to form saturated gaseous hydrocarbons. The laboratory-scale experiments on this oil hydrogenation process went so well that it seemed possible to make much quicker progress on the project for hydrogenating coal by building a commercial scale demonstration plant using an oil feedstock. Accordingly, a plant for the hydrogenation of oil was planned in 1957 at 7·5m. cubic feet per day. Design and chemical engineering problems which were common to both coal and oil could be studied by using a commercial-scale plant, and the conversion to coal hydrogenation would be expected to follow from further work. The oil plant was to be erected at Partington in the area of the North Western Gas Board, and to assist with process development a large scale pilot plant, for 1 million cubic feet per day, was built at Solihull at the same time.

The pilot plant for oil hydrogenation was not producing the desired results by 1958 and the Partington demonstration plant was delayed. Pilot plant tests showed that the process using a fluidised bed might be very much more expensive than previously calculated. In 1959 the Partington scheme was put into abeyance, but only in order that continued tests might be carried out on the pilot plant. It was three years later, during this second stage of the development work for the Partington coal hydrogenating plant that the breakthrough in oil processes came. In the meantime the Midland Research Station was ready to go ahead in 1959 with a demonstration plant for the conversion of LDF to methane under pressure in an atmosphere of steam. The process used a catalyst for conversion and was based on earlier work by Dent at Poole. It became known as the Catalytic Rich Gas process (CRG).

In the meantime projects on coal gasification, the Lurgi slagging gasifier, the deep-bed Lurgi plant and the fluidised bed coal hydrogenator continued at the Midland Research Station and were approaching the pilot plant stage. The slagging gasifier was an adaptation of the Lurgi process which, by allowing temperatures to develop at which the coal residue became a slag, reduced the consumption of steam and thus improved the economics of operation. Another experiment with the Lurgi process was the deepening of the coal bed through which the steam and oxygen were blown, the object being to increase the amount of methane production by hydrogenating the coal at the lower levels where the right conditions for the formation of gaseous hydrocarbons existed. The fluidised bed coal hydrogenator was really a three-stage coal gasification process. In the first stage the coal was prepared for hydrogenation by a partial distillation yielding liquid hydrocarbon by-products; the second stage provided the hydrogenation of most of the coal, and in a final stage the residual coal 'char' was gasified in steam to provide the hydrogenating gas.

Two other processes, both tried out by the North Thames Gas Board, should be mentioned briefly. The first was a plant to produce a lean gas from oil feedstock at atmospheric pressures by the reaction with superheated steam. A fairly large test plant, of 1 million cubic feet per day, was built at Stratford, but after a year of testing it was decided in 1959 that the output was uneconomic. The other project was again a process from Germany, the Otto-Rummel slag bath gas generator. Using low grade coal and blowing steam through the coal over a molten bath of slag waste, the generator was not unlike a steam-coke plant and it produced lean water gas. It had been developed for German brown coals and was found to be in need of modification when tried out at an experimental plant at Bromley in 1961/2.

In 1961 the first commercial-scale Lurgi plant in Britain was coming into use at Westfield, Fife. designed for an output of 30m. cubic feet per day, the plant produced a lean gas enriched by butane from Grangemouth refinery. At Coleshill the Lurgi plant planned by the West Midlands had been delayed by planning permission, and eventually started producing in 1963.

DECISIONS ABOUT SUPPLY

In 1960, despite the determined efforts to find an alternative feedstock to coal, the industry was still largely dependent upon it. Over 90 per cent of the gas supplies available were still produced from coal sources, compared to 98 per cent ten years earlier (Table 5.8). What had happened in the interim was that carbonisation as a source of supply had been exchanged for bought gases, mostly from coke ovens.

Table 5.8 *Gas Made and Gas Bought, 1950—61 (m. therms)*

	1950/1	*1955/6*	*1960/1*
Coal gas	1,889	2,085	1,706
Water gas	395	367	416
Producer, oil and other gases	52	31	90
Total gas made	2,336	2,483	2,212
Gas bought	326	419	678
(Coke ovens)	(320)	(410)	(509)
Total gas available	2,662	2,902	2,890
Coal based gas	2,604	2,862	2,631

Source: Gas Council, *Annual Reports*, 1956—62.

The wide-ranging programme of research and technical development had not led to the adoption of any new processes or new feedstocks on a major scale. The Segas and Onia-Gegi processes for oil gasification, which most Boards had taken up, were still only present as a minor intrusion and contributed output in the region of 50m. therms per year. Refinery waste gases and liquefied petroleum gas were adding some 170m. therms per year. The most important new source of supply in prospect was from the

North Thames Gas Board's project to import methane. By 1964 this source was to be supplying over 300m. therms per year.

The explanation may be found in demand conditions. Although the upturn had occurred, it was not yet marked and bought supplies of gas could be expected to increase. Indeed, when sales are examined at the level of the individual Boards, much of the reason for holding back investment in new types of plant becomes apparent.

As Table 5.9 shows, half the Boards were experiencing virtually no growth of demand and thus were not seeking to expand capacity. Of the other half, the Wales and East Midland Boards had access to ample supplies of coke oven gas, as had the Northern. The West Midland and the Eastern Boards did expand their gas-making capacity for demand reasons. However, in general the policy of the Area Boards was to wait until a process became available which would make large savings on cost, rather than investing heavily in innovatory plant of which the economics were unproven. This attitude was perhaps not fully understood at a time when, in other fields, such as nuclear power and aerospace, expensive projects were going ahead based on the hope, rather than the knowledge, that they would produce economic returns.[20]

Table 5.9   *Increases in Demand, 1950/1 to 1960/1, Twelve Area Boards*

Area Board	1950/1 (m. therms)	1960/1 (m. therms)	Area Board	1950/1 (m. therms)	1960/1 (m. therms)
Wales	71	105	South Eastern	276	290
East Midland	248	326	North Western	338	341
West Midland	297	345	North Eastern	144	143
Northern	146	168	Southern	114	111
Eastern	126	141	South Western	117	109
North Thames	380	405	Scottish	205	182

Source: Gas Council, *Annual Reports,* 1951/2 and 1960/1. Tables of 'Gas Sold and Used' in Appendix 'Area Board Statistics'.

The Boards' reasons for their policies up to 1960/1 were economic reasons and not in any way a reflection of narrow-mindedness, excessive caution or a lack of boldness in experimentation. Many different schemes and processes were under active consideration, but finding the one which offered positive benefits to the industry was a matter of being sure, not merely optimistic, about costs, by testing the performance of a process as thoroughly as possible. There was a very wide range of possibilities being explored, of which only two or three survived more than a few years' investigation.

The coal-based processes, such as Gaz Integrale, Rochdale and Rummel, were never able to offer promising levels of costs in demonstration plants and were not explored on a commercial scale. The Hall, Jones, Shell and Texaco processes were based upon oil and predictions of their full-scale operating costs suggested that the total cost of production would be 2d or 3d per therm below that of carbonisation. The Shell process, in particular, was installed at Isle of Grain on the expectation of production at 9·5d per therm when carbonisation plant was operating at about 12—15d per therm. However, special conditions of siting near a refinery applied to this calculation. The oil processes most widely used (all the Boards had installed one of them by 1962/3) were the catalytic reforming of oil of various grades by Segas or Onia-Gegi methods. However, they were cyclic rather than continuous methods, requiring a process run to alternate with the gas-making run. Costs varied considerably with the price of the feedstock and with the load-factor on the plant. They were low on capital cost but fairly expensive on feedstocks and most Boards built them to replace water-gas plant and to supplement carbonisation as a peak load process. Oil feedstocks were still more expensive than coal per therm of output. Thus, while the Boards were able to sell the by-products of carbonisation, cyclic oil-based processes were unlikely to replace the carbonisation plants for base load working. However, by 1961, the price of gas from cyclic plants reached a point where it was very similar to that from carbonisation, at about 10d to 12d per therm.

The Lurgi process was dependent on a site close to adequate supplies of cheap coal and costs were incurred for transmission. The Westfield plant was expected to produce gas after enrichment at 10·33d per therm. Coleshill was estimated at 10·93d per therm. Lurgi was, like carbonisation, dependent upon the price trend of coal for its cheapness.

Nevertheless, the West Midlands and the Scottish Boards went ahead with large Lurgi plants. For the West Midlands it was a question of gas demand. It needed extra capacity to satisfy industrial customers in the Area. For the Scottish Board the attraction was being able to use cheap coal from an open-cast site at Westfield. The further considerations were that the Coal Board was prepared to offer a special price for the Westfield plant's coal supplies; the plant was of the nature of a demonstration installation.

In 1957 the Gas Council set up a group to study the prospects of supplying all Area Boards through a grid based on Lurgi. One of the Group's studies (the Desford Study) suggested that the standard Lurgi process could be brought down to about 9d per therm, and the Coal Board suggested a delivered cost to Area Boards of 8·5d per therm. However, when the Gas Council proposed to Area Boards that an integrated production scheme be started, their replies were either that they could already see their way to procuring extra supplies, from coke ovens for instance, or else that they were not able to accept that the gas would be cheap enough.[21]

The scheme developed by the North Thames to import liquid methane natural gas was marginally more attractive. It promised to deliver methane to Boards for 7·5d per therm. Reforming for use would make the price up to 8·5d or a little more.[22] The margin for decision was very small, but, from the Boards' point of view, there was more prospect of the natural gas price remaining stable than of coal prices doing so.

GAS FROM OIL, 1962

Early in 1962, ICI announced a new process, the result of research for the production of fertiliser constituents, which produced a lean gas from the steam reforming of petroleum naphtha, the most common form of LDF. The catalyst in the process had actually been invented by Dr Dent in his earlier work on gas processes. The significance of this discovery by ICI was that it provided a cheap source of lean gas; the Gas Boards had sources of enrichment either immediately available or in prospect. One of these was liquid propane gas (LPG), a refinery product, and another was the imported LNG supply which would be arriving in quantity by 1964.

Carbonisation coals were being delivered to the gas boards in 1961 at about 4·5d to 5d per therm of the coal's total heat value. A ton of coking coal contains about 310—20 therms and its pithead price was just over £5 per ton at the time. Inclusive of delivery charges, its price to the Area Board was over 4d per therm for the gas works near to coalfields and about 1d more where transport was over some distance. Lower grade coals which could be used in the Lurgi process were priced at the pithead at between 3·3d and 3·6d per therm.

The range of oils which the Gas Council and the Area Boards were trying to gasify had a wider variation in price. Heavy fuel oil at the refinery, with a calorific value of about 420 therms per ton, could be obtained for about £8 per ton, and with the higher calorific value that gave a cost per therm of about 4·5d. Delivery added about 1d per therm. Waste refinery gases were available at about 6d per therm delivered to the Area Board, provided the distance was fairly short; gas oil used in carburetted water gas plant was 7·8d per therm delivered.

In 1961 the delivered price of coal and the delivered price of oil were edging closer together. Gas Boards which had lower transportation

Table 5.10 *Price Movements of Raw Materials for the Gas Industry, 1949—60 (indices 1957 = 100)*

	1949	1954	1957	1958	1960
Coal delivered	55	77	100	102	104
Gas oil delivered	67	87	100	87	87
Coke oven gas purchased	48	74	100	108	112
Heavy oil feedstock delivered	n.a.	77	100	72	75
Light distillate feedstock delivered	n.a.	n.a.	100	98	91
Average price received for coke	51	69	100	104	109

Source: D. E. Rooke, 'Developments in the Gas Industry', op. cit.

charges to pay for oil products than for coking coals would find the price of oil per therm marginally lower than that of coal. The increased refinery activity which was bringing down the price of oil feedstocks was also providing competition for the traditional by-products, other than coke, of the carbonisation process and this upset the economics of using coal even further. On the other hand the price which the oil companies were able to charge for petroleum naphtha was kept down by the knowledge that imported LNG was shortly to be available at 7·5d per therm.

In 1955 about half a million tons per year of naphtha feedstock was going to chemical companies and other uses, including gas works. By 1960 the total had risen to 2 million tons and in 1965 it was nearly 5·5 million. Interest in the use of naphtha was spread between the oil companies, to whom it was a by-product of refinery cracking of petroleum, the chemical industry, which saw it as a potential source of very cheap hydrogen, and the gas industry, which used it as a feedstock for the cyclical processes of gas making. When the Wilson Committee on Coal Derivatives reported in 1960, the potential of steam naphtha reforming for the production of pure hydrogen was already recognised.[23]

It was a simpler process than the Shell and Texaco partial oxidation of oil and potentially cheaper, because large-scale oxygen plant was not required. ICI's process operated in a manner no more complex than the Segas or Onia-Gegi cyclic reformers, but it was continuous and produced a higher thermal yield. Steam and vapourised naphtha were passed over a catalyst and formed a synthesis gas, which then went through a reaction to form hydrogen and carbon dioxide. When the latter was removed, the product was relatively pure hydrogen. No process run was required, because the heat of reaction was supplied directly from a furnace containing the reaction tubes.

The domestic heating boom took off in 1961 and gas sales began to increase at 4 per cent annually. Within a year of ICI's process being announced, plants for its use were under construction which had a total capacity, with the gas enriched to town gas standard, of 400m. cubic feet per day. This was equal to one-third of the capacity of carbonisation plants remaining in use. The process economics of the ICI steam reformer plus enrichment already promised to be an improvement on carbonisation for base load. The Gas Council's research programme produced two processes which improved it even further by providing cheap methods of enrichment.

The gas recycle hydrogenator (GRH) resulted from Council work at the Midland Research Station on the hydrogenation of oil under pressure. The simplifying of the fluid bed method of hydrogenating oils produced a way of using hydrogen and naphtha feedstocks together to enrich a lean gas. The pilot plant stage was demonstrated in March 1962 and the process was complementary to the steam reformer, because it required a cheap source of hydrogen. Naphtha and hydrogen were supplied under pressure to a reaction vessel in which the light distillate was hydrogenated to gaseous hydrocarbons which could be used to raise the hydrogen rich gas to town gas standards.[24] This process was exothermic (i.e. gave out heat), and was made self-sustaining by the gases recycled inside the vessel. This produced a high efficiency of conversion of the reactants into gas. With naphtha at a delivered price of 5·5d per therm, cheap hydrogen from the ICI steam reforming process and a high conversion ratio, the ICI/GRH combination was immediately acceptable to Area Boards as a basic process. As well as low material costs, it had negligible labour costs and the capital cost per unit of output was a fraction of that for carbonisation plant.

The second process was the CRG process, which had already been demonstrated at the Midland Research Station in the late 1950s. It was even more satisfying in its simplicity, since it used steam and naphtha in a simple reaction vessel containing a catalyst. Working at much lower temperatures (300—500°C) than were commonly thought necessary for methane synthesis, the CRG process produced a gas of 65 per cent methane, the rest being carbon dioxide and hydrogen, at a temperature of about 450°C and pressure of 25 atmospheres. By using three stages of CRG 'methanation' and removing the carbon dioxide, a gas of 98 per cent methane could be obtained. Although not so obviously important to the industry as a whole at the time, this was an invaluable result, because it allowed for the manufacture of SNG (substitute natural gas — natural gas is almost 100 per cent methane) at a later date, when the whole country was being supplied with North Sea gas. More immediately, the methane rich gas from CRG could be used as a source of enrichment for the lean gas from an ICI reformer.

Although the CRG process had been demonstrated several years earlier than the GRH process, it was not immediately installed in a commercial-scale plant. Both the West Midlands Board and the North Thames were interested in installing it and design studies to investigate the process were carried out in 1959 and in the early 1960s. The first order for a CRG process on a commercial scale was placed by Tokyo Gas in January/February 1965 and was in operation in November of the same year. However, the GRH process was developed more quickly, and the first order for a commercial scale GRH plant, providing enrichment to a steam reformer's output, was placed by the South Western Gas Board in late 1962 or early 1963.[25]

Adoption of the processes was stimulated by the growth of demand, just as it had been for the ICI process. With LDF prices remaining fairly stable at under 6d per delivered therm of heat, the high thermal efficiency (of about 80 per cent) gave the processes very low running costs. A bigger saving still was provided by reduced capital costs. Carbonisation plant was costing about £76 per therm of output per day in the middle 1960s. GRH or CRG plant combined with the ICI process were in the region of £10 to £15 per therm. The CRG process alone had a capital cost of £7 per therm of capacity. Run at 70 per cent load factor, the interest charges on ICI/GRH or ICI/CRG plant represented 1d to 1·2d on each therm, compared to 6·5d for carbonisation. The heavier labour, maintenance and repair charges of the latter favoured the oil-based processes even further. The overall output cost was possibly as low as 7·5d.

Before the South Western's plant at Avonmouth had come on stream, the West Midlands Gas Board decided to order an ICI/GRH plant at 50m. cubic feet per day and an order was received from Hanover in Germany for a plant of half that size.

By the middle of 1964 fourteen units of the ICI/GRH type had been oredered by Area Boards and five by customers abroad. A year later the CRG and GRH capacity on order was approaching 800m. cubic feet per day, equivalent to all the new plant installed from 1953 to 1961.[26] Table 5.11 shows the capacity of the various types of gas plant throughout the period 1955—75.

Table 5.11 *Plant Capacity, 1955—75 (million ft.^{3}/day)*

	1955/6	1960/1	1965/6	1970/1	1974/5
Coal carbonisation	1,532	1,341	970	96	0.7
Lurgi	nil	15	84	42	nil
Oil processes: cyclic	...[b]	167	521	794 ⎱	
Oil processes: continuous	nil	...[c]	1,231	4,793 ⎰	1,648
Other processes[c]	965	976	971	267	43
Total capacity	2,497	2,499	3,777	5,992	1,691

Source: Gas Council, *Annual Reports.*
Notes: [a] Mostly water gas.
[b] About 4m. ft.^{3}/day in operation at West Midland and South Eastern plants. Included in 'Other processes'.
[c] Experimental continuous process at South Western Board. Included under 'Other processes'.

There was no doubt about the massive impact of the continuous oil processes. The table shows how coal carbonisation plant, which had been declining since its peak of the mid-1950s at an annual net rate of 40m. cubic feet per day, suddenly dropped sharply in 1965, because old plant was scrapped and no new plant commissioned. Between 1965 and 1975 all the remaining coal plant was scrapped.

Cyclic processes also continued to be popular. The development of the domestic heating market had given the gas industry its own peak load problem, like that of the electricity industry. Cyclic processes had the advantage that they could use a wider range of feedstocks than the continuous processes.

Tables 5.11 and 5.12 reveal the progress of the oil revolution. Continuous processes for the production of gas from oil outstripped coal plant sometime during 1965 in terms of capacity, only three years after the announcement of the ICI process. After that the amount of new capacity installed averaged over 1,000m. ft.^{3}/day per year for three years up to 1968/9. At its peak, towards the end of 1969, continuous oil plant alone reached

Table 5.12   *Gas Available, 1955—75 (manufactured and purchased supplies, million therms)*

	1955/6	*1960/1*	*1965/6*	*1968/9*	*1970/1*	*1974/5*
Coal gas	2,085	1,706	1,269	665	238	
Water gas[a]	367	416	386	92	2	n.a.
Lurgi gas	—	4	69	52	30	
Oil gas[b]	31	85	692	2,134	1,208	
Total gas made	2,483	2,212	2,416	2,942	1,479	1,266
Gas bought[c]	419	678	1,424	2,063	3,106	
Natural gas[d]	—	—	—	160	2,157	12,426
Total gas available	2,902	2,890	3,840	5,165	6,741	13,692

Sources: Gas Council, *Annual Reports,* 1961/2—1973/4.
Notes: [a] Includes small amounts of other gas after 1961.
　　　　[b] Includes small amounts of other gas before 1965.
　　　　[c] By the mid-1960s the four main sources were coke oven gas, oil refinery gas, liquefied petroleum gas and imported Algerian methane. Each formed approximately, a quarter of supply in 1965/6 by heat content, but natural gas was 80 per cent of bought supplies by 1970/1, and an increasing proportion thereafter.
　　　　[d] Natural gas for direct supply to converted consumers.

5,000m. ft.^{3}/day, which was almost double the capacity needed by the industry in all types of plant up to 1961. Cyclic oil processing plants also experienced a boost in 1967 and 1968, reaching 1,000m. ft.^{3}/day.

One interesting feature is that it was supplies of purchased gas which catered for increased demand up to 1965/6, rather than expansion of manufactured gas capacity. The amount of gas manufactured in 1965 was no higher than ten years earlier, although the total supplies available had increased by 30 per cent. Supplies of refinery gas, LPG and LNG, wholly account for the upturn in the amount of gas available up to 1965.[27] Nor was coal gas as quick to disappear as might have been expected. Carbonisation gas and water gas (based on coke) still formed nearly 70 per cent of manufactured gases in 1965/6; the total capacity of oil plant, cyclic and continuous, was already greater than that of coal gas. Both the need of the mining industry to sell its coal and that of the coke market for a continued supply played some part in this, but much of the carbonisation plant still in use in the mid-1960s was of recent date or had been extensively refurbished in the 1950s, so that the industry was understandably reluctant to abandon it without extracting as much use as possible.

The year in which oil gas accounted for the highest proportion of gas manufactured was 1968/9. Over 2,000m. therms were manufactured by the two major types of oil process, cyclical and continuous. Cyclical processes did not contribute as much of the total in proportion to installed capacity as the continuous processes which met the base load. Water gas and coal production had shrunk to 760m. therms combined, and oil processes thus contributed 71 per cent of manufactured gas. Bought gases had by this time exceeded 2,000m. therms per year as well, and manufacture from oil met only 41 per cent of gas supplies available. The oil total was not as much in absolute terms as the total of coal and water gas in 1955/6; it was very much less significant as a proportion of total supply.

Oil-based manufacture thus never reached the same position of dominance which coal had held up to the mid-1950s. One reason for this was that the industry had developed such a variety of sources of supply in the late 1950s and early 1960s. The other reason was the discovery of North Sea gas in 1965. Without this latter source, bought gases, ready made except for enrichment or reforming, would probably not have risen much beyond 1,500m. therms per year, and oil processes would have been a dominant source of supply.

The Gas Council had carried out a comprehensive search for natural gas in the early years of public ownership. Dr Lees of the Anglo-Iranian Oil Company prepared a report on the geological prospects in 1952 and a subsidiary of the company was engaged to carry out field surveys from 1953 to 1958. Very little gas was found after five years' search and the expenditure of about £1m. Although a limited amount of work continued up to 1961, it was only when a large field of gas was found in Holland in 1962 that speculation about the North Sea as a source of gas turned into determined exploration. After a survey, the Council joined an American company, Amoco, in drilling for gas in the North Sea. During 1965 and 1966 a considerable number of finds were made; many of them turned out to have commercial quantities of gas. Most of them were in the area between 20 and 50 miles offshore, north of Lowestoft and south of Hull.

Bringing the gas ashore was accomplished very early. Before the end of 1968 supplies were flowing from the North Sea field of West Sole, the first to be discovered. They arrived at Easington, near Hull, and reached the main works of 8 Area Boards through the pipeline originally constructed for LNG from Algeria. In November 1967 the White Paper on fuel policy made it clear that immediate exploitation of the gas was required.[28] This entailed extending the gas grid to all Area Boards and converting the appliances of most consumers over a period of ten years.

Whereas carbonisation plant had been scrapped at an increasing rate in the period up to 1969, after that year oil plant was retired at a rate which far exceeded it. Between 1968 and 1975 capacity providing over 4,000m. cubic feet per day was put out of service. By the mid 1970s the gas industry had accomplished a second revolution in sources of supply. This second revolution was more far-reaching in its effects than the changeover to oil feedstock had been. Manufactured gases accounted for less than one-third of the total gas available by the middle of the 1970s, even though town gas was still used in some quantity. And instead of being primarily manufactured, the town gas supplied (for customers who had not been converted to natural gas) was made up mostly from natural gas and other purchased gases reformed to a suitable standard.

In spite of this, the industry never turned entirely away from research on manufacturing processes. Coal-based projects had mostly been abandoned in the 1960s because of economic considerations. The slagging gasifier, the modified Lurgi plant, was successfully run on a small scale, but the step to a pilot plant was not taken. Fully entrained hydrogenation, to produce methane from raw coal, was demonstrated in 1966.

Oil-based processes were still undergoing development in the period 1965 to 1975. Both the Gas Council processes, the catalytic rich gas process (CRG) and the gas recycle hydrogenator (GRH), had been developed to produce substitute natural gas (SNG) by 1966. The main plants to operate this process on a commercial scale have been built under licence in Japan and the United States. Since the processes can be operated on a wide range of oil feedstocks and produce a gas which is suitable for feeding direct to customers converted to natural gas, CRG and GRH manufacturing plants could be immediately applicable to supply gas to the regions in the British industry. The use of heavy oil and crude oil feedstocks in the manufacture of gas was made possible by a development of the fluidised bed hydrogenator. This was the plant which had originally proved difficult at Partington. By blowing the feedstock through a bed of fluidised coke particles it was found that a gas of 1,000 Btu/cu. ft. could be produced.

CONCLUSION

The gas industry's work in introducing new techniques of manufacture must be praised for its blend of inventive approach with a continued careful appraisal of the economics of new processes. In performing the delicate balancing trick of investigating new processes, undertaking experimental development and even commissioning demonstration plants, without taking the spirit of determined inquiry over the edge into unjustified optimism, the industry's technical personnel were undoubtedly fortunate that the pressure of demand waited until the processes were ready before making itself felt.

Yet it must also be judged that the innovative programme was well managed on its own merits, and not merely because the falling price of naphtha and the rising trend of demand coincided so fortunately. There was a thoroughgoing research knowledge as a basis for process development. The main objectives of the development programme were pursued by means of a number of parallel projects. Monolithic direction of R and D by a single authority was avoided, because of the federal structure of the industry. Good communications were kept up between the personnel responsible for the main programme and the members of the industry in the field dealing with the day-to-day production of gas. At each stage of a project (laboratory demonstration, pilot plant, commercial demonstration), evaluation took place and further work was delayed or cancelled if the results did not support the expectations. In this process of evaluation the Boards were able to be effective critics, because they had their own, more modest, efforts in technical development from which to judge.

It was because of the thoroughness of the groundwork that, when the time came for decisions on new types of plant, the industry was able to invest in new processes without having to trust to guesswork about how they would turn out.

NOTES

[1] Cited as source for Table 5.1.
[2] Gas Council evidence to Select Committee on Nationalised Industries, *Report on the Gas Industry, Session 1960/1* HCP280, HMSO, July 1961.
[3] Stimulated by the passing of the Clean Air Act, 1956.
[4] Select Committee, *Report on Gas Industry*, op. cit., Appendix 44. The comparisons (by the Gas Council) show fairly narrow margins in some cases, and they are based on ranged estimates which are not always easy to interpret. Nevertheless, they establish that gas still had a reasonably competitive position.
[5] When considering new methods of gas manufacture, it is often helpful to think of the town gas as being composed of three essential ingredients:
   (a) A lean gas with a calorific value of about 300 Btu/cu. ft. and containing a high proportion of free hydrogen.
   (b) A rich gas consisting of methane and other hydrocarbons with a calorific value of 900—3,000 Btu/cu. ft.
   (c) An inert or ballast component, consisting of nitrogen and carbon dioxide.
   A satisfactory town gas of traditional type can be obtained by the blending of three such components, which may all be derived from different sources (D. E. Rooke, 'Developments in the Gas Industry', *Institute of Petroleum Review*, February 1963). Cheap sources of supply for these components of town gas were made available by the discoveries and developments noted above.
[6] It was subsequently extended to Exeter, Wales, the north east and Scotland.
[7] However, the team which developed the processes in the Gas Council research laboratories received in 1971 the MacRobert Award, the highest award for engineering development given by Council of Engineering institutions. The team leader was Dr Dent, the Gas Council's Midland Research Station Director, originally of Leeds University and the Gas Research Board.
[8] 450 Btu/cu. ft. is only an approximate average calorific value for town gas. One therm is 100,000 Btu.
[9] *Report of Committee of Inquiry into the Gas Industry*, Cmd 6699, HMSO, 1945.
[10] At vesting day (1 May 1949) the Gas Light and Coke Company had thirteen gas works to supply an area in which total demand was approaching 300m. therms per year. All but one of the company's works were connected to the high pressure distribution grid. This degree of concentration of production and dispersion of distribution was not equalled anywhere else in Britain. The other two large systems were in Birmingham and Manchester, but the West Yorkshire grid acted as an important distribution system. Its major source of supply was bought gases from local coke ovens.
[11] Select Committee on Nationalised Industries, *The Gas Industry*, op. cit.
[12] Consultation machinery between the Gas Council, the Coal Board and the iron and steel industry, to cover all carbonisation activity, was considered in 1952.
[13] Carbonisation capacity increased by about 10 per cent over 1949—55, and gas industry coke sales reached 11m. tons in 1955/6, dropping to 8·5m. tons in 1959/60.
[14] The iron and steel industry also made a considerable amount of its own coke.
[15] Some Boards successfully developed processes for making solid smokeless fuel, which commanded a higher price than coke and thus allowed lower gas prices.
[16] Gas from carbonisation plant cost 12—15d per therm to manufacture in 1960.

[17] 'Carbonisation' is a way of making gas by releasing volatile hydrocarbons, but 'gasification' involves a chemical change in the feedstock. Thus 'complete gasification' means turning the whole of input substance, the feedstock, into gas.

[18] Later, between 1959 and 1964, all four did construct Segas or Onia-Gegi plants.

[19] A lean gas, for instance from Lurgi gasification at about 350 Btu/cu. ft., would need a pipeline capacity nearly twice as great as for natural gas to deliver the same quantity of heat and would need three times the pumping capacity.

[20] The Select Committee of 1961 thought the gas industry's attitude to new process research and development parsimonious and irresolute. However, they had not had the opportunity to see its results.

[21] When the scheme, to produce 120m. cubic feet per day, was being studied, it was found that there was only one coalfield location where enough coal of the right quality was being produced to supply a plant of such a size.

[22] The return on capital for the Lurgi plant would have been only 8 per cent, compared to 15—30 per cent on the methane supply.

[23] *Report of the Committee on Coal Derivatives,* Cmnd 1120, HMSO, 1960.

[24] GRH was later developed to produce a substitute for natural gas (SNG).

[25] CRG used a high-grade catalyst of nickel-alumina. The satisfactory development of the pilot plant and the operation of the catalyst caused some delay in the early 1960s.

[26] Delays arose in completing the orders, because of the load on the plant engineering industry. Thus demand shortages occurred in isolated instances. The GRH process also suffered a curious problem, although very temporarily. The feedstock naphtha used in some early commercial plants was too pure, causing soot to choke the reaction. Pure naphtha was needed for CRG to protect the catalyst, but the GRH process had been developed using naphtha which had sulphur impurities and these actually inhibited the secondary reaction which caused carbon to form.

[27] These gases were reformed to town gas standard before use, so that they were actually processed by the industry, while not being manufactured.

[28] *Fuel Policy,* Cmnd 3438, HMSO, November 1967.

6 Mechanised Mining and the Growth of Labour Productivity

Summary

In many ways the coal-mining industry experienced the antithesis of the good fortune which blessed the gas industry's innovation programme. The industry was in no state to guide an intricate process of research and engineering development at the time of nationalisation. Nor did economic conditions favour the efforts the industry made. Demand was strong in the early years, but had weakened irretrievably by the time that the Coal Board's programme of innovation began to take effect.

The industry's weaknesses in 1947 were such as to make it more difficult to formulate a long-term strategy for concentration and technical change. Coal mining had had one of the worst records of any industry in Britain for labour relations in the inter-war years. As well as the recurrent strikes over pay and conditions, the issue of colliery closure in order to concentrate production was an explosive one. It would have been difficult to put forward a reasoned argument for any radical change in the industry without arousing antagonism between colliery owners and the labour force. Even the degree of mechanisation achieved provoked bitter struggles.

The collieries themselves were for the most part in poor condition. Economic hardships in the 1930s had been followed by the war; the fundamental restructuring of the industry which might have been judged necessary, and which had taken place in some of the continental industries, had been side-stepped as an issue. Although there were a few larger and more progressive companies, particularly in Scotland, there was none that could be called an industry leader, and ownership was highly fragmented. The professional institution of mining engineers had not been able to take a leading part in guiding the affairs of the industry. There was no growing tradition of research and development, nor of its practical application as a general service in the interests of the industry.

The demand for coal was strong for at least ten years after nationalisation. It seemed that the nation could burn every ton of coal produced, and the forecasts were that demand would grow until at least 1965. No one added up the difference that would be made to consumption by improved efficiency in electricity generating and in the use of coke for making steel, by the demise of the coal fire and by the transfer of railway traction, gas making and some power stations from coal as a fuel to oil. Had the decline in demand which began as early as 1956 been anticipated, the long-term planning of the industry might have been very different. It would not have seemed so necessary to keep open relatively uneconomic pits in order to maintain output, although this does not mean that closure and concentration would have automatically followed.

The Coal Board's approach must be judged in the light of the particular difficulties which affected the mining industry in the postwar period, but there are grounds for arguing that the policy as it evolved over twenty-five years was not fully thought out. That policy was to modernise the machinery and update the working methods used in collieries, both underground and on the surface. In order to improve productivity, a major innovative programme was pursued over a period of more than twenty years to introduce total mechanisation at the coal face. Collieries were closed as their reserves ran out, or in order to rationalise the working of existing reserves between adjacent pits. Restructuring took place in the larger existing pits, sinking new shafts and driving new roads underground. A few new collieries were put into production.

Implicit in this approach to the problem was the judgment that the industry could be made viable simply by improving productivity at the existing pits. It is questionable whether this was at any stage a correct judgment, and experience has shown that the improvement in labour productivity which was looked for could not be achieved in this way. One must therefore consider whether the Coal Board's policy showed a correct appreciation of the problem which had to be solved.

The factors which affect the productivity of labour employed in collieries differ according to the main areas of work, at the surface, working below ground behind the coal face, or working below ground at the coal face. At the surface labour productivity is related to the amount of capital equipment installed for coal handling, preparation and transport, and to the efficiency of maintenance and engineering services. Gains in productivity are to be expected from increasing the amount of capital equipment, from improving the techniques it employs and from re-organising working methods. These gains will be the more substantial the larger is the colliery output.

Below ground behind the face, scope for using capital equipment exists in coal transport, the driving of new headings and roadway maintenance and repair. More equipment and the re-organising of working methods can be expected to produce productivity gains, but again the greatest return to the introduction of these measures will result from their application to the higher output collieries, if collieries of similar natural conditions are compared. At the coal face, labour productivity is again related to the application of capital equipment and it was in mechanising the operation of mining at the coal face that the Coal Board made its outstanding innovatory contribution. There are, however, limits to the length of face that can be conveniently worked. Labour productivity gains result from being able to use the capital equipment to the maximum intensity (maximum number of machine hours per day) and from being able to operate it with the minimum number of manshifts. High machine usage and low manpower requirements are associated with the better geological conditions at some faces; poor face conditions can cut efficiency at the face to a half or a quarter of the national average. Thus the productivity gains to be expected from scale are limited and the major determinant of efficiency is the nature of face conditions.

Labour productivity in mining is thus related mainly to the natural conditions encountered, the amount of machinery employed and the size of colliery output. Capital productivity of collieries is mostly affected by the capital costs of the pit and its associated workings. Difficult conditions encountered during sinking and development can cause forecasts of the capital costs of output to be upset, but, other things being equal, collieries planned and laid out for large outputs can be expected to have lower capital costs than those with smaller outputs.

The Coal Board tackled the issue of applying machinery to coal production, but did not adopt a clear-cut policy of concentration of output. Indeed it could be argued that the issue of concentration was once more avoided. There were several reasons for this. Up to the mid-1950s the policy objective was to maximise coal output, and only a few very small and inefficient pits were closed. Few very large new pits to assist in meeting the industry's output target were developed, partly on the ground that development was slow and uncertain. Some pits were enlarged and some concentration took place when falling demand caused pit closures, but by the 1960s the industry was facing such severe retrenchment that a faster rate of concentration was unacceptable. It remains to ask why the industry did not plan, in 1947, to produce from a much smaller number of much larger pits; perhaps as few as 200 collieries to produce 200 million tons might have been desirable by 1960, and a reduction to under 100 collieries by 1975 would have been needed to equal concentration in the mining industries of other countries.

The answer would appear to be that, for all the centralised structure of the Board, decision making on such matters of technical policy was diffuse. Mining engineers in colliery and Area managements all over the country would have had to favour concentration as a major priority in order to make it work. It may well have been the case that a consensus of opinion would have been against such a policy direction and it was certainly the case that no adequate machinery existed to sound out technical opinion, to present the issues so that the conflicts of objectives might be seen, and to resolve satisfactorily the question of what course of action was best for the industry.

The lack of an administrative structure to perform this function is in marked contrast to the gas industry, where the fourteen members of the Council could speak with considerable authority about the choice of production techniques. The Coal Board's difficulty in creating a technical policy structure stemmed from the nature of the industry. Cohesiveness, co-operative approaches to industry problems and the opportunity to resolve conflicts on technical policy had not been encouraged by the ownership structure, and they were not induced by the diversity of mining conditions to be met in Britain. A much greater degree of co-operation spread gradually through the industry under public ownership. One of the major mechanisms to bring about this change was the Board's innovative programme. The factors which marked the emergence of a more structured approach to technical policy making were the build-up of the research function, the launching by the Board of the mechanisation drive in 1956, the move to spread mechanisation practices through conferences, committees, working parties, etc., and the steady growth of the influence of the production department at headquarters. The decision in the mid-1960s to concentrate output on a much reduced number of high output faces was perhaps the most successfully executed technical policy decision ever adopted by the Board or the industry.

In areas other than the determination of overall technical policy the procedures of the mining industry showed greater strengths. A fairly wide range of technical solutions to face mechanisation was examined. The underlying federal nature of the industry in technical matters allowed different approaches to be developed thoroughly and tested in practice. Some aspects of the research programme, particularly the powered support concept and the refinement of the use of power loaders at the face, illustrated the successful application of research to the practical problems of production techniques. But there was some difficulty about deciding which types of coal cutter best suited the industry's needs; this did not only result from diverse geological conditions, but also from disagreement, which continued for several years, concerning the merits of large and small coal in the industry's output.[1]

The rapid reduction in the number of working pits during the 1960s and the failure of productivity to reach the anticipated levels by the early 1970s placed a severe strain on labour relations, which had been remarkably good during the previous history of public ownership. The future for miners looked insecure and their earnings were held back by low productivity. The two major strikes which followed were bad for the industry's mechanisation programme, but they had more serious effects as well. It had been becoming easier to achieve general agreement in the industry on the setting of technical priorities and more favourable conditions were appearing in which to re-examine the issue of concentration. The labour relations problem of the 1970s meant, however, that any determined effort to reduce still further the number of working collieries would have been resisted very strongly. Although the better prospects for demand for coal led to plans for the expansion of the industry, through the addition of new capacity on a large scale, the issues of productivity and concentration still remained as the major problem facing the industry.

The work of the miner and the nature of the tasks he has to carry out underground are difficult to visualise for anyone not familiar with the industry. Imagine that a section of the earth's crust can be removed to discover what is happening inside. A large coal mine may be exploiting the seams in its area for a radius of five miles from the location of the shaft. Looking down through the strata at relatively frequent intervals one can see the thin black layers of the coal seams, looking like jam filling in a layer-cake. Some of the seams lie near the top, but in the British coalfields being worked in the 1970s many of the important coal measures are more than 1,000 feet below the surface. Within the carboniferous strata there may be between ten and thirty separately identifiable coal seams, with layers of rock in between. The vertical distance between the top seam of the carboniferous series and the bottom seam may well be 1,000 to 1,500 feet, so that as the pit shaft drives down through the earth it will pass through different coal seams at levels which are a considerable distance apart. The seams are rarely horizontal, like the layers of a cake, but dip and rise irregularly. Gradients of one in two and even one in one are often experienced in coal seams, making the working of a face more difficult.

Nor are the seams always continuous. Pressures working on the earth's crust have caused the coal-bearing strata to crack over wide areas, and then to slip up or down along the line of the crack, so that a seam being cut may suddenly disappear if a fault of this nature is reached. The continuation of the same seam may then be found several hundred feet higher or lower than the previous working.

In Figure 1, the two shafts going down to the seam can be seen, but the points where the shafts formerly gave access to seams closer to the surface have been omitted. From the shaft bottom main roads run both ways to the different parts of the seams which are being mined. In the centre the exploitation of one seam is shown in detail. A major face can be seen at the upper end of the large space marked 'excavated area'. As the coal is brought down it is conveyed along the face, down one of the tunnels (called gates) serving the face and so by further conveyers or locomotive haulage to the upcast shaft. There it is 'wound' (raised) to the surface and prepared for sale in washing and grading plants.

British mining engineers use a system of extraction called longwall face mining, and the face shown in Figure 1 is a longwall face. Earlier mining techniques were simpler because they evolved from surface drifts. Where a coal seam which is near the surface has been thrust upwards by a fault, it crops out on the surface and its coal may be had for the picking. A drift is a tunnel cut into the coal at an outcrop such as this in order to dig out more of the coal as it lies in the strata. When the tunnel in the coal becomes inconveniently long for carrying the produce back to the surface, the miner drives a new tunnel, often at right angles to the first. These tunnels built in coal for the purpose of extracting the seam are usually called 'headings'. Systematic extraction of the largest possible amount of the seam would demand that the drifts and headings were driven in a grid pattern, leaving square pillars of coal between the intersections of adjacent drifts and headings (see Figure 2).

A proportion of the coal would thus be extracted in digging the criss-cross tunnels. Provided that roof conditions were satisfactory, the pillars themselves could then be extracted also, leaving the strata which had previously bounded the coal seam to converge. Naturally the extraction of pillars had to start from the point furthest inbye, which means furthest from the exit to the surface. The system of extraction is known as 'room and pillar' or 'bord and pillar'. Until the middle of the nineteenth century very little other than room and pillar mining was used in Britain; it was not always identical with the operations described above but the principle of quartering off the coal with tunnels into blocks for removal was usually employed.

As many of the best seams with coal near the surface and good roof conditions became exhausted, the coal engineers were forced to go deeper and frequently this necessitated a shaft being sunk to reach the coal. The seams which they wanted to reach either never cropped out or else were impossible to work from the outcrop. Mining from shafts was not new. The Cornish tin miners had evolved the techniques centuries before and

Figure 1 Cut-away view of coal mine.

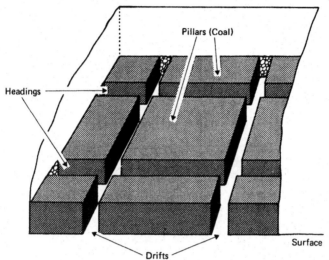

Figure 2 Drift mine working.

coal engineers had themselves previously employed a shaft where it provided a more convenient way of reaching a seam.

However, new developments of mining techniques followed from the working of seams that lay deeper in the earth. The greater stresses at increasing depths made it more difficult to extract all the coal without severely disturbing the strata. Convergence of the roof and floor in the areas excavated caused heaving and buckling in the areas which still contained coal.[2] Extraction of the pillars became hazardous and the amount of maintenance and support needed for the drifts and headings increased enormously.

In order to contain these forces, the techniques of building packs and stowing waste in the goaf were adopted. By replacing the excavated pillars and tunnels with thick walls of stone or other underground waste a measure of control over roof collapse became possible (see Figure 3). Better roof control improved the conditions for mining.

As roof control techniques developed, the need to quarter the coal into squares for removal one at a time was obviated. The whole of a long section comprising many pillars could be removed at one time, doing away with the work of making a number of headings. The longwall could be attacked by a team of men all at once, taking a slice off the full length in each shift, rather like slicing a piece off the long side of a loaf.

Cross headings became redundant. With room and pillar working two constraints had been imposed on the amount of extraction possible. The first was that the rate of extraction and the question of whether the seam could be removed in its entirety were dependent upon the conditions of

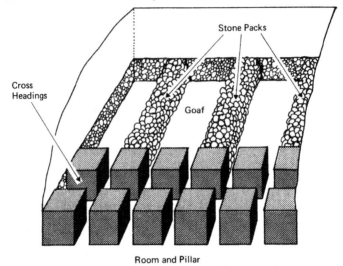

Figure 3 Roof control with stone packs.

roof and floor. Too much movement of the strata made mining impracticable. Secondly the economics of working a particular seam were affected by the need to spend some considerable time driving drifts and headings into the coal to develop it to the point where full-scale extraction of the pillars could be started.

Roof control techniques (or more properly strata control, since both floor and roof have to be considered) provided an opportunity to dispense with these development workings and to start immediately on excavation of the complete seam. Usually a single heading would be needed to expose the flank of the coal seam along the most suitable line for a longwall face (such as the heading at the bottom of the worked out area in Figure 4). One side of the heading or development road then became the coal face and a team of miners strung out along the face would cut or blast the first web.[3] Thus the work of tunnelling to the limits of the area to be excavated was eliminated and the coal was no longer excavated from inbye outwards.

The change to the advancing longwall face technique took many years to accomplish. If it was resisted by miners and engineers on occasions, then their reasons were probably that its effect was to replace the traditional skills, self-reliance and virtuosity of the individual miner underground, first with teams of men and soon with machines. The severe economic conditions of the interwar period and the abysmal labour relations in coal mining did little to soften the effects of change for the men or their taskmasters.

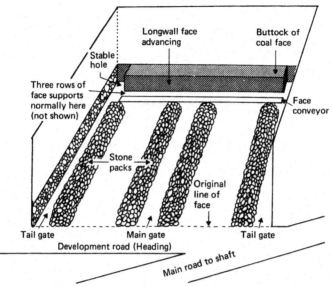

Figure 4 The advancing longwall face system of mining.

However, by the end of the Second World War longwall advancing had been adopted on all but a few coal faces in Britain and it was around the concepts of the longwall face that the technical innovations of the postwar period were evolved.[4] Figure 4 shows a longwall face in operation and the sequence of operations is described below. A three-shift system grew up, the tasks of each shift being distinct; considerable demarcation of skills between workers was thus maintained. The amount of work to be carried out by an individual or a team during a shift was called a stint.

The coal-getting shift would start by preparing the face to bring down a web of coal. Holes might be bored for shot firing, the coal would often be undercut with a machine to ensure a good fall and other cuts might be required as well. The coal would then be brought down off the face by shot firing, cutting, or by the use of manual labour and picks. When the coal face had been cleaned off the shift was finished.

Following this was the filling shift, whose task was to load the fallen coal for transport to the pit-bottom. Finally the third shift had to advance the face supports ready for the next coal-getting shift. This entailed setting new rows of pit-props to support the roof where the last web of coal had been removed, moving forward the face conveyor by threading it through the rows of props to a position as close as possible to the new location of the face, and attending to the problems of roof control behind the face in the goaf where the coal had already been extracted. Mainly this involved the care and maintenance of the roadways, which served the face with air, supplies and transport. Stone packs built alongside each roadway to support the roof and control the collapse of the strata would be extended towards the face. Ripping and dinting (cutting the roadway roof and levelling the floor) were required to bring roadways to a height which made transport and access possible.

THE IMPORTANCE OF OUTPUT PER MANSHIFT

Output per manshift (o.m.s.) is the main measure of productivity in the coal industry. Its changing value throughout the twentieth century charts the progress which mining has made towards increased efficiency (Figure 5). Labour is the largest single input to production in coal mining. In the earliest days of comparatively primitive mining, labour would have been practically the only production cost. The employment of machinery over the years since the mid-nineteenth century in increasing proportions obviously diminished the labour content of output, but the industry's conditions and methods of production were not such that machinery had reduced the labour input to a low level.

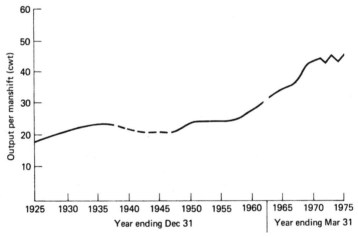

Figure 5 Progress of output per manshift (o.m.s.) 1925—75. *Source:* NCB *Annual Reports* and Cmd 6610.

During the 1920s, wage costs probably formed over three-quarters of the pithead costs of a ton of coal mined underground. At that time mechanisation (coal cutters, power tools and conveyors) affected less than 20 per cent of production. International trade competition drove down the proceeds of sale of coal from nearly £1 per ton in 1924 to about 13s 6d in the early 1930s.[5] This induced greater mechanisation at the coal face. But although by 1939 68 per cent of coal produced was mechanically cut and face-conveyed and a slightly smaller percentage also conveyed back from the face to the haulage road, o.m.s. at the coal face itself had risen only from 52 cwt to 60 cwt. The overall effect of this early mechanisation upon productivity (that is o.m.s. for all workers at the face, elsewhere underground and on the surface) was an improvement, from 18 cwt in 1925 to 23 cwt in 1938, but by 1947 the improvement in o.m.s. had only reduced wage costs to a point where they formed 66 per cent of the costs of production.

The disadvantage which a high wage proportion of costs gives to any industry is that it causes a close relationship between increases in wage rates and increases in the overall cost of output. Between the two wars the effect of falling prices was to drive down miners' wages, but in the period following the Second World War miners' wages rose as fast as or faster than the national average for a time.[6] In coal mining an increase in wage rates means either a coal price increase of approximately two-thirds the rate of the wage increase, or else a compensating increase in productivity. O.m.s. increased faster from 1947 to 1960 than it had done since the late 1920s, but not by enough to counter the effect of rises in wages and the prices of other inputs. Coal increased in price by about 85 per cent between 1950 and 1960 (compared with gas, which increased by about 65 per cent, oil by 30 to 40 per cent and electricity by 24 per cent). As well as being a disadvantage to coal mining, these price increases raised costs for the industry's main customers.

PROBLEMS OF THE 1940s

Towards the end of the war a general summary of the technical conditions of the industry was produced in the Reid Report.[7] The Committee was headed by Charles Carlow Reid and appointed in September 1944. Its members were technically qualified to a man, coming from the mining industry or the mining machinery companies. Its Chairman came from the Fife Coal Company. Their conclusions left little doubt that considerable government involvement was required in order to meet the industry's needs.

The worst problem was the large number of very small mines, a legacy of the days before the Coal Act of 1938; each part of the coal seams had belonged to the owner of the land above them. There were about 1,800 collieries at the start of the war, more than half producing less than 50,000 tons each year, and very few reaching an output of half a million tons. Small collieries, many of them individually owned, meant that resources for modernisation were also small; the chances of planning large efficient underground layouts were much reduced by the pattern of boundaries; even where a company owned several collieries, the mines were often kept separate because of land ownership problems.

Added to this, the ownership problem and economic hardships in the industry had produced more than a century of bad labour relations. New machinery and changes in methods had been resisted by the miners as one of their few weapons to try and obtain better conditions.[8] Fragmentation of the industry, lack of capital and the lack of the right spirit between the miner and the owner had caused the British industry to become out-of-date and uncompetitive. Competition had forced prices down and reduced the size of the output. Falling production had diminished the opportunities for improving organisation and working methods. A vicious circle was in operation.

The technical conditions of operation underground at the time of the Reid Report may be summarised as follows. Approximately 1,800 collieries produced 227 million tons in 1938. A majority of the output was gained by longwall methods, 68 per cent being won by using a cutter at the face. For the rest, although pneumatic picks and other machines were used in some mines, manual work with a pick provided over a quarter of production. Transport of coal from the face was by conveyor for 67 per cent of output, but in very small mine cars for most of the remainder.

The most inefficient part of British mining practice underground occurred between the point of filling the coal and its arrival on the surface. Gate-conveying (using a conveyor to take the coal back from the workings to the point where a main or district road was reached) began to be used in the later 1920s and had been applied to 40 per cent of output by 1939. After the coal reached the main or district roads it was handled by antiquated haulage systems. Manual haulage was still in use; pit ponies for main and subsidiary haulage still exceeded 20,000; endless rope systems, where the tub was clipped to a constantly moving line, were regarded as fairly modern and the number of main conveyors or underground locomotives was very small. Underground mine cars tended to be small, typically 10 cwt; the labour employed on haulage was about a quarter of all underground workers and each manshift was able to move only about 5 tons to the surface.[9] Winding of men, coal and materials up and down the shafts was hampered by small shafts, old-fashioned equipment for motive power and the need for extra handling of the coal.

NATIONALISATION AND RECONSTRUCTION

The number of coal mines still operating in 1947 was between 1,600 and 1,700, depending on whether the definition included some of the very small undertakings which might have employed only half-a-dozen men. The National Coal Board took over those in which employment underground amounted to thirty men or more; it was thus in control of about 980 collieries. Nearly 450 small mines continued to be operated under NCB licence by their previous owners.[10]

The industry was at a low point in its fortunes at the time of nationalisation. Wartime conditions had meant making little attempt to find solutions to the problems which were a legacy of the 1920s and 1930s. There were, however, two positive factors. The first was that ownership by a single public corporation provided the organisational opportunity to attend to the major failings pointed out by Reid. The second was that demand for coal was strong, and appeared likely to remain so.

The first task of the Board was to establish a management framework. The Scottish, English and Welsh coalfields were divided into eight main Divisions (and one subsidiary one) and subdivided into 48 Areas. The Board in London was clearly to be both the origin and the moving force behind policy, but yet the members of the Board, knowing how different problems, priorities and attitudes characterised each district of the coalfields, did not want to lose the benefits which regional management might bring by closer involvement. The Area was designated as being the optimum business unit in size and scope for day-to-day management responsibility. Its average turnover was about £10 million per year and its chief executive was directly responsible for production, being called the Area General Manager. But the Board retained departments which controlled industry policy on finance and marketing, production, the application of science, labour relations and personnel. There was no question of the Area being autonomous. Recognising that there might be severe delays in the administration of detail from headquarters, the Board used the Division to act with the delegated authority of headquarters and to form a two-way channel of communication between Area and HQ.

The last man in the management chain was the colliery manager. Many of these men stayed on from the days before nationalisation, and in them undoubtedly rested a great deal of the skill and knowledge which kept the industry going. A typical area might have an output of 5 million tons, coming from up to twenty pits; one Area even had sixty-six collieries. It was impossible for the Area Manager to exercise daily control over this number of units: he was very dependent upon his colliery managers. It was even common practice to have one or two further levels of delegated authority. An Agent and a Sub-Agent (titles which echoed the old days of the coal owner) would exercise the functions of the Area Manager in the case of individual collieries or a very small group.

Taking an admirably long-term view, the Coal Board at headquarters embarked on two quite new policies for the industry in 1947. The first was the preparation of a fifteen-year plan of resource development, and the second was the establishment of a structure for the application of science in the industry.

The Plan for Coal was produced in October 1950.[11] It was a product of lengthy consultations between all levels of management. Essentially it concentrated on capital development, rather than dealing with market forecasts or detailed proposals on techniques. Its major technical judgment was that the large-scale collieries of continental Europe were not strictly feasible in Britain; the development of new pits and the making of existing pits larger was to be aimed at producing outputs of 1·2 million tons to 1·5 million tons per year. Output, investment schemes, capital expenditure and manpower requirements for the period 1950—65 were set out for each Division. New collieries planned amounted to twenty-two deep mines and over fifty surface mines or drifts, most of the latter in Scotland. Reconstruction and amalgamation, including some new shaft sinking and the development of new workings, applied to another 250 collieries.

Technical developments were not ignored by the Plan. The need for new methods was re-stated, particularly the overhaul of underground transport; in this the Plan followed the recommendations of the Reid Report. The Plan did not specify any particular way in which the changes in underground techniques were to be brought about. Its main aim, the exercise of showing how a deep-mined output of 240 million tons per year could be achieved by the early 1960s, was achieved by the analysis of what new units and expanded collieries were required, showing which coalfields were to expand and which ones would contract.

The second new departure for the industry was the adoption of a research programme and the application of science in a systematic way to coal production. It is important to recognise that research, development and scientific method had been little used in mining before the 1940s. The reasons for this were to do with the nature of mining as a skill and the characteristics of people involved in the industry.

Coal mining is an old industry and mining of all types in Britain is even older. Coal owners were active in the industry in the early Middle Ages; some of their methods may have been learned from the tin miners of Cornwall and the industry was well established in its use of techniques in the early nineteenth century. Large mining companies were few; coal owners had little incentive to come together to form co-operative associations, or to examine their industry's problems in unison. Even well into the twentieth century, the mining village or community tended to be isolated, or at least cut off from the rest of society by its habits and its traditions. The fact that the work place was determined by the coal seams meant that the work force did not join the general drift towards city employment. The mining people's social parallels are the Cornish people, the navvies of the eighteenth and nineteenth centuries, canal boatmen and their wandering families, or the road construction gangs of the postwar era. They display the same closeness towards their own kind, a sense of belonging that owes more to their own past than to current social fashions and a sense of identity in their trades which the more general industrial and commercial employee probably does not experience.[12]

Mining engineers have thus a long history. Until quite recently their skills had to be self-taught, or would have been learned through association with other miners. Working often in great danger, and seldom for the most enlightened masters, their calling would require a spirit of risk taking and enterprise which bred a sense of independence. Although a professional body the Institution of Mining Engineers, was formed, as similar bodies were formed by other professional engineering groups, the coal engineer was not one who by his trade or his way of life would have wide-ranging professional contacts after the manner of civil engineers and power engineers.

During the twentieth century a few colliery companies introduced a measure of scientific day-to-day control, and an even smaller number set up a basis of research work. There was also the British Colliery Owners Research Association, set up in the 1920s with many of the other industry

Research Associations, but little research on techniques was conducted by these bodies. One of the main technical influences up to 1947 had been the implementation of the Coal Mines Act, 1911, and its enforcement by HM Inspectors of Mines, and this was an influence for caution rather than change. The Safety in Mines Research Board was perhaps the only research body which had any widespread influence on the techniques employed underground. Its mission was directed towards rather different objectives from those of the mine's owner and manager.

The NCB put air and dust sampling, coal quality control and routine safety testing into the hands of the Divisional Chief Scientists and the Area Chief Scientists. Their tasks were to codify local practices and local regulations, to enable uniform procedures to be established and to assist in controlling safety and the quality of working conditions.

Secondly, the Board set out to establish the nature, extent and location, of the country's coal resources, with major faulting to be charted. This had not been thoroughly done before; in the absence of experimental drilling, the exploitation of major seams was an undertaking having its share of surprises. The Coal Survey of pre-war days was now set to work under the Board, with eight laboratories conducting studies in the main coalfields.

Finally, a central research facility was established, together with a scientific and technical programme, under the Board Member for Science, Sir Charles Ellis. The first establishment, at Stoke Orchard, was founded in 1948. It covered scientific research into coal properties, technical research into coal products and coal production methods, as well as health and safety research.

RE-ORGANISATION, THE DRIVE FOR PRODUCTION

Demand for fuel rose rapidly at the end of the war and, although it was important to think about the long-term future of the industry, there was an immediate problem of a coal shortage, to which the Board had a primary duty to respond. Both on the question of colliery reconstruction and on the use of new techniques underground, the industry had to adopt the methods of production which promised short-term returns. In spite of the Reid Report's call for the amalgamation and closure of small collieries, the planning of big new units and new mining techniques, the collieries had to be geared immediately for increased output.

It required a major effort of organisation to take over the industry, bring it under national control and expand production by a few million tons. Few small mines were shut down at first. A number of producing units were amalgamated and pits were closed where the reserves were worked out. At the end of five years NCB units had been reduced by only 7 per cent and at the end of ten years they were 12 per cent less, at 840 collieries. Since the collieries closed were all smaller ones, the net loss of output was more than made up by expanding output in other pits. In 1954 the deep-mined output was at a peak of 211·4 million tons. Reconstruction programmes were also geared to keeping up output, and putting capital resources into the projects which would have a short-term product. About 150 projects of a major character, costing more than £100,000 each, were authorised up to the end of 1950. Only two of these were new pits (Rothes and Solway) and they had both been started before nationalisation. Of the eighteen to twenty schemes costing over £500,000 in all, more than a third of the expenditure incurred was on building coal preparation or treatment plant or coke ovens on the surface.

Table 6.1   *The Coal-Mining Industry, 1947—75*

Year ending [a]	Collieries open	Output (million tons) [b]	Inland consumption (million tons)	Exports (million tons)	Stocks (million tons)	Deep-mined output (million tons)
1947	958	197	185	5	18	184
1951	896	222	208	11	18	209
1955	850	222	215	14	20	208
1959	737	206	189	4	50	193
1963	611	198	193	5	32	189
1967	438	173	170	3	35	165
1971	292	142	148	3	20	133
1975	246	125	125	2	21	115

[a] Year end was 31 December to 1962, subsequently 31 March.
[b] Including open-cast output at an average of 11m. tons a year in 1947—59, and 8m. tons a year in 1960—74.

In order to raise productivity in the collieries, the Coal Board concentrated in the first few years upon the installation of more machinery underground and at the face. The policy followed was very much in line with the recommendations of Reid. Underground roads were re-organised, new shafts and drifts were sunk, new equipment for haulage underground and for raising coal was installed, more power machinery was used at the face. These were the measures which attracted most of the funds and kept output growing slowly towards 210 million tons. In the three years 1946, 1947 and 1948, the industry purchased large quantities of underground mining machinery, particularly coal cutters, conveyors, powered loading machines and haulage locomotives.[13] Transport of coal underground had been one of the barriers to higher o.m.s. and conveyor installation was the major policy used to raise the output of transport workers; by 1953 the total mileage of conveyors in use underground had doubled in five years, to 1,734 miles.

Short-term reconstruction of existing pits was not just a policy dictated by economic pressures. Technical opinion in the industry was not in favour of more radical change. Major re-organisation, such as took place for instance in the gas industry, would have been more disruptive of both the technological and the sociological structure of coal mining. The detailed information base about the exact location and extent of British coal seams, which would have removed a large element of risk from any planned extraction involving extensive areas underground, was lacking. As a fourth factor, the technical methods available at the time to mining engineers for the rapid exploitation of coal reserves on a large scale were woefully inadequate.[14] Thus the economic necessity to adopt short-term measures was compounded by a lack of ability to adopt a more long-term strategy.

The machinery programme had its effect. O.m.s. grew from 20·6 cwt in 1946 to 24·5 cwt by 1951, but for various reasons it could not go on growing at this rate for very long. The returns to underground mechanisation were limited and the number of new installations of machinery began to drop off by the early 1950s. In particular, the conditions for using the early type of powered cutter/loader, the Meco-Moore, were difficult to find. Nor did many locomotive haulage schemes prove attractive.

By the early 1950s o.m.s. had stuck at 24 cwt and it did not rise above 25 cwt until 1958. The limits of the existing concepts of mechanisation underground had been reached, at least in so far as productivity could not be raised further in the range of existing collieries. New pits were planned to achieve overall productivity rates of up to 50 or 60 cwt per manshift. Reconstruction could raise output to near this level in some collieries, but to get o.m.s. climbing again in the average run of mines in use in the 1950s a technical innovation in underground mechanisation was needed.

THE ORIGINS AND DEVELOPMENT OF THE FULLY MECHANISED FACE

Even after the struggle had been won in the 1920s to introduce machinery into coal-getting and the longwall face had become an accepted method of working, underground mining was still a largely manual operation. Rates of production at the face were still tied to the muscle power of men, because they had little apart from muscles with which to prepare the coal face and clean it off after firing, to load the coal on to the face conveyors and to advance the pit props to the new line. The advancing longwall face imposed a rhythm of cyclical working and the cycle was the three-shift system.

The rigidity of three-shift working and the lack of mechanisation at the face had begun to exercise the thoughts of mining engineers before the second world war. The problem was that, should an unexpected technical snag, or the non-appearance of key workers, lead to delay in one shift's task being completed, the work of the next shift was disrupted, because the shifts carried out successive tasks. This difficulty sometimes caused collieries to adopt a forty-eight-hour cycle of operations, in order to provide adequate margins for shift completion. In other circumstances the amount of progress to be made by each shift would be set deliberately below the normal level, to allow for contingencies. One of the first serious

NCB strikes was sparked off at Grimethorpe in 1947 over the size of stint that the filling shift should do. It eventually spread to sixty-three collieries. The immediate cause was negotiation over work loads in introducing a shortened week, but the three-shift system was the basic cause.

Mechanisation of coal-getting at the face and the reform of the shift system were two objectives which were pursued concurrently. Logically, the first step was to remove the need for the filling shift, by cutting the coal down from the face so that it fell directly on to the face conveyor. A machine which could travel sideways along the length of the face, cutting down the web and loading it aboard a conveyor, would allow several coal-getting operations in one shift.

The first machine to put this technique into practice was the Meco-Moore, which had trial operations before the war. It worked by making a cut with two jibs (looking like a large version of a motor-powered tree-felling saw) at the middle of the seam and underneath. At the same time a following jib took a vertical cut up the back of the web being dislodged, and the falling coal was loaded on to its own small conveyor set at right angles to the Meco's direction of travel. The Meco travelled along in the buttock, the space between the pit props and the coal face, but the face conveyor to carry away the coal was separated by the front row of props. To have the conveyor beside the machine would require too large an unsupported area of roof between the props and the face. As it was, the Meco needed good roof conditions to encourage the coal to break cleanly, rather than caving, and it needed a good floor to establish the path for its next run. As the Meco progressed, its own small conveyor had to be kept clear of each prop and a new line of supports had to be set behind it. When the run was completed the face conveyor had to be dismantled and threaded through the lines of roof supports, then reassembled ready for the next run. A number of Mecos were in use at the end of the war and about 30 installations were taken over by the NCB in 1947. For some years it was the most widely used power loading machine and it could be used to good effect, but its range of application was not very wide and it did not provide the general mechanisation system which mining engineers were seeking. Its peak year was in 1956/7, when approximately 125 were in use; however, by then it had already been overtaken by the Anderton Shearer and its use gradually declined.

The Meco-Moore scarcely got away from the shift system. What was needed was a conveyor to run alongside the face in the width of the buttock, to be used in conjunction with a cutter which would load directly on to it. One British experimental design, supported by a programme of finance from the Ministry of Fuel and Power, was close to the right concept. It was a stripping machine, employing a wedge action to split the coal off the face, in the way that a steel wedge is often used for splitting lengths of timber. The steel wedge halfway up the cut forced a passage through the coal, and ploughshare blades following burst off the web, which fell on to a conveyor running underneath it.

This technique of ploughing coal was extensively used in Germany, where seams were of a softer nature and had a harder floor than British seams. The face conveyor was a critical component. It had to be versatile enough to operate in rough conditions of installation and robust enough to be advanced with the face by being pushed forward bodily, without dismantling. The stripper only split off a narrow web from the coal, and advances had to be made several times per shift to achieve high output, leaving no time for dismantling the conveyor in the course of the advance.

Λ prototype conveyor for this application was being developed at the end of the war. However, it was thought that special conveyors of a type which might be suitable had been in use during the 1930s in Germany. Soon after the end of the war in 1945, a British Commission visited Germany to examine the coal industry there, and found that such conveyors did exist. The type brought back to test in England was called the Panzerfoederer armoured conveyor. Built of heavy steel, it was composed of several short and semi-independent conveyor sections, which were connected with a simple joint. Not only could it be mechanically pushed forwards towards the coal face, but it could be installed over a twisting track and on uneven floors with varying gradients. Its third advantage was that the conveyor provided a track for the cutter to run on top of it. Instead of having to spend the third shift preparing a level floor, the miner had a ready-made road available beside the coal face as soon as the conveyor was pushed up to it.

With the appearance of this conveyor, the basic elements of a simultaneous-operation mining system became available. The Meco-Moore was not really suitable to being adapted as the conveyor-riding cutter. Various types of cutter were being tried out experimentally during the early 1950s, some of them stemming from the engineering work founded by the Ministry of Fuel during the war. One was a slabber which took a fairly thin web off the face. There were also the Huwood Slicer, the Gloster Getter, the Joy Continuous Miner and the Dosco Miner. The last two were developed on the other side of the Atlantic. Considerable interest had been shown in American mining methods during the war. The Reid Report had recommended their intensive room and pillar method of working as the bset for high productivity. The Joy Continuous Miner was a multi-chain jib-head cutter of massive proportions, which cut the coal, loaded it and then conveyed it on a second jib some distance to a mine-car or roadway conveyor. This type of mining could be employed only in fairly thick seams of 5 or 6 feet, and not in the 2-, 3- or 4-foot seams being worked in many of Britain's collieries.

In the early 1950s a new type of cutter was invented by an Area General manager of the North West Division. Called the Anderton Shearer, after the inventor, Mr Anderton, and the cutting method, shearing, the machine attacked the buttock of the coal face with a set of picks fixed in a rotating drum. The drum or cylinder containing the picks was rotated with its spindle at right angles to the line of the face, and as it was dragged along it broke up the face, by subjecting the coal to a series of small shearing or chipping forces from each of its picks. Although subject to some opposition from the industry, the Shearer was the forerunner of most of the power loaders successfully used during the next twenty years. It was first tried at Ravenhead colliery near St Helens in 1953 and soon after at the nearby Cronton and Golborne pits.

Figure 6 shows the time scale of the introduction of mechanisation at the face. It can be seen that the Meco-Moore predated all other types of machinery by some years. The use of ploughs began in 1948/9 but did not start to increase until the mid-1950s. The Anderton Shearer was adopted very quickly and built up to its first peak in use on 350 faces in 1958. However, the stripping machine and the slabber, the Huwood Slicer and Gloster Getter, were being used mainly experimentally on a small number

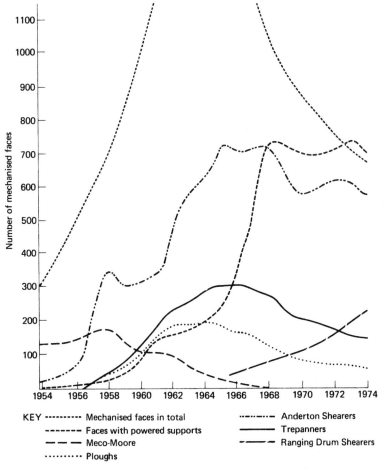

KEY ⋯⋯⋯ Mechanised faces in total ⋯⋯⋅⋯ Anderton Shearers
        ------- Faces with powered supports ——— Trepanners
        — — — Meco-Moore ⋯—⋅— Ranging Drum Shearers
        ⋯⋯⋯⋯ Ploughs

Figure 6 Development of types of mechanised face.

of faces in the period 1950—6. The types of coal upon which they could be applied most successfully had to be discovered. It was necessary to try out different thicknesses of cut, different rates of advance and various blade geometrics.

Most of the types of power loading equipment being tried out in the early 1950s were dependent on the Panzer conveyor, as a basis for mounting a cutter of one nature or another. Apart from the cutters mentioned above, which employed special techniques, more conventional coal cutters of the type introduced in the 1920s and 1930s were also used. They were adapted so that the machine could run on top of the conveyor, with its blade angled to cut into coal as low down as possible, or even with a swan-neck curve. A second cutter was sometimes mounted above the first to help bring down the coal. Chutes, guiding fingers and scoops were attached in different configurations to the conveyor-mounted cutters, to guide the coal on to the Panzer for conveying as it fell.

These developments, which took place between 1947 and 1956, were being undertaken simultaneously in different geographical locations, by different groups of mining engineers and without a clearly co-ordinated plan of campaign. Thus the Meco had some of its most successful applications in the Nottinghamshire coalfields, the Panzer may first have been tried out with a riding cutter at Frickley pit in Yorkshire, the Shearer appeared in Lancashire and the different types of plough were used in a number of coalfields. Most of the mining engineers taking a leading part in the advancing of techniques knew what other groups of engineers were doing, but the work of the groups was not directed towards co-ordinated ends. The Production Department at HQ in London was in charge of technical methods and their development, but, as well as being very fully occupied with the drive for more production, it was too remote from the collieries to be able to exercise a continuous monitoring and controlling function.

There was therefore an element of disjunction, which makes it difficult to look upon the early years of experiment as a programme. No centre existed to which schemes were put up for approval, or which assembled and communicated information about the results of work all over the country. The industry had not reached a stage of centralisation and control which made that strategy of development practicable. It was effectively colliery managers. Area Engineers and other technically competent personnel at the end of the management chain who determined the rate and direction of technical change. The research function, however, was gradually gathering strength. Although the Coal Board's main establishment at Stoke Orchard, the Coal Research Establishment, had many areas of scientific responsibility to oversee, it extended its interest into roof control and thus began to assist a new development which became part of the face mechanisation concept.

The removal of seams of coal at depths of some hundreds of feet or more below the earth's surface sets up considerable repercussions for some distance in the surrounding strata. Some movement of the rock layers above and below the coal seam is necessary in order to relieve stresses set up by excavation, but not so much upheaval that the process of coal getting can not go forward or that the roads supplying the face become damaged. The control of heavy loads in the strata was seen to be analogous to the landing of heavily loaded aircraft. Discussions started early in the postwar period between the Coal Board and the makers of hydraulic aircraft suspension units.

Although at first the hydraulic pit prop looked too expensive for ordinary applications underground, the concept was taken up by the managing director of one of the mining machinery companies and experiments were carried out in co-operation with the Board's research laboratory at Stoke Orchard for several years, beginning in 1948. When it was established that hydraulic roof supports had other advantages, they were developed more specifically as an aid to the fully mechanised face. The Safety in Mines Act of 1911 set out conditions for the maximum area of unsupported roof under which men could be allowed to work, but mining engineers wanted to establish a prop-free front face in order to assist machine mining. Technically, this could be achieved by using a cantilevered support system over the front of the coal face, of roof bars set at the heads of props and linked to the bars and supports at one row's remove. The use of a cantilevered support would provide room for the conveyor and cutter to travel along the face unimpeded. A test case was fought in order to establish that the cantilevered support would be allowable under the 1911 Act. Hydraulic pit props, which could be pre-set to yield at a given load and then take up again, and which could be very quickly set and removed, thanks to the hydraulic operation, made the linked-bar prop-free front much easier to use. By 1952 it had been accepted by the Board and 300,000 yielding props were quickly ordered, in order to set up faces where hydraulic strata control could be put into practice.

In 1952 a second research facility, the Mining Research Establishment (MRE), was set up at Isleworth, in west London, to co-ordinate data on machinery for mechanised mining. Its work included development of the new plough-type coal cutters, powered hydraulic supports for the roof at the coal face and other underground machinery. Ideas for mechanisation were developing so rapidly that by 1955 a third centre, called the Central Engineering Establishment (CEE), was brought into being in order to tackle, in a laboratory environment, the problems of machine mining which were questions of design engineering and testing. CEE developed closer links than Stoke Orchard and MRE with mining engineers in the collieries. It was in the charge of the production department at HQ, whereas the research programme was still in the care of the Board Member for Science.

FACE MECHANISATION, 1955—65

Having assembled most of the necessary elements, the mining industry began the process of applying power-loading machines to coal production. The number of machine loading faces grew steadily and exceeded 400 of one kind and another by 1955. Some hundreds of Panzer armoured conveyors had been delivered and the yielding pit prop was being installed in a number of collieries.

The coal industry's situation at this time was problematical. The failure of productivity to grow was one source of concern, and the falling level of deep-mined output was another. The Coal Board had set itself a production target of 250 million tons per year by 1965. With output from opencast sites averaging about 10 million tons, this meant that the collieries had to expand output to 240 million tons, an increase of nearly 40 million tons above the 1950 level. At first output had grown quite satisfactorily, from 184 million tons in 1947 to 211 million tons in 1951. By 1955 it was 208 million tons.

It was at this stage that mechanisation became the subject of a much more coherent plan, drawn up by the production department at HQ and backed by the new Chairman, James Bowman, an ex-miner himself. The second research station, MRE at Isleworth, was made responsible for monitoring the installation of power loaders in order to collect data on the effectiveness of the different types and to identify the technical problems associated with them from a wide variety of experience in different collieries. The Central Engineering Establishment was brought into the campaign, working alongside MRE to determine how increased output and productivity could be obtained. The need for a centre at which to conduct development tests of machinery was recognised and plans were made for a test coal face to be established. As well as testing machinery which mining engineers were designing, CEE aimed to achieve better liaison with the NCB's main manufacturing suppliers (represented by the Council of Underground Machinery Manufacturers). In the early 1950s new ideas on mining equipment were advancing so quickly that manufacturers had very little chance to define the specifications of a standard model which they could build, and it was hoped that CEE would provide a channel of communication through which the mining industry and the manufacturers could achieve understanding.

The object of the plan was to apply the concept of mechanisation as widely as possible over the coal industry. The total number of coal faces still in operation was over 4,000. The 400-odd mechanised faces thus formed a small proportion of the total; their contribution to output was only 11 per cent in 1955 (Table 6.2).

It is clear that one of the major problems which the industry faced from the start was how to implement this technical programme. The highly federated structure of the industry gave managers and engineers at local levels considerable freedom to decide what machinery they would use, and whether they believed in using it at all. Apart from the many levels of responsibility between Board and coal face, it is essential in the mining industry that the man on the spot should make the important decisions about techniques. Every mine confronts different problems; trying to generalise from the experiences of a dozen collieries in order to provide detailed information and advice about the way to introduce machinery over the whole industry was not a reasonable approach. In the final analysis the mining engineer underground would use his own judgment. If mechanisation of face operations was going to succeed in raising output and productivity, it would have to do so through the adoption by thousands of mining engineers of its ends and its methods as their own.

Table 6.2   *Growth of Output and Mechanisation, 1950—60*

31 Dec.	Collieries (no.)	Deep-mined output (m. tons)	Productivity (cwt/manshift)	Power-loaded output (%)
1950	901	202	24·2	4
1951	896	210	24·5	4
1952	880	211	24·2	5
1953	875	210	24·9	6
1954	867	211	24·9	8
1955	850	208	24·7	11
1956	840	207	24·8	16
1957	822	207	24·9	23
1958	793	199	25·6	28
1959	737	193	26·9	31
1960	698	184	28·0	38

Source: NCB *Annual Reports.*
Note: A change of definition affected productivity in 1952. The value under the previous definition was 24·6 cwt.

A mechanisation drive thus assumed the proportions of something like an education programme for the mining engineers and officials, plus the hundreds of thousands of miners. The task was made more difficult by the fact that the profession was one which had never been rooted firmly in the formal educational system of university or technical college. The mining engineer was rarely a degree holder, and he might have attended only a few evening classes since leaving school at 14 or 15. While no worse an engineer for this fact, he was not one to change his ways in response to the conclusions of an erudite paper read to a learned society. His background and self-taught skills made him ingenious, independent and hard to convince.

The production department held a national power-loading conference in 1955, a pioneering approach to the problem of technical change. It anticipated the conferences more widely held by business groups during the 1960s, to spread such techniques as 'management by objectives'. Machine mining in all aspects was discussed by people who had had experience of its application, both successfully and unsuccessfully. A series of articles, 'Machines to Aid Men', was published in the industry's house magazine *Coal*, with the intention of bringing new techniques to the notice of workmen in the many different trades, employed underground and on the surface. A machinery exhibition was staged, so that people who had never seen the equipment in their own pit could examine the new machines at first hand.

The Anderton Shearer Loader was already beginning to receive special attention by 1955, as one of the machines most adaptable to different conditions underground. The No. 3 Area of the NW Division, where the Shearer was invented, was power-loading 35 per cent of output in 1955 and occupied a leading position. The effects of the Coal Board's campaign to get mechanisation accepted can be seen in Figure 6. As an exercise in the diffusion of new techniques it was reasonably successful. Power-loading was introduced at a rate approaching ten new colliery faces each month. Within two years the proportion of output which was power-loaded had doubled. The Shearer was widely used, as one of the first of the specially developed machines available. More commonly used were the conventional cutters mounted on Panzer conveyors. The Meco-Moore reached its peak of application in 1957.

In addition to the application of power-loading, hydraulic supports for the face were making progress. Initially adopted as yielding supports, they had been developed to fulfil a more complicated function by the time the power-loading drive was under way. With hydraulic and pneumatic power available at the coal face, it was a natural development to apply it to rams, which were introduced to perform the function of pushing the Panzer armoured conveyor up to the face. This operation no longer had to await the completion of the whole cut along the face, but could be performed after the power-loader had passed, because of the strength and flexible joints of the Panzer. In order to complete the concept the powered supports were then re-designed, so that they were capable of being self-advancing. Cantilevered roof beams were already used in conjunction with the powered supports, providing the prop-free face for running the cutter. The powered supports were set in pairs, close enough together for one of the pair to be pushed forward while the other one held the roof load. The self-advancing powered support was considerably more sophisticated as a design than the original hydraulic prop and it continued to be refined in the 1950s and 1960s. The first faces began to be equipped experimentally in 1956. Although a number went into operation during the mid-1950s, detailed re-design based on continuous assessment by the CEE and MRE, working with the co-operation of the manufacturers, enabled the self-advancing operation to be achieved more neatly; it was not until the mid-1960s that these more developed types began to be widely used.

In 1958 the rate of mechanisation was temporarily slowed down. Powered loaders of the types being used tended to produce a great deal of small coal and fines. It was feared by a number of people in the industry that this was a deterioration in the standard of product, which would have an adverse effect on the market. A programme was started to increase the proportion of large coal produced. This objective gave an impetus to the coal ploughs, which had been under development since the 1940s, but which had been little applied. It also gave birth to a new type of coal cutter, the trepanner. Like its counterpart in metalwork, the trepanner used a cylindrical cutter to take out a circular section of coal.[15] Larger coal was produced by the coring action. Subsidiary cutters then squared off the section. Trepanners and ploughs increased in use, being applied to some 300 and 200 faces respectively, by the mid-1960s.

FALLING DEMAND AND INCREASED MECHANISATION

The programme of introducing face mechanisation prevented any further significant fall in output from 1955 to 1957. It did not have time to achieve its intention to raise output. Demand for coal began to slacken by about 1956 (Table 6.3). Although the impact of new methods of heating and new types of fuel was hidden for some time, and inland consumption reached a peak in 1956, the underlying trend of movement away from coal had already started.

The downturn in demand showed itself in exports first. Inland consumption of coal was maintained at a level above previous years in 1955 and 1956, because of the demand from the electricity, coke making and gas making markets. But it had already turned down in the domestic and other inland markets by 1955 or 1956, mainly because of the influence of electric heating in the home, the start of the trend to central heating, and the replacement of coal-fired by oil-fired boilers on industrial premises.

The industry's forecasts of demand had not predicted the move away from coal. When the trend began to appear in the late 1950s, it was hoped that it might be temporary or reversible. New forecasts of demand were made, and incorporated into a new industry statement of policy, the *Revised Plan for Coal* (NCB, 1959). This envisaged some reduction in the 1965 forecasts, particularly in the space heating markets. It set 1965 consumption at 206 million tons. There was a revival in 1960, which appeared to confirm this expectation, but it was mainly a product of cyclical stock effects.

The actual level of demand during the 1960s remained fairly buoyant considering the strength of the trends towards other fuels. It was sustained by a rapid increase in the coal burned at power stations, against a steady fall in other areas. Beneath the figures for the early 1960s there were again a number of trends which promised to reduce demand rapidly from 1965 onwards.

Nuclear power stations were coming into operation from 1962 onwards. As the output of the Magnox stations built up to a peak in 1969 they replaced eight million tons of coal annually. Oil replaced even more, but the actual amount varied according to price changes and the policy of the Government towards support for coal. In the gas industry a major revolution in techniques started in 1962. New gas processes based on oil cut the industry's consumption from 25 million tons in the late 1950s to 9 million tons by 1968/9. The improvement of processes for iron and steel

Table 6.3   *Demand for Coal by Sector, 1952—75*

Year to *31 December*	*Electricity*	*Gas and* *coke*	*Domestic*	*Other* *inland*	*Total* *inland*	*Exports*	*Total*	*Stock* *change*
1952	35·5	52·8	37·6	80·9	206·8	18·5	221·7	+ 3·0
1953	36·7	53·0	37·9	80·2	207·8	21·7	224·4	− 1·4
1954	39·6	53·9	38·0	82·3	213·8	21·2	229·8	− 2·6
1955	42·9	54·9	37·0	80·4	215·2	17·9	229·1	+ 3·8
1956	45·6	57·1	38·0	76·8	217·5	13·1	227·2	+ 0·5
1957	46·5	57·1	36·1	73·2	212·9	10·5	220·8	+ 6·3
1958	46·2	52·6	36·8	66·8	202·4	6·5	207·3	+ 9·9
1959	46·0	48·2	34·0	61·2	189·4	5·5	193·7	+12·8
1960	51·9	51·4	35·5	57·9	196·7	7·3	202·2	− 7·4
1961	55·4	49·5	33·3	53·6	191·8	8·2	197·5	− 5·5
1962	61·1	46·1	33·8	50·2	191·2	7·7	196·0	+ 3·4
Year to *31 March*								
1963	63·8	45·9	34·0	49·7	193·4	8·1	198·4	− 8·5
1964	66·9	46·4	30·7	45·8	189·8	13·1	197·7	− 1·6
1965	69·2	46·0	28·6	43·5	187·3	8·7	192·6	+ 1·7
1966	68·8	43·8	27·8	40·7	181·1	5·9	184·7	− 0·6
1967	67·4	40·5	25·7	36·3	169·9	4·2	172·4	+ 3·2
1968	69·9	37·3	24·2	34·1	165·5	3·5	167·5	+ 6·2
1969	75·2	34·6	22·8	32·4	165·0	5·6	168·1	+ 4·6
1970	76·0	31·4	21·0	30·5	158·9	6·5	162·4	−11·9
1975	71·0	20·0	14·0	19·0	125·0	2·0	127·0	

Source: National Coal Board.
Note: Before 1960 Northern Ireland appeared under 'other inland'.

making meant that less fuel was required per ton of metal output, even though production was increasing. Gas sales in the central heating and space heating market took away 10 million tons more. The railways abandoned steam traction in the middle of the 1960s. The cumulative effect of all these tendencies was that demand fell very rapidly after 1965.

The timing of the fall in demand was doubly unfortunate for the mining industry. If it had occurred earlier, re-organisation of the industry might have taken a different direction. If it had been later, the industry might have been better prepared to meet it. Coming in the middle of a major change in mining methods, the changing demand conditions caused uncertainty about the direction in which the industry was going.

Before the power-loading innovation, productivity had remained static at between 24 and 25 cwt per manshift. It began to show an upward trend in 1957 and this was confirmed by steady growth into the 1960s. This meant that the industry was able to produce approximately the same output per year (deep-mined output remained above 190 million tons until 1960) from a steadily decreasing number of collieries with a diminished labour force. Although the power-loading installations of the 1950s did not immediately revolutionise the rate of output per face, they did have the effect of reducing the number of men required on face work to produce a given output.

Employment in the industry began to fall in 1958, dipping permanently below 700,000 men. A net total of 22,000 men left the mines in that year. In 1959 the serious downturn in demand began to be recognised and not long after the publication of the *Revised Plan for Coal* work started on a new plan for the 1960s. At least as serious as the threat from technical change (in the steel industry, gas industry and railways) was the threat which falling oil prices offered.

By contrast with the forms of fuel in which prices promised to decrease, or were actually doing so, coal had a poor outlook. Prices generally had risen by about 90 per cent during the 1950s and were to go up another 6 per cent in 1960. From 1961 to 1966, several factors fortunately combined to hold overall coal prices fairly steady, but prices were bound to go up again to the extent that productivity failed to keep pace with rising costs.

Although keeping its prices as low as possible, the Coal Board found it hard to deliver coal at a per therm to the power stations which would be competitive with oil. Electricity generating was one of the only markets in which, when more realistic forecasts of the prospects were examined, coal expected to be able to achieve growth. The newly adopted plan for the industry was aimed at keeping prices from rising any further during the period of increasing competition from oil. It therefore had to be a plan which reduced mining costs, and that meant the achievement of higher productivity.

Alfred Robens, afterwards Lord Robens, took over as Chairman of the Coal Board in 1960. He brought to the job a sense of dedication to the issue of the industry's survival which few heads of public corporations have equalled. Robens adopted the campaign of spreading mechanisation throughout the industry as his own. Again the Coal Board adopted the approach of trying to win the support and co-operation of miners through conferences, persuasion and exhortation. This kind of appeal was necessary because the successful introduction of face machinery depended so much upon the team spirit and co-operation the miners displayed.

The new approach to face mechanisation was not different in nature to the previous one, but it was intensified. It was marked by the much wider introduction of the types of cutter loader which had been developed specifically for the fully mechanised face, i.e., shearers, trepanners, ploughs or developments and different types of these machines. In the years 1960 to 1965 the number of faces which employed these machines increased from about 500 out of 1,000 mechanised faces to about 1,200 out of 1,450 mechanised faces (Table 6.4).

Table 6.4 *Proportion of Output Power-Loaded*

Year to 31 December	*NCB deep-mined output (m. tons)*	*Power-loaded (%)*	*Faces using powered supports (%)*	*Face o.m.s. (cwt)*	*Overall o.m.s. (cwt)*
1950	202·3	3·8	—	63·7	24·2
1953	209·8	6·0	—	65·8	24·7
1956	207·3	15·5	—	67·0	24·8
1958	198·8	27·8	2	70·7	25·6
1960	183·8	37·5	4	79·5	28·0
1961	179·6	47·7	6	83·5	28·9
1962	187·6	58·8	6	91·0	31·2
Year to 31 March					
1963	188·3	61·2	7	92·9	31·7
1964	187·2	68·4	9	99·1	33·4
1965	183·7	75·0	12	103·6	34·8
1967	164·6	85·7	50	113·7	36·6
1969	153·0	91·8	75	132·4	42·5
1975	115·4	95·0	92	155·4	45·0

Source: National Coal Board.

The trend is shown in Figure 6. Shearers increased rapidly from 1961; trepanners continued on a steady rate of growth to 1964; ploughs reached over 190 faces by 1964. The specialised machines replaced the conveyor-mounted power-loader adapted out of the more conventional cutter on many faces where the latter had been in use.

The other feature which distinguished the intensification of face mechanisation was that it was accompanied by a higher rate of colliery closings. Table 6.5 shows that there was a net loss of 260 collieries from 1947 to 1960, a rate of twenty per year. Nearly 700 collieries remained in 1960, but ten years later there were just under 300, a net loss of 400. The rate of closure had nearly doubled during the 1960s and the annual net loss was forty collieries.[16] It was almost invariably the smaller and the less efficient collieries which closed down, either because of exhaustion of reserves or because of high costs and falling demand. Closures therefore had the effect of raising the average level of output of all collieries (Table 6.5). In the period 1947 to 1960 the average size of producing unit had risen by only 36 per cent. In the next ten years it rose from 262,000 tons per year to 468,000 tons per year, an increase of 79 per cent. The fact that the pits closed were less efficient, with a lower-than-average output per manshift, meant that closure helped to raise the level of productivity throughout the industry.

Table 6.5   *Reduction in Number of Producing Collieries, 1947—75*

Year ending	NCB producing collieries	Deep-mined output (m. tons)	Average annual output/colliery (000 tons)
1947	958	184·4	192
1955	850	207·8	244
1960	698	183·8	262
1963	611	188·5	308
1965	534	183·7	343
1967	438	164·6	374
1970	299	139·8	468
1975	246	115·4	468

Source: National Coal Board, *Annual Reports.*

RESEARCH AND DEVELOPMENT APPLIED TO MINING TECHNIQUES, 1960—75

During the 1950s the research function had been establishing itself in the industry, fitting into an environment which had scarcely contained such an element before. By 1960 the Coal Research Establishment had been in existence for twelve years, the Mining Research Establishment for eight years and the Central Engineering Establishment at Bretby for five years. One major element of the work of MRE and CEE had been to identify, by collecting information and testing equipment in use, the problems which hindered the successful introduction of face mechanisation. Another major part of the work the establishments carried out was directly innovative.

From the experiments in the late 1940s on yielding supports, the two establishments and the production department at headquarters had evolved the idea of self advancing supports, first tested in the mid-1950s.

The use of self advancing supports, which were set and controlled hydraulically, led to the idea that they could be operated remotely. Improving the design and testing the equipment took several years, but in 1963 remotely controlled longwall faces were tried out at a number of collieries in the east Midlands. The machinery used was a sophisticated development of that which was being introduced throughout the coalfield. A power-loader and a set of self advancing supports were installed at the face; controls for the hydraulic equipment and electrical drive of the loader were set up in a control room some hundreds of yards away. Cables carried controlling signals from the operating room to the pumps and drives at the face. Monitoring of the cutter's progress, the loading of the coal, the snaking of the conveyor and the advance of the groups of supports was conducted by viewing them over a closed circuit television network. Instrumentation was introduced progressively, to report on operation and performance at various points in the equipment.

The remotely operated longwall face (ROLF) was Bretby's (CEE's) most advanced and most important project during the 1960s. There were a dozen ROLF test installations at work in the east Midlands by 1965. They were being used to improve the technique of steering the cutter through the coal, to test the effectiveness of different types of cutter under conditions of remote operation, to identify the causes of machine non-operating time and to develop further the design of supports. ROLFs were worked at first with small teams of men at the face to assist control and monitoring; they were particularly needed to investigate the causes of any snags and report quickly to the operation centre. The intention, however, was to develop the equipment so that most of the interruptions to mining could be detected by the television system and the instrumentation. When delays to mining and difficult conditions could be detected and cleared from the control room, each ROLF would be cutting coal with no manpower at the face.

In 1964 it was decided to equip a complete colliery at Bevercotes with remotely operated longwall faces. While continued advances were made at the experimental faces, ROLFs were installed at Bevercotes colliery. Operations started in February 1967. The gains which could have been achieved by operating coal faces with no manpower, other than for the control room and for maintenance, were those of a very high rate of output per manshift for the colliery as a whole. The intention was to work the faces seven days a week and twenty-four hours a day, in order to keep the equipment in use for the maximum time. However, it proved difficult to bring Bevercotes to a fully operational level.

The many difficult conditions experienced during mining were highlighted by the ROLF experiment. Coal seams are irregular in their characteristics; variations in the seam height and minor faulting require delicate steering of the cutter. Roof and floor conditions are also critical to the steady advance of the face through the seam; the face equipment must be responsive to variations which otherwise cause mining to be halted. Severe conditions for machinery exist in all deep underground seams and mechanical breakdown is to be expected as a result. The combination of these factors prevented the ROLF equipment at Bevercotes from actually being in operation enough of the time to raise output and productivity to the levels necessary. It is probably true that the equipment itself was adequate to the task in a situation where the mining conditions were predictable and consistent. But mining conditions are very rarely thus. Although the ROLF experiment did not lead to coal getting by unattended machines, it had the virtue of laying emphasis on the major factors which inhibited high rates of mechanised output.

Automatic techniques of mining did not suffer eclipse with ROLF. A second innovation of the CEE at Bretby was the use of nucleonic instrumentation to steer the coal cutter through the seam. One of the disadvantages of mechanised power-loading was that machines, being less able than men to distinguish between coal and other substances, were inclined to cut more dirt and stone where minor variations occurred in the coal seam. Nucleonic sensing was developed to distinguish between the coal and other substances, the information providing automatic steering of the cutting. An early application of coal-sensing instrumentation was to the Collins Midget Miner, a machine developed for cutting in very thin seams; by the 1970s nucleonic steering was being applied with some success to power-loading machines.

The research effort which was mounted on mining techniques probably achieved a greater impact on productivity through its assistance to the successful introduction of the powered-support mechanised face than it did through more radical innovations. The stepping up of the mechanisation programme which began in 1960 was accompanied by systematic efforts to understand and counteract the factors which prevented high outputs per manshift from being achieved on all mechanised faces.[17] The NCB's production department used the data collected and analysed by MRE and CEE in the later 1950s, and their experience of the experimental face set up near Bretby, in order to improve the effectiveness with which machinery was being applied.

The general problem which the mechanisation programme faced was that the results produced by applying machinery varied widely between one face and another and were essentially unpredictable. Instead of being able to forecast that mechanisation of one or all the faces at a colliery would yield a predictable increase in output per manshift and in the total output per face per day, the Coal Board found that some projects fell far short of their potential, and many resulted in productivity increases which were significantly less than forecast. Consequently, rational decision making, based on criteria such as the capital rate of return, was an exercise whose ends were frustrated.

The major symptom of the problems which the research establishments were being called upon to solve was the slowness of the rate of growth of productivity. Although nearly 50 per cent of output was mechanised by 1961, face o.m.s. had gone up by only 30 per cent and o.m.s. overall by less than 20 per cent (Table 6.6).

Table 6.6   O.m.s. by Place of Work, 1950—75

31 December	Mechanised (power-loaded) output (%)	Overall (cwt)	At the face (cwt)	Elsewhere underground (cwt)	Surface (cwt)	Major capital expenditure (£m.)[a]
1950	4	24·2	63·7	64·0	99·5	10
1957	23	24·9	69·3	58·5	115·0	50
1961	48	28·9	83·5	66·4	132·3	48
31 March						
1965	75	34·8	109·7	77·7	159·9	28
1969	92	42·5	132·4	93·7	189·3	14
1975	95	45·0	155·4	92·3	201·0	n.a.

Source: National Coal Board.
Note: [a] Capital expenditure covering new collieries and major reconstruction. Maximum in 1959 at about £68 million.

The reasons why o.m.s. failed to grow at a rate consonant with the increase in mechanised output are as varied as the many different conditions which are met underground in British collieries. First, there were the problems on the face itself. Major faulting of seams can usually be predicted by survey, and production can be planned to avoid it. But minor faults are often undetectable, so that the mechanised face team comes upon them unexpectedly. Then they are involved in long and difficult labour to arrange a way of working the face in spite of the fault, or in some cases the face may have to be abandoned. Seams do not always form a good roof, so that there are constant delays while different methods of strata control are tried. Many of the coal seams being worked were inclined, had changing gradients and excessively wet or dusty conditions, and these characteristics place a strain on all the equipment at a fully mechanised face, which may make it break down more frequently than it should. The seams were too narrow or too faulted, too deep in the ground or surrounded by unpredictable strata. Many of them just did not have the reserves of workable coal or a rich enough coal content to make mechanisation pay. The tunnels and shafts connecting the coal faces to the surface were tortuous, often narrow, difficult to open up initially and to maintain. Many of the collieries themselves were too small ever to be high productivity units, their locations in relation to the largest reserves of coal were against them and the scale on which they had originally been laid out, in late Victorian or Edwardian times, made the introduction of mechanised mining more a question of 'mend and make-do' than of modernisation. Then there were the problems of work behind the face. Many essential jobs are required in a colliery to service the coal output. They include transport, electrical work, maintenance, opening up new headings and supplying the faces being worked. All of them are unproductive, in the sense that increasing manshifts in these areas with no increase in face output decreases the overall productivity of the colliery. And o.m.s. elsewhere underground (Table 6.6) had grown much more slowly than at the face. By 1961 it had increased only 4 per cent above the 1950 level, and by 1965 it had achieved no more than a 20 per cent increase.

The rate of driving tunnels underground to open up a face for exploitation was slow. One hundred yards per week was a record in 1959, while the average rate at all collieries was 14 yards per week. Once development headings had been opened up, they were difficult to maintain in a usable condition at depths of 400 to 700 yards below the surface. A disproportionate amount of the manpower which had been saved at the face was necessarily employed in securing the access from the district roads to the face, particularly if the rate of advance was high. In order for the power-loader to attack the coal face sideways on and cut a web off the length, a heading in advance of the face had to be driven at each end (the headings were called stable holes). Cutter-loaders had to be returned to the starting end of the face after each cut. Before the successful development of self advancing supports in the mid-1960s, a good deal of labour was employed in setting supports, as the face itself went forward.

The solution to many of the problems in making the mechanised face more successful was progressively seen to lie with the painstaking application of engineering development; the years 1960 to 1975 saw a steady improvement in the concept being evolved between the production department at HQ and the research establishments at Isleworth and Bretby. In 1955 the Coal Board had instigated an internal inquiry into organisation and the resulting Fleck Report had recommended that there should be a stronger technical policy-making agency. The first research and development committee was formed, with the Chairman, Bowman, at its head. Although it was able to identify problem areas it was not successful in getting solutions adopted. During 1961 and 1962 (under Robens) this rather broadly representative R and D committee was replaced by a smaller Board-level committee to determine important issues of technical policy; a conference of Divisional production directors provided a channel of communication from the coalfield's mechanisation problems. One of the major tasks was to persuade the colliery managers and Area production directors that the problems they faced were potentially soluble by Isleworth and Bretby, and to get closer co-operation between the engineers in the field and the engineers on the research and development side.

However, MRE and CEE began to tackle the day-to-day problems of producing coal at an early stage, undertaking development of a tunnelling machine to improve rates of drivage during the late 1950s. In 1962 MRE at Isleworth was transferred from the science department to the production department at HQ. Work on the self-advancing face was at a stage in 1962 where it was nearly ready for wholesale application to existing faces.

Experiments were under way to improve productivity in the maintenance of roadways. Machinery for driving the stable holes at each end of longwall faces was being tested.

By concentrating the attention of production departments at Area and Divisional level and the research efforts of MRE and CEE, the industry was able to reach a more generally agreed view of the main problems. During the years 1962 to 1966 the requirements of high outputs from mechanised faces began to be clearly understood. The most radical result of the concentrated application of research was that it became accepted that many of the longwall faces in the collieries were not actually suitable for mechanisation. The mining conditions which they presented were harsh enough to tax the ingenuity of the best mining engineer; the addition of machinery provided only a marginal benefit. The major limitation on face outputs in these cases was not the amount of power which could be applied, but the rate at which the ground would allow coal to be removed.

POWERED-SUPPORT MECHANISED COAL FACES, 1965—75

The recognition that geological conditions were a major constraint was a most important decision for the powered-support face. Although power-loading affected 75 per cent of output by 1965, the performance of the industry was still held back by collieries and coal seams in which higher o.m.s. was not practicable. The best collieries and Areas, where power-loading was eminently applicable, were already in the early 1960s achieving face outputs of 120 to 150 cwt per manshift, compared to the average for the industry of about 93 cwt in 1963. Similarly, overall o.m.s. was as high as 45 to 50 cwt, where the collieries with poor conditions were struggling to achieve 20 cwt.

The result of recognising these facts was, first, that the number of faces being worked was drastically reduced, and, secondly, that efforts were intensified to get very high daily outputs from the faces which remained. As a result of colliery closures during the early 1960s, the total number of faces being worked had come down from over 3,000 to about 2,400 by 1965. 1,680 of these were mechanised. By 1969 the number of mechanised faces had been reduced below 1,000, with the total number of faces in operation down to about 1,200. By 1975 there were about 650 major longwall mechanised faces and fewer than 750 faces being worked in all. The 246 collieries remaining in operation on 31 March 1975 had an average of only three faces each in operation. Average annual production per colliery (Table 6.5) increased rapidly from 1965 to 1970. Output per face increased dramatically, from 300—320 tons per face per day in 1965 to approaching 650 tons per face per day by 1975.[18]

These improvements in colliery and face rates of output were brought about with the assistance of the techniques worked out and applied by the production department and the research establishments. The self-advancing powered-support face was increasing in use very rapidly before

1965, over 250 faces having been fitted. By 1967 over 700 faces were equipped and during 1968 and 1969, as the total number of mechanised faces in use came down rapidly towards 850, the proportion of output which was provided by self advancing faces approached 80 per cent (Figure 7). Development of the powered support face equipment continued, to produce machines which could cope better with varied conditions.

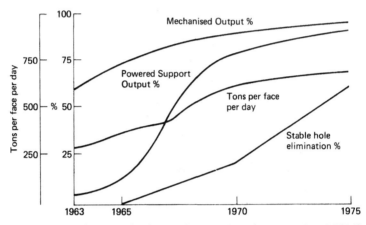

Figure 7 Progress of mechanisation and output per face per day (1971/2 and 1973/4 excluded).

The second programme which was based on work from Bretby was the improvement of methods of making stable holes. In some cases a face would be worked with the stable holes driven by a separate heading machine. More commonly two power loaders were employed, one being used to cut a short distance into the coal at one face-end and thus create an entry for the other machine, which took the main coal-getting cut. Reducing the work of stable hole formation was important, because it allowed a significant reduction in manpower to be made on a face. In Figure 7 the stable hole programme has been represented as affecting 20 per cent of output by 1970 and 62 per cent of output by 1975; the progress made, however, was not necessarily steady.

Further progress was made in the design of cutters. The number of trepanning cutters used failed to grow after 1963 and ploughs declined in popularity (Figure 6). A new cutter was introduced, called the ranging drum shearer. Developed as a variation of the original Anderton Shearer, it was more adaptable in its application to a range of cutting needs. Programmes were started by the production department to raise the daily output per face. The programme of 'spearhead faces' originally covered 19 faces, where an objective was set to produce 1,000 tons per machine shift. One of the purposes was to provide an example of the rate of output which was possible using the equipment developed. The programme also led to important experience being gained of the degree to which intensive mining on this scale was dependent on co-ordination by management. Eventually the programme was extended to some 150 faces, which were able to achieve daily outputs of 1,000 tons.

An attempt was also made to increase the amount of retreat working. A retreat face reverses the order of operations used in longwall advancing. Two headings are driven into the coal from the district roads and are pushed forward to the furthest limit to which the seam is to be extracted. Then a coal face is established, by driving a cross drift to connect the headings at their further ends. Extraction of the coal takes place by working back from the furthest extent of the headings towards the district road where they were originated. This method can produce very high rates of output, in the right geological conditions. The need for stable hole formation is eliminated, because of the existence of the headings already driven; the work required behind the face supports of an advancing face, controlling the collapse of the roof into the goaf and maintaining the tunnels which serve the face, is also eliminated, because the face is working back to the district road and not away from it.[19] Where manning levels of eighteen to twenty men were required for most advancing faces, a retreat face could use as few as eight men and the gains in o.m.s. were very substantial.

With improved power loaders, self advancing supports, the elimination of time-consuming face work, high productivity programmes, concentration on a much smaller number of faces and the closure of most high cost collieries, it seemed in the late 1960s and early 1970s that the rewards to be expected from mechanisation were about to be reaped. The Annual Report of 1969/70 summed up the feeling as follows:

'The last ten years have seen a substantial investment by the coal industry in mechanisation. This has already brought large returns but further large benefits still remain to be won. The need in future is to concentrate management effort on obtaining the best possible utilisation of the modern machinery now available. This calls for the highest standards of management and of engineering expertise, for enthusiasm from the mineworkers and for the closest co-operation with the unions.'[20]

It was expected that overall productivity in the remaining collieries would rise from the level it stood at in March 1965, of about 35 cwt, to reach approximately 75 cwt by the mid-1970s (cf. Figure 5). The days of large numbers of colliery closures were over by 1970. Only fifty-three pits were closed in the next five years, the lowest rate of closure since nationalisation.

Somehow the expected failed to happen. The technological advance which the development of the fully mechanised face represented failed to register itself in any startling increase in productivity. Instead of being able to control costs and keep coal prices steady as a result of improvements in output per manshift, the Board found itself forced to raise prices because productivity grew too slowly.

Output per manshift had been increasing since 1958 (Figure 8). The rapid reduction in the number of faces in production, which reached its peak between 1964 and 1970 (Table 6.7), helped o.m.s. to climb rather more quickly for a few years. In 1970, however, the trend began to flatten out. By 1975 o.m.s. had reached only 45 cwt, instead of the 75 cwt which had been the objective.

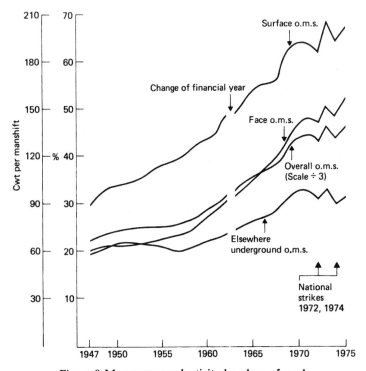

Figure 8 Manpower productivity by place of work.

It is naturally impossible to say what would have happened to the industry if the price of oil had not risen so quickly in 1973. Productivity was failing to grow fast enough to provide for regular wage increases and prices would presumably have had to go on rising in step with the increases in the Board's costs.[21] As it was, the increase in oil prices prevented coal from becoming uncompetitive and probably saved the industry from further contraction. However, the events of the oil crisis and the two miners' strikes of the early 1970s only served to divert attention temporarily from the real problem, which continued to be that of productivity.

Table 6.7 *Reduction of Working Faces, 1960—75*

	Collieries in production	Faces in use (estimated)	National output per day (estimated) (000 tons)	Output per face per day (3 — 2) (tons)
1960	698	3,050	736	241
1964	576	2,300	750	326
1965	534	2,070	750	362
1966	483	1,770	710	401
1967	438	1,600	675	422
1968	376	1,260	665	538
1969	317	1,060	625	590
1970	299	940	585	622
1973	281	770	530	689
1975	246	680	480	706

Source: National Coal Board and author's estimates.

CONCLUSION

There were three general reasons why the face mechanisation innovations did not solve the problem of low productivity in the mining industry.

(1) The potential of mechanisation in terms of face productivity. The mechanisation equipment was complex to operate; its performance was critically determined by the skills and ingenuity of the men on the face. The equipment was also subservient to geology; face conditions primarily determined output rates. Hostile geology could prevent the best installation and the most skilful team from raising output significantly.

(2) Productivity elsewhere underground. The very low rate of growth of productivity at work places underground, other than at the face, acted as a brake upon the effect which face improvements could achieve. If o.m.s. elsewhere underground had increased at the same rate as o.m.s. at the face, overall productivity in 1974/5 would have been 55 cwt instead of 45 cwt.

(3) The scale and nature of British collieries. Small collieries use labour less efficiently than larger collieries, particularly labour employed at the surface and below ground, but not at the face. British collieries in 1975 were still significantly smaller in terms of average output per year than German, Dutch and Polish collieries had been before the last war. Antiquated layout underground also reduces labour efficiency; the majority of British mines were planned to exploit reserves of coal long since exhausted and have had to adapt the imposed layout as well as they could to reach new reserves.

The major difficulties of implementing the powered support and power loader equipment have been dealt with above. Even in 1975 it remained an open question by how much the mechanisation concept could be expected to raise productivity at the face. The extent to which each team of men learned to apply the face machinery so that its potential for raising output was fully realised was one factor. Given further time and additional improvements to the system, some measure of greater success could be expected. What was much less clear was the extent to which continued concentration on improving the application of techniques would produce more uniform results over all the faces in operation. Table 6.8 shows how the Coal Board planned to raise the average output per face so that, compared to 1974, it would be relatively evenly distributed about an average value of approximately 900 tons per face per day, instead of being unevenly distributed about an average value of between 600 and 700 tons per day. The unknown factor was whether output per day on each face was mostly dependent upon the standard of labour skills in applying the machinery, or whether it was really determined by the natural conditions on each face. Such an increase in average output per face might require that the number of faces being worked was reduced by as much as 50 per cent, in order to concentrate on those faces which allow really high rates of output. It is worth noting that the German industry, in which daily face output reached 900 tons in 1971, was at that time working on less than 500 faces, in seams that were on average thicker than British ones and provided better mining conditions.

Table 6.8   *Planned Distribution of Face Output, Late 1970s*

Face output (tons per day)	1974 (% of faces)	Late 1970s (% of faces)
0—400	39	16
401—800	36	30
801—1,200	15	32
above 1,200	10	22

Source: National Coal Board.

Raising face productivity only tackles part of the problem. Even if it could be increased to 1,000 tons per day on average for all faces, the effect upon overall o.m.s. would be much diminished, unless productivity elsewhere below ground and at the surface also increased. A determined assault by the industry during 1969—73 on reducing the number of underground manshifts worked on transport, roadways, engineering services, etc., did not reveal promise of really startling improvements in the output per manshift elsewhere underground. The jobs that are not directly productive are always going to impose the same kind of servere brake upon advances made in face productivity. If the average colliery in 1975 was running three production faces at about 600 tons per day each, about 200 manshifts every day were required at the face to produce the coal. At the same time 390 manshifts had to be worked elsewhere underground, to get the coal to the winding-shaft and keep the mine working. Another 180 manshifts were being worked at the shafts and at the other surface installations. It is the number and nature of these other manshifts that holds back the effects of improved coal face productivity.

The complexity of even a mechanised colliery, the interdependence of the groups of men and equipment which keep it going and the extent to which it constitutes a complete system, are things which it is hard for the outsider to appreciate. At the average size colliery, with an output in the region of 1,800 tons per day, the day-shift might have the following type of personnel distribution. About twenty-five to thirty men would be working on three high-production faces, in charge of the cutter loaders, operating the powered supports, advancing the maingate and tailgate tunnels in step with the face and performing other more or less immediately productive jobs. Between the faces and the bottom of the shaft there might be as many as thirty-five or forty transport workers, beltmen, transfer point supervisors, loco. operators etc. In addition, there would be about twenty electricians, fitters, lubricators and other maintenance or engineering services personnel. Employees involved in bringing up supplies, salvaging equipment and other miscellaneous jobs would make up another fifteen men. Twenty-five extra men might be distributed around the workings, driving headings for new faces, building roadways and repairing existing tunnels. Finally, about twenty supervisors, under-managers, deputies and overmen would be in charge of work underground. On the surface would be another dozen men, involved in bringing up the coal and winding men and supplies in and out of the pit. In addition, there would be twenty-five more maintenance, transport and ancillary workers, half-a-dozen men working the coal preparation plant and several more officials.

With other odd tasks to be performed from time to time, the total number of workers employed during the shift would approach 250, of which less than a third, but probably over a quarter, would be face-workers. The job which each man does is an important one, and the skills employed have evolved over a long period. The management, direction and control of the whole working unit is a demanding task. Much of the time the main enemies are the forces of nature, in their unexpected manifestations. It can seem an uphill task to keep productivity merely at a standstill. Trying to increase productivity, particularly that of the many workers employed away from the face, is a problem for which an immediate prescription is seldom apparent.

Raising face output from 700 tons per face per day to 1,000 tons over a five-year period, supposing it were achieved, at the size the industry was in 1975, with no increase of manshifts at the face, would have the effect of raising face output per manshift to approximately 190 cwt, compared with 155 cwt in 1975. The effect of this on overall productivity, if the output per shift of other workers did not increase, would be to raise o.m.s. from 45 cwt (1975) to just less than 55 cwt. But if wage increases, capital costs and material prices were to increase the costs of deep mined output by only 5 per cent annually, then productivity improvements of this order would not obviate the need for higher coal prices. If the benefits of face mechanisation are to lead to control over costs, then productivity behind the face has to grow as well. At best it has grown only slowly up to 1975 (Figure 8), and at times it has declined.

In the past, o.m.s. both elsewhere underground and at the surface has risen most quickly during periods of colliery closure, when the average size of colliery was increasing. The jobs which are performed at those locations are more efficiently done when the scale of the colliery is large than when it is small. In the twenty-five to thirty British pits which have an annual output of over 1 million tons, o.m.s. elsewhere underground is some 25 per cent higher than the average for the industry, and in the West German industry, where the average colliery size is over 1·5 million tons, the level of o.m.s. elsewhere below ground is 30 per cent higher than in Britain.

As well as being affected by size of colliery, o.m.s. elsewhere underground is affected by colliery layout. Excessive distances or complex patterns of underground workings create lower productivity, because they require greater manning levels and more maintenance. Only about 15 of the 246 collieries which remained by 1975 were new constructions, planned from the start on the basis of reaching the coal in the most efficient manner. Some 200 of the other mines were sunk between 65 and 100 years previously. Originally the sinking was intended to exploit coal reserves which have been long since exhausted, but the collieries have been adapted and their lives extended by driving new headings to reach other parts of the coal. The result is that a colliery frequently consists of the original shaft or shafts, perhaps subsequently enlarged, other shafts, associated with formerly separate workings, but later incorporated into the surviving colliery, abandoned drifts or headings from worked-out seam sections, adapted headings from old workings subsequently utilised for access to new coal, several miles of main road to the current working areas, a number of new district roads where the coal is being worked, development headings to new coal, and a number of other underground shafts and headings which provide intercommunication, facilities for transporting materials and routes for ventilating air patterns. Complex layouts such as these do not lend themselves to efficient levels of output.

The uncomfortable conclusion which has to be drawn from the experience of face mechanisation from 1950 to 1975 is that if the 'further large benefits' of which the Coal Board spoke are to be won, then they will have to be accompanied by further significant concentration of the industry. It is an uncomfortable conclusion because the mining industry has already experienced great stress during the programme of concentration during the 1960s. The further strain on labour relations of more colliery closures might cause considerable damage to the industry and that factor undoubtedly weighs with the Board in its consideration of policy.[22] One cannot help feeling sympathy for a public corporation which has to implement harsh policies such as these for the long-term health of the industry, especially since the failure of the private owners to concentrate production is the main cause of the present problem.

However, concentration is the biggest issue which faces the Coal Board. In order to get productivity to increase faster than costs, the Board might have to aim for a total output, excluding new collieries, of 120 million tons from 400 faces by the 1980s, an average of 1,200 tons output per face per day. To get productivity moving in work locations behind the face and to keep it increasing on the surface, the 400 faces might have to be located in no more than 100 collieries, producing 1·2 million tons output per year on average. Whether the Coal Board, given the nature of the industrial relations problem, really has the opportunity to choose that kind of policy is extremely doubtful.

NOTES

[1] Decisions to invest in underground machinery at individual pits were also difficult to make, but this was because of uncertainty about the production rates which would result from mechanisation. Diverse geological conditions meant that the production results of mechanisation at one colliery were not an accurate guide to expectation at another. Colliery engineers who knew their local conditions often did not have the experience of mechanisation needed to predict its effect on their own pits and forecasting of production costs after the installation of face mechanisation was frequently unreliable, making the application of investment analysis techniques unfruitful.

[2] The excavated area is called the goaf.

[3] A slice taken along the length of face.

[4] About 85 per cent of output was cut on longwall by 1948.

[5] *Coal Mining: Report of the Technical Advisory Committee,* Cmd 6610, HMSO, 1945.

[6] Average weekly earnings were £9 2s 4d for miners in 1950 and £15 1s 8d in 1960, an increase of 75 per cent, when allowance is made for reduced working hours. Nationally, wage rates increased by 69 per cent.

[7] *Coal Mining: Report of the Technical Advisory Committee,* op. cit.

[8] G. W. Ditz, *British Coal Nationalised,* Edward W. Hazen Foundation, New York, 1951.

[9] Underground haulage in Holland moved 25 tons per manshift and in the United States, 50 tons, *The Future of the Coal Miner,* Ministry of Fuel and Power, HMSO, 1946.

[10] Some small mines in the Forest of Dean were left to be worked by the 'free miners' under ancient rights. Total output of the licensed mines averaged under 2 million tons annually.

[11] *The Plan for Coal,* National Coal Board, Hobart House, October 1950.

[12] Ditz, *British Coal Nationalised,* op. cit. See also, Mary Craddock, *A North Country Maid* (Hutchinson, 1960), the autobiography of a miner's daughter who went from a Durham pit village to university, which gives an insight into the miner's independent attitude to his skill.

[13] Over 2,500 cutters, 4,200 belt conveyors, 2,600 scraper and other conveyor types, 300 powered loading machines and cutter loaders and 160 locomotives were bought.

[14] For example, Calverton New pit in Nottinghamshire did not reach coal until some five years after sinking had started on 1 January 1947, and that was after the previous owners had dug the first shaft before the war. Difficult conditions were encountered. Slow rates of drivage on main roadways and development headings also delayed mine construction in general.

[15] The action can be visualised as the same as coring an apple, the machine cutting a continuous core along the coal face.

[16] The actual rate of closure in the 1950s was about twenty-one per year, but new openings brought the net loss down to twenty p.a. In the 1960s fewer new collieries were opened and the rate of closure was about forty-one per year.

[17] *Power Loading in Difficult Geological Conditions* (NCB Production and Reconstruction Department, January 1961) showed how many different types of hazard could strike face output.

[18] Figures refer to all faces. At major longwall faces, output was in the region of 680—700 tons/face/day by 1975.

[19] There are, of course, disadvantages associated with retreat working. It takes longer to open up the faces. Geological stresses are more severe and the headings serving the face have to be very stable. Retreat working has never been popular among British mining engineers, because the geology in British seams rarely favours it.

[20] NCB, *Annual Report 1969/70*, HMSO, 1970, p. 5.

[21] Mining wages were falling below national averages. Average earnings for miners increased by 65 per cent between 1963 and 1971, compared with 83 per cent for all weekly earnings. To make power loading easier to introduce, the payment scheme had been reformed between 1966 and 1970, but this brought home to all mineworkers the earnings consequences of the low growth of productivity. An extended strike over pay followed in 1972 and was repeated in 1974.

[22] The opening of the large-scale colliery at Selby which will employ miners from smaller pits in the area is an attractive way of resolving the dilemma but one which is not unfortunately available everywhere.

7 Productivity and Technical Change

What effect did the programmes of technical change described above have upon the industries, or corporations, in which they occurred? The cases studied are interesting enough just as examples of innovation or the diffusion of new technology; however, the purpose of technical change is to produce economic benefit and the programmes were worth pursuing only if they could be shown to have a beneficial effect upon the economics of operation in their various spheres.

A change in the technology employed in an industry improves operating economics, because it increases the number of units of output obtained from each unit of input. Other things, such as the price of inputs, being equal, operating costs are decreased. The new technology employed may represent a saving of manpower, or of raw materials. Or it may be that the price paid for capital equipment or for other goods and services declines proportionately to the output produced. Some technical changes will bring about savings in all cost categories.

Table 7.1 shows the proportion of expenditure on revenue account in each organisation which was paid to various factors of production in 1950 and in 1975. The figures are derived from the published accounts of the corporations, but some assumptions have had to be made about the category to which each item of published expenditure belongs.

It will be seen that payments to labour formed the largest single category in 1950 for the Coal Board, for the telecommunications department of the Post Office and for BEA. Labour payments include wages, employee welfare, national insurance and pension payments. For the gas industry and the generating industry, on the other hand, it was fuel for conversion to gas and electricity which was the greatest cost, amounting to over half of revenue expenditure in 1950.

We shall, therefore, look primarily at the effect which new technology had upon labour and fuel productivity, rather than trying to estimate the effects upon all categories of cost. The productivity of capital is also an important issue, particularly in the generating industry and in telecommunications, where payments of interest and depreciation accounted for 20 per cent and 40 per cent respectively of all costs throughout the period. However, the simple measure of capital productivity which are

Table 7.1 *Five Corporations: 1950 and 1975 Compared* (percentages of expenditures on revenue account paid to input factors)

		Labour related costs	Depreciation and interest	Process materials or fuel	Other	Total
BEA	1950	45	7	11	37	100
	1974[a]	42	14	9	35	100
British Gas	1950	16	11	56	17	100
	1975	22	34	18	26	100
Generating industry	1950 (estimated)	12	18	57	13	100
	1958	12	23	57	8	100
	1975	10	22	56	12	100
National Coal Board	1950	66	7	27		100
	1970	50	6	44		100
Post Office telecom- munications	1950	43	36	21		100
	1975	37	41	22		100

Source: Accounts of the public corporations.
Note: [a] BEA is not separately distinguishable after 1973/4.

available do not seem to provide a satisfactory basis for intertemporal comparisons within the industries. The development of more satisfactory means of measuring capital productivity is a major task in itself and so only passing reference can be made below to the effects in this area.

In measuring labour productivity, it is fortunate that the industries covered have certain features which serve to make the figures which can be produced more credible. In the first place, the output of each industry is reasonably homogeneous. There are, of course, different grades of coal and different types of airline seat, but no great departure from realism arises by expressing the output of each industry in terms of a single unit.[1] Secondly, the nature of the products and services produced is such that they sustained comparatively little change in the period covered by the study. Thus the difficulties of comparing the output of an industry in which the 1975 product is vastly more advanced than that of 1950 are largely avoided. By the same token, the new technology adopted by the industries in the interim has been embodied mostly in process improvement rather than in product innovation, so that technical changes and productivity changes may be more simply related. Thirdly, the definitional framework and statistical coverage of the industries and corporations has remained fairly stable in spite of slight changes in some of the organisations (see Chapter 1).

Even so, the figures produced below must be interpreted with caution. The prevalent difficulty which besets the exercise is that of attributing factor saving to particular technical changes, except where the most detailed statistics are available. Too often, several changes are taking place concurrently, and the effects of the introduction of new equipment or new techniques cannot be separated from the consequences of concentration of producing units, rationalising of distribution or selling arrangements or increases in the scale of operations.

COAL

In the British coal mining industry it is labour productivity which exercises the dominating influence upon the industry's fortunes. If this judgment needs emphasis it is provided by the fact that statistics of output per manshift (o.m.s.) have been recorded for the industry since the early part of the twentieth century.

Overall labour productivity has increased from 21·5 cwt of output per manshift in 1947 to 45·0 in 1975 (Table 7.2). This represents a rate of growth of just over 2·5 per cent per year from the time of nationalisation, a record which was certainly a great improvement over the performance of the industry before it passed into public ownership. Up to the end of 1959, o.m.s. grew at just below 2·5 per cent; for the ten years from 1960 its rate of growth advanced to reach 5 per cent annually, dropping back in the 1970s.

Within the overall picture of changes in o.m.s., there are significant variations according to the place in the colliery at which the manshifts were being worked. Table 7.3 gives details of the number of shifts worked daily at each of the three main locations, the coal face, elsewhere underground and on the surface. Although the table provides only partial coverage, it can be seen that the ratio of face manshifts to the manshifts worked elsewhere underground and at the surface has substantially improved in twenty-five years. Approximately two men working a full shift at the face and three men working elsewhere were on average required in 1949 to produce nearly 6 tons of coal (i.e. five manshifts at 23·4 cwt each equals 117 cwt). In 1975 the same amount of coal could be produced by 2·6 manshifts altogether, about half the number previously required, but the ratio between face workers and others was 2:5. Two manshifts at the face were producing on average about 15·5 tons in 1975, instead of about 6 tons twenty-five year earlier. But whereas the output of two face workers in 1949 (6 tons) could be supported by three manshifts behind the face and on the surface, for the output of two face workers in 1975 (15·5 tons) five other manshifts were required.

The figures in Table 7.2 for productivity at the three main places of work support this conclusion. Coalface o.m.s. increased by a total of 167 per cent over the period while surface o.m.s. was not far behind, with a total improvement of 133 per cent. But o.m.s. elsewhere underground, that is to say on the part of transport workers, heading drivers, repairers

Table 7.2   *Progress of Coal Output per Manshift, 1947—75*

Year[a]	Deep-mined output (m. tons)	Manpower[b] (000s)	Producing collieries at year's end	Power-loaded (mechanised) output (%)	Productivity (cwt/manshift)			
					Overall	At the coal face	Elsewhere underground	On the surface
1947	184	704	958	2	21·5	58·4	56·9	86·1
1949	201	713	912	3	23·4	61·9	61·6	97·1
1954	211	702	867	8	24·9	65·6	62·7	111·2
1959	193	658	737	31	26·9	75·0	62·7	127·4
1964/5	184	491	534	75	34·8	103·6	77·7	159·9
1969/70	140	305	299	92	43·4	137·7	95·4	189·6
1974/5	5	246	246	94	45·0	155·4	92·3	201·0

Source: National Coal Board, *Annual Reports.*
Notes: [a] Year ending 30 December, 1947—59, 31 March, 1964/5—1974/5.
   [b] Manpower refers to wage labour on the books at collieries. Staff labour and workers in non-colliery activities varied between 50,000 and 75,000.

Table 7.3 *Coal: composition of Manshifts Worked Daily by Place of Work* (000s rounded)

	1950[a]	1960[a]	1968/9	1971/2	1974/5
Face					
Mechanised production faces			78	62	51
Other face manshifts			18	15	11
Total face	210	190	96	77	62
Elsewhere underground					
Officials		n.a.	22	20	19
Transport		79	42	37	33
Roadway development		20	13	13	12
Roadway repair		5	14	11	10
Engineering services		28	24	18	17
Other underground manshifts		63	20	17	14
Total elsewhere underground		n.a.	135	116	105
Surface					
Officials		n.a.	4	4	3
Winding & banking	339	13	17	13	11
Coal preparation		17	10	8	7
Maintenance		26	19	16	14
Other surface manshifts		32	18	16	13
Total surface		n.a.	68	57	47
Total Overall	549	523	299	250	214
Daily output (000 tons)	817	736	625	525	480

Source: National Coal Board, *Annual Reports.*
Note: [a] Estimates produced by applying an attendance factor to the number of workers on the NCB books divided by type of worker. The 1950 totals are not further broken down. In 1960 it is not possible to allocate shifts to the 42,500 officials and foremen, underground and on the surface. 'Roadway repair' shifts may be included in 'other underground' for 1960.

and engineering services, etc., increased by only 62 per cent in twenty-eight years. The coalface increase represents 4 per cent per year, that at the surface represents 3·5 per cent and the increase in o.m.s. elsewhere underground represents a rate of just over 1·5 per cent annually.

Both concentration of output and mechanisation of operations at the coal face contributed to improved o.m.s. Productivity at the surface is dependent upon the nature of the capital equipment employed in raising coal and preparing it for sale, and upon the efficiency with which management organises for functions such as maintenance, repair and administrative duties. It would appear that these activities are likely to have been improved during the period since nationalisation by two factors; first, in the early period to about 1958 the replacement of surface facilities and re-organisation of colliery layout would provide the main source of productivity gain. As reconstruction schemes at the surface began to be completed, however, the rate of colliery closure went up and incidentally increased the average size of colliery from 260,000 tons output to 470,000 tons output annually. Productivity gains in the second half of the period are largely attributable to the increased efficiencies of scale which attend most surface jobs.

Productivity underground elsewhere than at the face showed least tendency to improve and there is little evidence that it was affected by innovation. Work elsewhere underground is widely varying in nature, largely labour intensive, not conducive to system and difficult to plan and manage. O.m.s. improved marginally while conveyors and improved transport were being installed in the late 1940s. Otherwise productivity appears to have increased steadily only during the programme of large-scale closure from 1958 to 1969. This is consistent with o.m.s. underground but not at the face being related mainly to the scale of colliery operations.

Gains in face productivity may be estimated to be attributable equally to face mechanisation and concentration of production. Full-scale mechanisation was capable of reducing the manpower requirement on a face by a considerable amount, but the faces to which it was applied, representing only 15 per cent of the number in operation in 1947, were the best faces for mining operations. Their level of face productivity without mechanisation would have been well above the 58 cwt per manshift of all faces in 1947.

GAS

Productivity comparisons in the gas industry are difficult to interpret, because of the two major changes in the source of supply over twenty-five years. Table 7.1 shows that the proportions of revenue expenditure going to labour, capital, fuel and other costs altered radically. In 1950 fuel costs were by far the most important component, with capital costs at a fairly low level. Twenty-five years later capital costs were a third of total costs, fuel had shrunk to less than one-fifth and labour costs had actually increased as a proportion of total costs. This reflects the transition from the fuel conversion process to direct natural gas supplies, with its high rate of investment in the transmission network and accelerated depreciation of old plant. The trend was accentuated by the diminishing cost to the Gas Boards of both manufactured and purchased supplies of gas. The approximate cost per therm, before allowing for inflation, was around 12—15d for gas from the most efficient carbonisation works in the early 1960s; oil-based gas in the mid 1960s was estimated at 6—7d and the supplies of North Sea gas in the early 1970s were contracted at around 4d per therm.

Labour costs also became an increasing part of total costs because of the reductions in the cost of gas supplies, but labour productivity showed steady improvement. In crude terms, in 1954/5 there were 18,400 therms sold per employee; in 1974/5 over 126,400 therms were sold per employee. Part of this increase in productivity can obviously be attributed to the fact that production workers were reduced to a tenth of their former numbers because of the switch to North Sea supplies (Table 7.4).

Table 7.4   *Trends in Gas Sales, Production and Numbers Employed in the Industry, 1955—75*

Year ended 31 March	1954/5	1959/60	1964/5	1969/70	1974/5
Gas sold per employee (therms)	18,400	20,200	26,400	44,200	126,400
All gas sold[a]					
(m. therms)	2,636	2,591	3,188	5,267	13,019
gas made	2,502	2,231	2,373	2,220	1,266
gas bought	376	590	1,147	2,787	12,426
Employment					
production	60,217	46,065	37,309	21,278	6,220
conversion	nil	nil	nil	4,981	1,506
distribution		15,752	14,893	15,939	18,213
customer service	83,161	38,755	43,172	45,799	41,452
customer accounts		11,217	10,251	11,084	12,548
administrative etc.		15,171	15,663	20,394	22,114
Total	143,378	126,970	121,288	119,475	103,053
of which manual	106,783	89,567	74,414	54,723	41,686

Source: Gas Council and Gas Corporation, *Annual Reports.*
Note: [a] The total of gas sold includes gas used in gas works for processes. 'Gas made' and 'gas bought' together amount to more than sales because of process and distribution losses.

The number of production workers required to produce the output of manufactured gas demonstrates the contribution which the newly invented methods of gas manufacture made to reducing labour costs in the industry. In 1954/5 the gas made per production worker per year was 41,500 therms, in 1959/60 it was 48,500 and in 1974/5 204,000 therms (Table 7.5).

The improvement in output per production worker between 1954/5 and 1964/5, about 4 per cent annually, is mainly attributable to the process of concentration of supply and rationalisation of distribution which had been made possible by public ownership. Productivity then grew at just over 10 per cent per year until 1969/70, as a result of the transition to oil-based methods of manufacture; during the next five years, in which productivity

Table 7.5   *Productivity of Gas Production Workers*

	Therms per production worker per year	Gas made (m. therms)
1954/5	41,500	2,502
1959/60	48,500	2,231
1964/5	62,500	2,373
1968/9	123,400	2,942
1969/70	105,000	2,220
1954/5	204,000	1,266

grew at 14 per cent per year, there was a high rate of scrapping of plant, even of relatively recent oil-based process plant. Concentration of supply in the most recent plants took place and process plants used a wide range of feedstocks, natural gas, oil and refinery products.

If the 13,019 million therms of gas sold in 1974/5 had all been produced as town gas from process plants, at the efficiency ruling for actual production in that year, instead of being for the most part piped to the consumer direct, the effect upon employment would have been to increase the number of production workers required to about 64,000. Total employment would thus have increased to 160,317 (conversion workers can be excluded) and overall productivity would have stood at 81,500 therms sold per man year, compared to 26,400 therms in 1964/5. The rate of growth of productivity of labour which this implies for new gas processes is just over 11 per cent per year over the ten years.

The comparison of fuel productivity for the carbonisation process with that for the oil-based processes introduced in 1962—5 is difficult because the former process resulted in a product part gas, part coke and part other materials. It seems that carbonisation was approaching an average of 78 per cent overall thermal efficiency of products in the late 1950s. Oil-based methods of producing gas had thermal efficiencies of 75—80 per cent, and they resulted in total gasification. In terms of gas products, thermal efficiency improved from 0·33 therms of gas per therm of fuel bought in the early 1960s to 0·64 therms per therm of fuel in 1969/70.

Table 7.6 shows how the capital costs of gas plant were reduced by new process discoveries. Some of the processes, such as Shell (enriched) Onia-Gegi, Segas and cyclic catalytic uniflow, had capital costs very close to those of the ICI, GRH and CRG processes which most Boards adopted; fuel costs were higher for Shell, due to the need for enrichment. Cyclic catalytic uniflow processes were very close in overall costs to the ICI + GRH process, since each used the same fuel.

The overall effect of improved labour productivity, the conversion to oil processes and reduced capital costs was that the average price of gas stayed nearly constant for a ten-year period from the early 1960s, while other fuels increased by 40—60 per cent in price.

Table 7.6 *Specific Capital Costs of Gas Making Plant*

Process	Feedstock Primary	Feedstock Enriching	Calorific value (Btu/cu. ft.)	Capital cost (£/therm/day)	Equivalent capital charges 70% load factor (d./therm)
Continuous vertical retorts	coal		500	76	6·48
Carburetted water gas	coke	LPD	500	15	1·28
Lurgi—lean gas	coal		310	60	5·12
Lurgi—enriched	coal	LPG	500	38	3·24
Shell partial oxidation 92% hydrogen	HFO		305	60	5·12
Shell partial oxidation enriched	HFO	refinery gas	500	23	1·96
Cyclic catalytic—regenerative					
Onia Gegi or Segas	HFO		500	27	2·30
Cyclic catalytic—uniflow	LPD		500	14	1·19
ICI—lean gas	LPD		340	16	1·36
ICI—enriched	LPD	methane	500	8	0·68
ICI + gas recycle hydrogenator (GRH)	LPD	LPD	500	14	1·19
ICI + catalytic rich gas (CRG) in parallel	LPD	LPD	500	12	1·02
CRG followed by tubular reformer	LPD		500	11	0·94
CRG alone	LPD		650	7	0·60
CRG followed by methanation	LPD		970	10	0·85

Source: D. E. Rooke, 'The Development of New Sources of Gas for the British Gas Industry', International Gas Union 10th Annual Gas Conference, Hamburg, 1967

Notes: Plant size at 20—30 million standard cubic feet per day.
Capital charges equivalent to 6½ per cent and depreciation over twenty years (i.e. 9·076 per cent p.a.).
LPD = light petroleum distillate.
LPG = liquefied petroleum gas (butane/propane).
HFO = heavy fuel oil.

BRITISH EUROPEAN AIRWAYS

Labour related costs form a surprisingly large part of total expenditure on revenue account in BEA's operations. The airline business is labour intensive mainly because of the large number of employees needed for engineering maintenance, aircraft overhaul, ground handling and traffic purposes.

There are two main measures of the efficiency with which airlines employ labour, the capacity ton mile (CTM) per employee per year and the load ton mile (LTM) per employee per year. The latter takes into account the labour input required to provide each ton of load and thus the airline's success in selling the capacity which it decides to provide. The former measure covers only the labour input per unit of capacity provided, taking into account the efficiency which applies in engineering, flight operations, ground handling, etc. CTM per employee is used here to measure productivity changes.

Labour productivity in BEA grew from 6,205 CTM per man year in 1949/50 to 35,720 CTM per man year in 1974/5 (Table 7.7). The annual rate of growth which this represents is over 7 per cent for the twenty-five-year period. Growth of productivity was faster up to the early 1960s, at 9 or 10 per cent per year, and then slowed to below 3 per cent annually.

Table 7.7 *Employment and Output in British European Airways, 1950—75*

Year ending 31 March	1949/50	1954/5	1959/60	1964/5	1969/70	1974/5
Personnel employed	6,479	9,143	12,170	17,685	23,228	19,023
Aircraft—effective fleet	87	101	102	88	102	82
CTM produced (million)	40	98	192	436	661	679
Cost per CTM (current prices)	49·2d	41·8d	43·0d	35·5d	43·9d	n.a.
Cost per CTM (constant 1950 prices)	49·2d	33·4d	30·2d	21·8d	22·5d	n.a.
CTM per effective aircraft (000)	462	973	1,880	4,916	6,277	8,285
CTM per employee	6,205	10,755	15,776	24,629	28,471	35,720

Source: BEA, *Annual Reports.*

In the earlier years the rate at which airline traffic as a whole was growing was high, in the region of 13 per cent per year for a long period. It was consequently in BEA's interest to introduce aircraft which represented large successive increases in size and in the rate of production. The Comet and Vanguard, introduced in 1960, produced nearly four times as many CTM per year as the aircraft of the early 1950s (see Table 4.12). A number of factors contributed to the large increases in output which took place. Productivity rose because there were only relatively modest increases in employment. There were scale gains to be made in operating procedures and ground handling as the volume of passengers increased. The amount of engineering work required per CTM performed decreased with the increasing size of aircraft and increasing reliability of turbo-propeller and jet engines and their airframes. The rate of output of aircrew and other staff was immediately increased by the larger sizes of aircraft.

However, after the early 1960s it was not so easy to increase the rate of output of aircraft, partly because of BEA's position as a short-haul operator. The Trident 3 introduced in March 1971 had a yearly rate of output only 30—50 per cent higher than the Comet and Vanguard of 1960. The vast improvement in CTM per hour which the big jets made possible for other airlines were achievable only on long-haul routes. BOAC increased its average rate of aircraft output from 3,612 CTM per hour in 1960 to over 9,000 in 1967, while BEA's rose only from 2,030 to 2,670 during the main period of introduction of jets. The actual increase which BEA achieved in labour productivity in the 1960s and early 1970s was mostly attributable to organisational changes reducing the size of labour force needed, to increasing the number of hours worked by each aircraft and later to the replacement of older types of aircraft with the Tridents 2 and 3 and the BAC 1-11. The traffic densities and aircraft technologies which made possible further significant steps in the rate of output of aircraft did not appear until the middle 1970s.

Evidence of the movement of fuel productivity and capital productivity is contradictory. Turbo-prop aircraft appear to use more fuel per CTM provided than piston-engined aircraft of the same capacity. Jets of the same capacity also use more fuel per CTM than piston-engined aircraft, but the advantage of the latter types diminishes with range. With increased size the jet becomes more efficient than the turbo-prop or the piston-engined aircraft. There are a number of ways of measuring capital productivity, but the ones used in Chapter 2 for BEA aircraft (Table 2.12) are the capital outlay (new price) per CTM per year and the annual overhead cost per CTM. On these measures the tendency displayed was for aircraft to show a decreasing capital cost per CTM up to 1960 (Comet and Vanguard), but for increases of 25—50 per cent to show up in the Trident 1 and BAC 1-11. This feature is almost certainly explained by the fact that the jet aircraft used by BEA were not able to show the advantages on their short stages which were demonstrable by jets on longer stages. The trends in fuel and capital productivity were such that the gains made by BEA due to aircraft innovation were mostly in the field of labour productivity.

THE GENERATION OF ELECTRICITY

Fuel is the largest component in the cost of generating electricity, accounting for over half the cost of each unit. It is followed by depreciation and interest charges at approximately 20 per cent of total costs, and labour, which accounts for about 10 per cent. These figures should be understood as relating to generation and main transmission only: if the costs of general distribution, selling and servicing at Area Board level were included as well, then the labour proportion of costs would rise to over 20 per cent, as in the gas industry, depreciation and interest would be slightly lower and fuel costs would drop below 50 per cent.

Labour productivity in electricity generating is shown in Table 7.8. There are two figures, for electricity generated per power station employee and for electricity generated per generating industry employee. Both, however, follow approximately the same trend. The productivity of all employees in the industry grew at 6 per cent per year from 1949/50 to 1959/60 and then grew more slowly, at 4 per cent annually, to 1974/5. Productivity for power station employees started out at 7 per cent but dropped back to 5·5 per cent growth after 1959/60.

During the first ten or eleven years of public ownership, output per employee grew rapidly because demand was expanding at a time when it was possible for the industry to rationalise supply. The smaller and older stations which had been part of the industry before public ownership were being closed, with consequent manpower savings, and many new stations which were more economical in their use of labour were being commissioned. In the period from 1959/60 to 1969/70 technical troubles delayed the commissioning of much of the new plant in the system. At first, while maximum demand maintained a high rate of growth, much of the older plant planned for scrapping had to be used and the trend towards supply by stations of increasing size was checked. Although the load growth rate diminished in the mid-1960s, so that plant scrapping could be resumed, much of the new plant of large size ordered in the early 1960s was not fully commissioned until 1970 or later, and it was not until then that productivity again approached its earlier rate of growth.

Most of the labour productivity improvement must be attributed to scale increases. In 1955 about 35,400 employees were needed to man 19,000 MW of installed capacity and twenty years later approximately the same number of employees were manning nearly 65,000 MW of installed capacity.

Fuel productivity also grew more rapidly in the first ten years of the period than in the next fifteen (Table 7.8). Increases in fuel productivity, or thermal efficiency, are dependent upon technical change and the improved characteristics of new plant. Thermal efficiencies of 35 per cent were being achieved by 1964 by stations with advanced steam conditions and re-heat, compared to a system average of 21·5 per cent in 1949/50. But where plant has a long expected life, as do power stations, other factors affect the impact which new techniques have on the system's efficiency. The amount of old plant which is used on the system is one of these. Thermal efficiency in the CEGB's system actually dropped during 1965 and 1966, because new plant was late in commissioning and the system's capacity had to be maintained by increased use of plant with a

Table 7.8 *Output, Employment and Fuel Use in Electricity Generation, 1950—75*

Year ended 31 March	1949/50	1954/5	1959/60	1964/5	1969/70	1974/5
Electricity generated (million kWh)	45,717	69,077	100,556	151,301	195,093	227,226
Electricity supplied (million kWh)	43,036	64,860	94,488	141,022	180,719	210,968
Employment						
at power stations	(31,000)	(35,400)	36,123	40,437	42,548	35,584
total generating industry	43,099	50,837	53,027	68,580	72,895	66,099
Fuel used[a]						
total coal equivalent (m. tons)	27·1	37·4	50·0	73·2	81·9	91·3
Productivity						
heat consumed per kWh supplied[a] (btu)	15,900	14,310	12,870	12,415	11,317	11,765
thermal efficiency[a] (%)	21·5	23·8	26·5	27·5	28·3	30·6
Electricity supplied						
per power station employee (mkWh)	1·39	1·83	2·69	3·49	4·26	5·95
per generating industry employee (mkWh)	1·00	1·28	1·78	2·06	2·49	3·20

Sources: CEGB, *Annual Reports, Statistical Yearbooks*; Electricity Council, *Handbook of Electricity Supply Statistics.*
Note: [a]Coal, oil and gas-fired steam stations only.

thermal efficiency below the average level. Thus the rate of scrapping and the rate of addition of new plant to the system are also of considerable importance.

Changes in capital productivity have been fairly regularly surveyed by the electricity supply industry. There are conceptual difficulties about measuring the productivity of the whole plant and equipment stock, and the most commonly reported figures are in terms of the construction costs of new power stations per kW of installed capacity. In the late 1940s the commonly quoted price was £50 per kW; inflation caused increases to £68 per kW by 1952, but this had been reduced, despite further inflation, to about £55 per kW by 1960 as a result of technical improvements. By 1970, as a result partly of inflation and partly of unexpected technical difficulties in development, costs were about £65 per kW. Put in terms of 1958 prices, power station output was about 13 watts per £ of expenditure in 1948, 18 watts in 1960 and 20 watts in 1970.

There was therefore a steady improvement in the output to be expected from each £ of expenditure on new power stations. Both changes in scale and changes in the techniques used contributed to this. The size of the typical new turbo-alternator increased from 30 MW in the mid 1940s to 500 MW in the mid-1960s; technical changes in the boiler, the turbine and the alternator raised the thermal efficiency, and thus the output per £, at each frame size.

THE TELEPHONE SERVICE

Labour costs form a fairly large proportion of the revenue expenditures of the telephone service, given that a great many calls are automatically connected. In 1975 labour costs were 37 per cent and in 1950 they were even higher, at 43 per cent of total costs (Table 7.1). There are three general reasons for this. In spite of the automatic connection of 14,500 million calls annually in the mid-1970s, there were still some hundreds of millions of calls per year made to operators for manually controlled calls, for information and for assistance. The demand for telephone services in this area outstripped the ability of the system to automate, operator calls having grown faster than automatic calls in the 1950s.

The type of automatic equipment in use, the Strowger switching system, has a heavy requirement for maintenance; service and maintenance engineers are also needed for subscribers' equipment. The Post Office maintains a fairly large staff to install new capital equipment, extend exchanges and connect new subscribers.

Unfortunately, in view of the importance of labour productivity, significant measures of the trends which have been developing since 1950 are not publicly available. In Table 7.9 the growth in the total number of calls made from 1955 to 1975 is shown. From 1955 to 1965 growth was at 5 per cent annually, rising during the 1960s to 7 per cent per year by the end of the decade and approximately maintaining this rate up to 1975.

Table 7.9   *Employment and Traffic Handled in Telecommunications*

	1955	1960	1965	1970	1975
Originated effective calls, local, inland and external (millions)	3,923	4,290	6,342	9,638	15,596
employment[a]	n.a.	(160,000)	n.a.	228,000	247,000

Source: Post Office, *Annual Reports.*
Note: [a] 1960 estimated.

However, all types of call are included in this total of output, which begs the question of whether a dialled local call should be counted as equivalent to a manually connected international one. On the labour side it has been estimated that there were 160,000 employees in 1960,[2] giving a rate of production of 26,800 calls per employee in 1960 and 55,000 calls per employee in 1975.

The causes of productivity growth in the telephone service are more complex than in the other industries. In a fully manual system the growth of calls made cannot much exceed the growth of operator employment. In a fully automatic system it depends upon the provision of talking circuits between subscribers and the calling rate per subscriber; the latter depends on the social and business habits of subscribers and on the proportion of the population converted to the system. For a system in transition from manual to automatic, the two most important factors may be the degree of automation and the degree of telephone penetration in the population.

The number of people needed to provide the service will depend on the degree of automation, but operators cannot be dispensed with where the service expects to provide operator assistance as a back-up to the automatic system. The level of employment will depend upon service and maintenance efficiency, and this may be directly affected by the type of capital equipment employed. The contribution of technical change to improved labour productivity is thus far from clear, but it would appear that the rate of adoption of automatic equipment and the requirements of the equipment for service and maintenance are of fundamental importance.

NOTES

[1] Probably the least satisfactory measure is that of the output of the telephone service, where a local call differs substantially from a trunk or an international one, and the mix of calls varies systematically with time. Some measure such as a call-minute-mile might be better, but is not available; there would in any case also be reservations about its accuracy in reflecting output.

[2] Administrative, professional, clerical, etc., 26,000; operating, etc., 59,000; engineering, 75,000.

8 Conclusions

The policies of technical development pursued by the five corporations were ambitious and largely original in their conception. They were designed to have a radical effect upon the production process in each industry. They were executed with a considerable degree of independence from outside sources of technical assistance. External technical help, where it was sought, came in the main from the manufacturing industry supplying capital equipment and only occasionally from the diffusion of techniques developed elsewhere than in the immediate environment of the industry. Research, where it was necessary, and the essential engineering development of new techniques, were functions in which the user industries took a remarkably active role. Indeed, in all the developments described in the preceding chapters, the customer corporations took the leading role in advancing techniques of production. The dominance which the user industries displayed in the evolution of techniques must inevitably be associated with their position as the major customers for the types of capital equipment being developed.

CAUSES OF TECHNICAL CHANGE

The most important motivation which can be identified in each of the publicly owned industries for seeking new or advanced techniques was the desire to control costs. Although very different circumstances of plant organisation and concentration affected each of them, they were all faced by the prospect of the steeply increasing price of one or more of their main factors of production.

For the coal industry, the labour cost per unit of output was the most important determinant of total costs and it was inevitable that the price of coal would be closely related to the price of labour. The introduction of machinery to improve labour productivity had been adopted as a policy for controlling labour costs in the early part of the century and the National Coal Board continued this approach, making a highly innovative contribution to underground mechanisation.

Capital costs and the productivity with which capital was employed were both difficult to measure, but it would appear that capital costs were a small part of total costs. Where capital costs form a low proportion of the cost of output, the productivity of capital is of less importance than the productiveness that the form of fixed capital used imparts to the other

234

factors of production. The indications were that very large units of capital, collieries with outputs of one-and-a-half million tons per year and over, would have been more efficient in their use of labour than small ones; the average British colliery in the 1950s was producing about a quarter of a million tons and very few exceeded half a million tons annually. The larger colliery route to reduced labour costs was not chosen, however; among the main reasons for this were the lack of a consensus of technical opinion in the industry and the difficulties in labour relations which concentration would have caused.

Cost control in air transportation also depended mostly upon the improvements made in labour productivity. Again labour costs formed a large proportion of total costs. The labour input to each flying hour consisted of aircrew labour, engineering and maintenance labour, flying operations and ground handling labour and the labour employed in sales, administration and other central functions. The type of capital employed, however, and the efficiency with which it permitted labour to be employed, was what really determined the overall costs of production, the significance of capital costs themselves being relatively low.

If the type of capital employed (of which 90 per cent or more consisted of aircraft) had remained unchanged, the increasing price of labour would have forced up the price of air travel. However, technical changes in airframes and engines produced substantial increases in the carrying capacity of aircraft and the average speed at which they could complete journeys. The rate of production of the aircraft was dependent upon the product of capacity and average speed, so that the amount of output potentially achieved by one aircraft in one year multiplied rapidly, as size increased. Capacity ton miles per aircraft year went up by more than ten times over a period of less than twenty years and the increased scale of output raised labour productivity.

This was because increased rates of aircraft output did not require proportional increases in labour inputs, and for this reason the use of aircraft which were larger and faster was a sure route to steady improvements in productivity. Labour productivity increased so rapidly through steady improvement in the type of capital employed that the price of air travel in real terms fell every year over a long period in which technical advances were being made.

Specifying new aircraft which were larger and faster and embodied techniques not previously used in airliners provided improvements in labour productivity, because the aircraft output per hour approximately trebled with each new aircraft introduced, while the labour input required to produce that aircraft hour increased only fractionally. Some of this reduced labour input per unit of output was due to the fact that new techniques in airframes and engines actually required less frequent servicing, but productivity improved mainly as a result of the scale increases which new techniques permitted. The aircrew, ground staff and headquarters staff required per flying hour for a larger aircraft were not much increased over the manning levels used on smaller ones.

Capital costs, however, did not follow the trend of labour costs. New aircraft were expensive to design and build and they proved to have heavy introductory costs for the airline. It would appear that the capital costs and capital-related costs of a unit of output remained approximately constant as aircraft increased in size and speed, but since capital costs were a small part of total costs this tendency did not upset the general trend towards steadily reducing costs in air transportation as a whole.

Technical change in the electricity and gas industries was closely associated with the problem posed by the increasing price of coal. In each industry fuel accounted for more than 50 per cent of costs. The prospect of steadily rising fuel prices implied steady increases in the prices of electricity and gas. Capital costs were also a significant part of total costs in each industry, and any solution to the problem of fuel costs had to take into account the need to hold capital costs in check.

The difference between the two industries was that gas making by carbonisation had been developed to its technical limits, whereas the basic electricity generating process had not; there was no prospect with carbonisation of higher thermal efficiency, nor that increases in plant scale would substantially reduce the capital costs. The problem of fuel costs therefore pushed the gas industry towards a new process. In the electricity industry rising fuel prices and a tendency for capital costs to rise rapidly in the postwar inflation caused generating techniques to be advanced to the limits of scale and thermal efficiency.

In both the gas and the electricity industries the technical advances which were achieved produced big improvements in fuel productivity. Approximately two and a half times as much gas and 50 per cent more electricity were produced from each unit of fuel after the technical changes as had been produced before. More remarkably, savings in capital costs lay in the same direction and were at least as significant in controlling costs in general as the savings in fuel. Gas plant which used oil as a feedstock was much cheaper to build than carbonisation plant, and it had the advantage that its product was wholly gaseous, instead of being partly of coke, as in the case of carbonisation plant. Scale increases in generating plant produced lower capital costs per unit of output and made technical advances, re-heat, higher operating temperatures and pressures, alternator cooling, etc., more worthwhile. For reasons that were partly to do with scale of operations and partly to do with the added simplicity of new plant, both industries also recorded steady improvements in labour productivity.

The considerations which lay behind the development of electronic switching were also those of factor prices. Both labour and capital costs form a large part of costs in the telephone service, together amounting to as much as 80 per cent of the total. The standard form of automatic exchange was technically inelegant and cumbersome. Its capital costs were related to the large quantities of equipment necessary to serve each subscriber and to the space needed to house the plant; its labour costs arose from the need for frequent servicing and maintenance. Knowledge of electronic techniques made it seem possible that exchanges with a much greater degree of common equipment could be built, thereby saving on capital costs and space. At the same time the reliability of electronic devices, when used in functions such as switching, was recognised to be higher than that of electro-mechanical equipment, so that there was a reasonable expectation of reduced labour costs.

Conceptual problems in measuring output in physical terms, combined with insufficient statistical detail, make it difficult to estimate the overall effect which new types of switching have upon costs in the telephone service. Technical change in telephone systems takes an extremely long time to permeate through the network; the need for old and new equipment to work together during any transition period slows down the realisation of the effects of new techniques. The improvements in labour productivity which were observable in the period 1950 to 1975 were probably related to changes in the working methods introduced for technical staff, to managerial changes in the employment of administration and sales staff and to the near-complete conversion of the local and long distance service to automatic working. Scale of operations, not in the capacity of the individual exchanges, but in the increase in the number of telephone calls made annually on the whole system, must be regarded as the primary cause of improvements in productivity, both for labour and capital.

FACTOR PRICE CHANGES, TECHNICAL CHANGE AND PRODUCTIVITY

In the light of the conclusions of the previous section, some further comments are in order about the way in which changes in the relative prices of factors of production lead to changes in factor productivity. The basis which is used here for the examination of these relationships is the theoretical formulation and empirical analysis of movements of productivity and technical change originally suggested by W. E. G. Salter in 1960.[1]

Salter points out that the classical prescription for increased labour productivity is the substitution of capital for labour. He might also have pointed out, if he had been writing ten or fifteen years later, that conventional wisdom attributes low levels of labour productivity and low rates of economic growth in countries such as Britain to the low rate of fixed capital formation. But examination of the sequence of events in the five important sectors of the economy covered by this study gives no ground for the belief that simply increasing the amount of capital inputs to production output, compared to the amount of labour inputs to the production process, is the shortest route to higher labour productivity, nor that factor substitutions generally are the main cause of productivity gains.

In rejecting the simple version of the prescription, Salter argues that it would imply that industries which were most successful in improving labour productivity, and thus in reducing labour costs per unit of output, would also reflect the greatest increase in capital costs per unit of output. The empirical evidence which he produced pointed in the opposite direction. The data available from the present study of only five industries suggest no consistent relationship between the movements of labour costs and of capital costs. The industry achieving the greatest change in labour productivity, air transportation, showed very little improvement in unit capital costs. Coal mining recorded the lowest gains in labour productivity; data on capital costs are sparse, but the trend in capital productivity was probably gently upwards, as mechanised mining spread. In the gas and electricity industries labour productivity grew fairly quickly, even compared with air transportation, capital productivity increased rapidly and there were also gains, although of a smaller nature, in fuel productivity.

The explanation of factor productivity changes which makes most sense of the data in the study is one which includes scale increases, technological change and, to a lesser extent, some factor substitution, as the causes of productivity improvement. In the cases studied, labour and capital productivity are determined by the scale of operations and by the production techniques which are employed. Scale increases lead to improved labour productivity, either because the basic technique is more efficient in its use of labour when employed in a larger unit of production (electricity generating plant), or because new techniques make possible a larger size of productive unit which results in labour savings (air transportation). New techniques unaccompanied by scale changes can also result in the improvement of labour productivity (oil-based gas making plant and electronic exchanges).

However, labour productivity gains associated with scale increases and technical change were frequently accompanied by gains in capital productivity of the same order of magnitude. There was no generally observed tendency for capital inputs per unit of production to show an increased proportion to labour inputs with the scale changes and the changes in techniques, even though the price of labour was commonly increasing faster than that of capital. The substitution of factors, of capital for labour or other inputs to production, appears only as an incidental and occasional effect of technical advance and not as a main cause of factor saving.

The evidence from this study is thus that improvements in factor productivity result mainly from scale increases and from technical change. The use of a higher proportion of capital inputs to production, even where associated with scale or technique changes, was of some significance only in coal mining and air transport. Elsewhere 'more capital intensive' methods of production scarcely figure as a contributory cause of factor saving. Thus the quality rather than the amount of fixed capital has a greater effect in determining the improvements in factor productivity.

This result accords with Salter's explanatory hypothesis of inter-industry productivity changes over time:

'the analysis has suggested that the variation between industries in the extent of increases in labour productivity can be explained primarily by the uneven impact of three influences: (i) improvements in technical knowledge, (ii) potential economies of scale and the extent of their realisation, and (iii) factor substitution. Although analytically distinct, these three influences are highly inter-related: realisation of economies of scale depends upon increases in output which are in part induced by technical advances; while factor substitution is prompted by changes in relative factor prices which to some extent originate in technical change itself.'

And again:

'The analysis has suggested that, to explain the data, primary emphasis must be placed on technical progress and economies of scale. These are causes of labour productivity which extend their influence to all factors and so can account for the behaviour of costs. Increases in the personal efficiency of labour and factor substitution can not explain the data by themselves.[2]

IMPROVEMENTS IN FACTOR PRODUCTIVITY

It is therefore argued that improved factor productivity (improvements in the output obtained per unit input of labour, capital, fuel and other materials) owes more to changes in techniques than to factor substitution, at least for industries similar to the ones which are the subject of this study. Although factor substitution may accompany technical change, it is not a necessary accompaniment even to the most far-reaching changes producing major savings in all inputs to production.

It is fair to regard the objective of the technical policies studied as being the improvement of factor productivity. The industries studied may be considered as process industries having a product which is in itself relatively unchanging. Although some technical effort and research was directed towards product change, the major effort was devoted to production improvements.

In general it may be supposed that the contribution of changing techniques and increases in scale to improvements in factor productivity in any industry would be determined by the following:
(1) the availability of knowledge suitable for advancing the techniques of the industry (affected by applied research, scientific discovery, the transfer of knowledge from other industries);
(2) the effectiveness with which this knowledge is translated into techniques which improve the production process or which make possible larger scale production methods (affected by engineering skill, the choice of new techniques, development policy);
(3) the growth of demand (affecting the viability of increases in the scale of production and determining the amount of new investment which takes place and which may incorporate new techniques and scale increases);

(4) constraints imposed by the ownership pattern, size of producing unit and other institutional factors upon the diffusion of techniques and the adoption of large-scale methods of production.

Structural constraints to the spread of techniques or increases in scale, the last factor mentioned, may be an important influence in industries with many firms which are not large enough to make use of scale or technique changes. In the public industries studied here their influence was minimal. Ownership under nationalisation was organised on a scale which allowed productive units to be of the largest size practicable. Only in the gas industry was the new form of organisation under public ownership less than fully centralised; the twelve Area Boards were autonomous so far as production was concerned, but even so the scale of production operations for each Board was well above that level at which the largest scale of plant was viable. The unified ownership structure of the five industries also meant that the best techniques available were not prevented by division of ownership among a number of rival firms from spreading to all the units of production.

There were, however, one or two examples of the operation of other institutional constraints upon the contribution made by scale and technique advances. One noteworthy instance was the decision taken by the Ministry of Supply in 1947 to limit the size and steam conditions of turbo-generators, which temporarily delayed the potential contribution of advanced generating plant factor productivity. Of a similar nature was the political restraint exerted on the telephone service to keep investment in switching equipment at a very low level after the war. This delayed the completion of the conversion of the system to automatic working, reducing the gains to be expected in labour productivity. Thirdly, the size of productive unit in mining appears to have remained below the level at which factors of production were most efficiently employed and institutional reasons must be considered among the possible causes. Problems of labour relations and divisions of technical opinion reduced the rate at which mining output was concentrated upon larger collieries. Generally, however, the role of structural and institutional constraints must be regarded as very limited, certainly far less important in determining factor productivity improvement than demand and the effectiveness with which new techniques were advanced.

DEMAND

Although factor price changes must be regarded as stimulating the technical developments described in this study, it would misleading to suggest that relative changes in the prices of input factors are a sufficient condition for the introduction of new techniques to an industry. In the industries studied here, although cost control was the objective of the programmes of innovation, demand considerations were more influential in bringing about the introduction of new techniques into the capital equipment.

Demand effects can be seen relatively easily in air transportation. Without the steady increase in traffic density on its main routes during the 1950s and 1960s, BEA would have found it uneconomical to introduce larger aircraft of the type which made best use of new techniques. Only a small part of improved factor productivity in air transportation arose from the use of techniques which were intrinsically labour saving (e.g. jet engines were simpler to maintain and had longer overhaul lives, but the labour saving involved was scarcely significant compared to the total improvement in labour productivity achieved by trebling the rate of aircraft output). Without scale increases there would have been very little opportunity to save on factor inputs and the growth of demand must be regarded as the predominant cause of the introduction of factor saving techniques.

In electricity generation demand growth was the main factor which influenced the rate of introduction of factor saving new techniques. Had demand remained static, there would have been only a minor opportunity to replace old and small power stations with new larger power stations which employed capital, fuel and labour more productively; such opportunity would have depended on the concentration of supply made possible by the Grid. But the growth of demand approximately quadrupled the total capacity on the system during the twenty years in which the main advances in size, techniques and operating conditions were taking place. Thus it was possible for relatively advanced plant to constitute approximately three-quarters of total capacity, simply because additions to capacity were necessitated by new demands.

Increasing demand for gas can also be credited with being the main factor leading to orders for new gas manufacturing processes. While demand was static, between 1949 and 1960, the industry consolidated production in the more efficient carbonisation plants and experimented with a range of new processes, but it did not invest in them. Orders for new plant on a large scale came only when demand began to grow after 1960. The savings in input factors which were provided by the oil-based gas making processes were so great that some replacement of carbonisation plant would have taken place in any case. Demand growth increased the rate at which the new techniques were incorporated in capital equipment. This process did not run its full course because oil was so soon eclipsed by natural gas.

Growth in the telephone system became very rapid during the period 1955 to 1975, the number of connections approximately trebling. To begin with this expansion took place with the established Strowger technique, but by the middle of the 1960s it became urgent that new switching techniques be installed. Both local and trunk switching capacity were by that time under pressure to expand even faster. If the extra capacity needed had been installed using only Strowger, the predominance of that technique in the system would have hampered the technical and economic performance of the service in the long term. So important was it to advance techniques during this time of expansion, that the Post Office invested in a considerable amount of switching equipment which was not of the preferred type of new technique, the latter not being ready for commercial use at the time. Demand thus forced technical change in the system to be adopted rather more quickly than the industry would have wished.

The coal mining industry presents the unusual circumstance that most of the advance in techniques was being implemented while production was falling. It is more difficult to introduce a change in techniques at a time of static or falling production, because new units of capacity employing advances in scale or techniques are not so likely to be introduced.

THE EFFECTIVENESS OF POLICIES USED TO ADVANCE TECHNIQUES AND INCREASE THE SCALE OF OPERATIONS

The efforts which were made by the public industries to introduce innovations and improve factor productivity in their capital equipment met with a reasonable amount of success. The only programme which suffered a major reversal was the development of the time-division multiplex exchange by the Post Office. In this case a number of factors could be said to have contributed to the programme's weakness: the method of choosing the project, the executive agency formed to carry it out and the role which the manufacturers of telephone equipment played in the development.

Project choice was also one of the weakest aspects of the innovations made in transport aircraft. Although the Viscount was an extremely successful aircraft, the airline (BEA) subsequently found itself in considerable difficulties in trying to determine what type of aircraft was required to meet the needs of the market beyond the 1950s. Again, the role of the manufacturers of aircraft was in question.

Thirdly, development of two major programmes in the generating industry, the AGR and the 500 MW generator, suffered serious interruption because of technical difficulties. In both cases the disruptions to the work could be described as being the fault, not so much of the CEA and the CEGB, but of the agencies responsible for the design concept or for the more detailed aspects of engineering design.

All three cases provide evidence that the relationships between the public corporations and their suppliers, and the role which each side plays in advancing technology, are a potential source of trouble in innovative programmes. This implies that some special aspect of the customer—supplier relationship creates unsatisfactory conditions of trading, such as the fact that the public corporation is frequently in the position of being the only purchaser, or by far the most important purchaser, of one type of equipment from the industries supplying capital equipment.

It is necessary to be satisfied that the evidence produced does not arise merely because of chance factors in what is, after all, a very small sample of innovation programmes, and it is also important to sketch out a causative hypothesis linking the nature of the market structure with the tendency for technical development to go awry. The first requirement is difficult to satisfy; statistical comparisons of the incidence of poor performance in innovative programmes in monopsonistic market situations compared to non-monopsonistic ones would be difficult to produce and easy to disagree with. It is therefore up to the individual observer to decide whether there is an unsatisfactory aspect about the performance of innovative programmes in the cases referred to above and also perhaps in other cases where a monopsonistic purchaser is involved with a supplying industry in making decisions about an advanced technology programme.[3]

The market structure conditions which applied to the cases studied here would not be considered as pure monopsony; the situation affecting the telecommunications industry was that only one large domestic customer existed for public exchanges; in the aircraft industry the nationalised airlines and the defence agencies were by far the most important domestic customers for large aircraft, while in the heavy electrical and plant industries the dominant domestic customer for large generating equipment was the CEA/CEGB. In these circumstances the manufacturers of capital equipment would run the risk of being put out of business, or of sustaining serious commercial damage, if they were not able to agree on contracts with the dominant domestic purchaser. It may be argued that awareness of this dependence would make the supplying companies much more amenable than they would otherwise be to build to the orders of the public customer. Nothing disadvantageous might be expected to follow from this reasonable response when the orders were for conventional equipment of established design, but dangers may arise where the work which comes from the public customer includes the advancement of techniques or other engineering development.

There are often perfectly valid reasons for disagreeing about advances in technology, conflicts of opinion which need to be resolved by the process of objective project evaluation, or by submitting alternative solutions to market forces. Where the manufacturing supplier has a number of customers he has greater freedom to voice differences of opinion over technical policy. Where there is one dominant domestic purchaser, the conditions are not naturally favourable to conflicts of technical policy being brought into the open and resolved by competitive means. Each supplier knows that if he is not amenable to the requests of the public customer, another supplier may be willing to take the contract instead.

The pressures are stated here more explicitly than they are actually felt by the manufacturers or expressed in negotiations; the hypothesis is that the existence of a dominant customer creates a tendency for responsibility for technical decisions to pass from the supplier to the customer. The second point concerns the actual responsibility for carrying out the research and engineering development work necessary to bring about the chosen advances. The tendency of the public corporations to perform some R and D themselves on technical advances in capital equipment reinforced the abrogation of responsibility from the manufacturers for decisions on the choice of techniques.

Nor was the type of market structure necessarily more satisfactory from the point of view of the public corporation. Its dominant position in the market could mean that it faced a narrower range of choice where technical advance was concerned than would be available to a larger number of purchasers. Since supplying companies would find it highly risky to develop new types of capital equipment unless the dominant customer had expressed a preference for the type, the public corporation would find itself unable to order fully developed equipment of the type it preferred unless it had already indicated that preference at an earlier date. The obligation imposed upon the dominant customer to express a preference for one new technique or new type of capital equipment in preference to another, at a point early enough in time to allow the supplying industry to develop it, was perhaps the central influence creating a complicated and sometimes unmanageable relationship between the supplier and the customer. It further reinforced the transfer of the responsibility for making decisions on technical developments from the manufacturer to the customer. Its second effect was to transfer also some of the responsibility for conducting R and D. One of the motivations which caused the public corporations to conduct applied research or engineering development on the techniques employed in their capital equipment was the desire to base the choices they made on their own experimental results.

The unsatisfactory features of the market structure for public corporations' capital goods were that conditions existed in which there was confusion about the responsibility for making decisions, there was division of authority for carrying out the R and D needed for a project and there was a failure of the two sides, customer and manufacturer, to together identify the most important economic and technical objectives and to work towards them in concert. The manufacturers, on the one hand, were inhibited in their negotiations with such large domestic customers, while the public corporations were ambivalent on the issue of whether the supply industry should be independent and self-determining or whether it should work under direction from the public sector.

Thus the aircraft industry was prepared to agree to proposals for building aircraft, not because they were the soundest commercial projects, but because they were the projects for which a domestic source of funds was available. The telecommunications industry was prepared to join the Post Office in a development programme for new exchange types, not because it believed it was the best technical choice on all-round criteria, but because the Post Office made it clear that it was not prepared to order other types of exchange. The heavy electrical and plant industries were prepared to accept series orders for 500 MW generators and AGR power stations based on commercially unproven designs, not because the industries themselves had judged their prospects to be good, but because they were in no position to refuse the business.

It would be incorrect, however, to reach the conclusion that it was a failure of technical policy on the part of public sector customers which caused the supplying industries to accept these shortcomings, just as it would be wrong to blame the suppliers for working on ill-favoured projects. It was, rather, the structure of decision making forced upon both sides by the market circumstances which caused the difficulties. In fairness, it should be pointed out that the creation of those market conditions which made technical choice difficult and project responsibility confused also made possible the implementation of other successful technical advances and scale changes, leading to improved factor productivity, to an extent which would have been impossible if fragmented ownership had continued.

If the market structure led to difficulties of technical choice and confusion about the responsibility for development in the cases of air transportation, electricity supply and telecommunications switching, how was it that similar results did not follow in the coal industry and the gas industry? The answer is, on the one hand, that the market conditions were not identical, and, on the other hand, that the strategies of technical choice and project development followed in the coal and gas industries, consciously or unconsciously, avoided the hazards encountered by the other industries.

The degree of centralisation in forming technical policy was less in the coal and gas industries than it was in the other industries. Developments in the mechanisation of coal face operations received comparatively little direction from the central headquarters, new ideas being tried out in different coalfields. Thus a committing decision to one type of solution was not taken before a good deal of experimental development of types of conveyors, power loaders and powered support had been carried out. The manufacturers of equipment were faced not by one single customer, but by a number of customers represented by the different Areas or Divisions, which had their own ideas about the equipment which was needed. This meant that it was worthwhile for the manufacturing suppliers to invest some effort in developing their own ideas, with a greater chance that one of the potential customers would be interested. The important features of this system of technical development were that the technical decisions made to determine the best types of equipment resulted from evaluation of competing solutions on which considerable development work had been done and, further, that the suppliers were called upon to exercise their commercial judgment about the capital equipment they were to manufacture.

In the gas industry there was again more than one customer. Each of the Area Boards ordered gas-making plant separately and many tried out different new techniques experimentally on a small scale. There was also an industry policy of Boards evaluating each others' technical developments. The plant manufacturers were in a stronger position than their confederates supplying switching equipment, aircraft, etc. Not only had they a wider opportunity of finding a customer for gas making plant, without the constraint that only one main type of plant was acceptable, they also had other customers among major industries in Britain, notably the oil industry and the chemical industry. The plant suppliers were thus not inhibited by the market structure from backing their own judgment of the best new techniques. On the other hand, the federal structure of the gas industry, and the way in which the research programme reflected that federal structure, assisted the evaluation and development of a number of new techniques to replace coal carbonisation. The make-up of the programme of applied research and experimental development reflected a wide variety of interests, of individual Area Boards, of university-based engineers and of the gas engineering profession as a whole. The resultant quest for new techniques produced a genuine comparison between alternatives. The projects pursued had to perform well enough to satisfy a range of discerning authorities in order to gain wide acceptance; conflicts of technical opinion tended to be resolved by experiment, rather than by the balance of power in the industry.

CONDITIONS NECESSARY TO THE SUCCESSFUL PURSUIT OF TECHNICAL
POLICIES INVOLVING A CHANGE OF TECHNIQUES OR SCALE

It has been argued above that the market structure for capital equipment in the electricity supply industry, the telephone service and air transportation produced an unsatisfactory relationship between customer and supplier where technical change was involved. Exaggerated dependence on the part of suppliers, premature choice on the part of the customers, confusion about the responsibility for technical decisions and diminution of the exercise of the suppliers' sense of commercial judgment, all were likely to follow from the situation where a single customer dominated the market in one product area. Conversely, multiple-customer conditions in gas and coal encouraged suppliers to back their judgment, relieved customers of the desire to foster special developments and allowed a reasonable amount of competition between alternative technical approaches at the experimental development stage.

However, the disadvantages of large-scale public monopolies organised on a centralised basis have to be weighed, in questions of technical change as in other areas of policy, against the advantages which are conferred by their size and structure. Problems arising out of the relationships between the industries supplying capital equipment and their dominant customers are relevant only to one aspect of the process of technological change. In other aspects the scale of the public enterprise was its great strength, while the form of organisation ensured that the benefits of new technology were widely spread. The unification of ownership under nationalisation provided the opportunity for scale increases, both in the average size of production unit employed and in the size of the whole corporate activity, and this, combined with the growth of demand, was what made possible the use of more productive types of capital as well as the more efficient use of labour and materials.

The second area in which the size and system of organisation made an important difference to the industries coming under nationalisation was in the use which was made of applied research. The availability of knowledge is the fourth of the factors (alongside institutional constraints, the growth of demand and the effectiveness of development policy) put forward above as determining the contribution of technical change to improved factor productivity. Applied research is one of the main mechanisms by which new knowledge is created or existing knowledge applied to problem areas. Interest in applied research as a corporate function had grown in industrialised countries during the latter part of the nineteenth century; in the early part of the twentieth century the beginnings of a national policy had emerged in Britain. Among its manifestations was the move to establish research as an industry-wide function, through the creation of research associations. What these associations lacked was the authority to direct large-scale, adequately funded programmes of applied research into important problems of the industries they represented, with the backing and cooperation of the constituent parts of the industry. By contrast, the nationalisation of an entire industry provided the opportunity to put into operation programmes of applied research having just these characteristics.[4]

The research programmes put into operation by the gas industry, the coal mining industry and the Post Office underpinned much of the technological development of their production processes, as well as of their products. The generating industry developed a substantial programme in one area, that of transmission techniques, although nuclear generation and turbo-alternator development were left largely to other agencies. BEA's applied research effort was of a modest nature, because public support for aerospace research was already maintained at a substantial level in government facilities and in the aerospace industry.

The tendency of the public corporations to enter the field of applied research and experimental development for the production processes which they used has already been mentioned as one of the factors which created a difficult relationship with the industries supplying capital equipment; the difficulties which were experienced when the customer corporation had a large research effort in the field of process equipment may seem to suggest that process R and D should remain as the preserve of the supplier. This view is difficult to support, because the large-scale user of technically complex equipment has a number of legitimate motives for maintaining its own research competence. As a large-scale user it may be in the best position to identify important gaps in the research or technical development conducted by the suppliers. This latter was indeed the major reason why the Post Office and gas industry (before it was nationalised) each initiated serious efforts in R and D. In each case the important gap identified (transmission techniques in the early twentieth century by the Post Office and process research in the 1930s by the gas industry) was one which the user of the technique was perhaps best placed to fill, by reason of its special interest in its development and by reason of having the expertise and the resources to make an effective contribution.

In the second place, the demand which the large-scale user generates for new technical developments will have a material effect upon what new types of equipment are developed by suppliers. The user needs to conduct experimental work and some research, as an information input and as an aid to making the choice for the next generation of capital equipment. In addition, some monitoring of technical development is important in order to keep pace with the work of manufacturers. The use of applied research to fulfil these functions was practised to some degree by four of the corporations, that is, all excepting BEA, which had access to the results of publicly funded aerospace programmes. The need for applied research to fulfil this role is also demonstrated by the tendency for the government and the armed services in many countries, as purchasers of advanced defence equipment, to build up a complex and comprehensive research capability in weapon technology.

There was one industry, electricity supply, which took the view that applied research and development in generating techniques were functions which the plant manufacturers could quite adequately fulfil, and as a consequence did not develop a programme of its own. It was indeed true in the pre-nationalisation world that the R and D undertaken by the plant manufacturers had been the source of most technical advance, and that up to the 1930s the British generating plant industry had been highly innovative. However, in some aspects of design and technical advance the British industry was already falling behind before the war. The CEA tried to plug some of the gaps by encouraging more manufacturer-based research and the CEGB belatedly established a co-operative approach to power engineering research. These measures were inadequate to provide a sound basis for the rate of advance of generating techniques planned by the electricity industry. The lack of a well formulated applied research programme in the CEA/CEGB left the supply industry in a position where it was responsible for making judgments about the viability of future types of power plant, but lacked the knowledge of the problems involved to enable it to exercise that judgment correctly. In conventional generating plant the effect of this was to cause some interruption of the programme of building the 500 MW generators, but in the nuclear programme the consequences were more critical. The lack of a supply industry nuclear development programme meant that its engineers lacked first-hand experience of designing new types of nuclear power plant. The absence of a programme of demonstration plant building contributed to the shortage of information, leaving the electricity authority, at the beginning of the building programme of second generation reactors, in an invidious situation. It was up to the authority to determine whether the advanced gas cooled reactor was at a stage of development where it could be ordered commercially, and to distinguish its merits from other types of nuclear power systems. The absence of an applied research effort in the field left it unprepared for a decision of this magnitude.

The fact of nationalisation, which brought into existence the very large customers for process equipment, created special conditions in the area of applied research, just as it brought about the more general problem of the relationship between customers and suppliers. What was needed was for these special conditions to be recognised and for arrangements to be made which would mitigate their effects. Thus the public corporations needed to define their legitimate and necessary interest in conducting applied research. At the same time, both they and the capital equipment suppliers needed to recognise that the existence of a substantial applied research effort on the part of the customer, together with the need for the customer to indicate his equipment requirements at a fairly early stage, together brought about an obligation to review and to reorganise the role of each side in creating technical advance.

The Post Office had made a serious effort in the 1930s to institutionalise the arrangements for bringing about technical change in switching equipment. Although these arrangements were associated with a system of market-sharing among an exclusive group of equipment suppliers and although, when they were extended to encompass the electronic research project, the arrangements broke down, nevertheless the attempt was deserving of consideration by the other public industries. Its particular virtue was that it provided a forum in which coverage of the applied R and D necessary for a particular advance could be agreed between the public customer and its suppliers. The other public corporations did not, however, follow this example and negotiate formal arrangements for comprehensive coverage of the field of applied research.

The reorganisation of research roles required, of course, that it should be agreed what project objectives were to be served by the applied research programme, and this definition of objectives was dependent upon the choice of development project, which was what proved to be the main area of difficulty. The approach which most of the public corporations adopted towards the difficult task of selecting the most promising new techniques showed even less recognition of the special circumstances which applied because of the market structure than was evidenced by their approach to applied research. It would appear in retrospect that there was a clear need to establish a system for the experimental development and evaluation of alternative new techniques, as part of a system for resolving conflicts of technical opinion, either within the public corporation or between the corporation and its suppliers. What actually happened was that the corporations confused their legitimate need to conduct R and D and to identify their capital equipment needs at an early date with the quite separate and distinctive function of examining alternative forms of technical advance and choosing between them. The conduct of applied research to inform the corporation and thus guide its choice led very quickly, in the absence of a structured system to compare alternatives, into the stage at which one preferred solution emerged in an unsystematic way and became established as the chosen technique or equipment type for the next generation of capital equipment, without any deliberate attempt to compare alternatives.

The conditions which applied in the gas industry's applied R and D programme, and to a lesser extent also in the coal mining industry, give some indication of what was required. In these cases a relatively comprehensive collection of alternative solutions to the technical problem in hand was formed. These were then put through development to a prototype or a laboratory model, and finally underwent some form of testing in commercial applications or as a commercial demonstration plant. The production of reasonably accurate cost and performance projections of technically novel equipment is an essential requirement for the application of investment appraisal or comparison techniques, but this information is available only at a fairly advanced stage in the project. In the gas and mining developments, such comparisons and evaluations were made, although the reason was largely the accident of a multi-customer structure rather than the design of a procedure for choice. The need to replace the functions performed by the multi-customer structure with some other structure for comparing alternatives and establishing firm data on performance was not clearly seen in the other industries.

The reasons usually given for this lack of attention to procedure in the matter of technical choice refer to constraints either of time or of resources, or both. However, reference to the preceding chapters, describing technical developments in detail, shows that the time constraint was often a perceived one which did not turn into an actual one. The need for speed of decision nowhere appears to have effectively precluded the adoption of a procedure which would have backed choice with more information. Nor does the argument that scarcity of resources prevented the collection of reliable projections of cost and performance data, and inhibited the comparison of projected developments with other prospective ones, bear close examination on the evidence of actual cases. In the situations where prototype development or commercial demonstration models would have been most expensive, those of short-haul aircraft and nuclear power stations, quite other reasons than cost, usually in fact an underlying assumption about the unsuitability of alternatives, provided the justification for simplifying the questions of technical controversy or market disagreement.

In examining the resources devoted to test models, experimental prototypes, the development of engineering methods, etc., in the fields of aerospace, nuclear engineering, telecommunications equipment and generating sets, it becomes clear that they were quite sufficient to allow considerable expenditure to be incurred on the production of information as an input to a decision procedure. What was absent was any attempt to set up an ordered process of decision making, and this omission can best be attributed to the unsatisfactory customer-supplier relationships which followed from the market structure for capital equipment.

NOTES

1 W. E. G. Salter, *Productivity and Technical Change*, 2nd edn, Cambridge University Press, 1966. Salter analysed the statistics of output, employment, factor prices and employment in a large number of industries in the UK and US between 1924 and 1950.

2 Salter, *Productivity and Technical Change*, op. cit., ch. X.

3 Defence programmes are one obvious example, and individual cases such as the Concorde programme might also be considered as coming within the category.

4 It is not intended to suggest that the opportunity to conduct applied research in this way was foreseen as a benefit of the nationalisation programme; it was scarcely referred to in the Acts, but it so happened that public ownership provided favourable conditions.

Index